THE 13 ORIGINAL CLAN MOTHERS

Medicine Cards™ (with David Carson)

Sacred Path Cards™

The Sacred Path Workbook

Other Council Fires Were Here Before Ours (with Twylah Nitsch)

THE 13 ORIGINAL CLAN MOTHERS

YOUR SACRED PATH TO DISCOVERING THE GIFTS, TALENTS, AND ABILITIES OF THE FEMININE THROUGH THE ANCIENT TEACHINGS OF THE SISTERHOOD

JAMIE SAMS

HarperSanFrancisco
A Division of HarperCollins*Publishers*

THE THIRTEEN ORIGINAL CLAN MOTHERS: *Your Sacred Path to Discovering the Gifts, Talents, and Abilities of the Feminine Through the Ancient Teachings of the Sisterhood.* Copyright © 1993 by Jamie Sams. All rights reserved. Printed in the United States of America. No part of this book may be used or reproduced in any mannner whatsoever without written permission except in the case of brief quotations embodied in critical articles and reviews. For information address HarperCollins Publishers, 10 East 53rd Street, New York, NY 10022.

FIRST EDITION

Library of Congress Cataloging-in-Publication Data

Sams, Jamie.
    The thirteen original clan mothers : your sacred path to discovering the gifts, talents, and abilities of the feminine through the ancient teachings of the sisterhood / Jamie Sams.
      p. cm.
    ISBN 0-06-250759-1 (alk. paper)
    1. Women—Religious life. 2. Indians of North America—Religion and mythology—Miscellanea.   I. Title.
BL625.7.S36 1993
299'.7'082—dc20   92–53910
                                                          CIP

93 94 95 96 97 ❖ HAD 10 9 8 7 6 5 4 3 2 1

This edition is printed on acid-free paper that meets the American National Standards Institute Z39.48 Standard.

For
Aida Hinojosa
who encouraged me to write,
seeing my heart's song through my words,

and to the memory of my
Ancestors of the Long Hair Clan
Mary Ross Sams
and her father
John Ross
of the Cherokee.

Contents

Note to Readers

For those of you who are reading this book and find it confusing that so many names are capitalized, I would like to give a further explanation. In the Seneca language and in most Native American languages in the original form, certain words are holy or sacred to Native American People. These words are always capitalized in our written languages.

Until recently, few Indian writers were published and those who were, did not have a say as to how the manuscript was dealt with. HarperCollins has shown respect for my work, by printing it in our preferred form. For this kind consideration, I am deeply grateful.

In Native American culture, we see everything as being alive. Each living thing has a specific role as a teacher and family member. Everything on Earth, whether stone, tree, creature, cloud, sun, moon, or human being, is one of our relatives. We capitalize the names of each part of our Planetary Family because they represent the sacred living extensions of the Great Mystery who were placed here to help humankind evolve spiritually. We capitalize Traditions and Teachings because these words represent the equivalent of another faith's holy books.

In Tribal Traditions, we do not consider Grandfather Sun as a deity. We do not worship trees or rocks. We do, however, see the Eternal Flame of Love that the Great Mystery placed in all of Creation and we honor that spiritual essence. In the Seneca language, we call it *Orenda*. This is the spiritual essence or creative principle called the Eternal Flame of Love that is found inside of all life forms. There is only one Original Source and we call that Creative Source, the Great Mystery.

The Thunder Chief, *Hinoh* (Hĕnō), is capitalized because of his role in bringing life-giving waters, without which we could not survive. Grandfather Sun and Grandmother Moon are capitalized because we see them as living beings. The Great Mystery gave them their missions of dividing day from night, bringing light and warmth to our world, as well as pulling the tides of our oceans. In all cases, the words that are capitalized are given respect because of the sacred missions they carry and the extension of the Great Mystery's love that they represent. We teach that all life matters and we honor the Medicines of all life forms as sacred extensions of the Great Mystery's loving plan.

NIGHT WIND

The night wind came crying,
Knocking at my door,
Squeezing
Through the cracks
In the ancient adobe,
Bringing the spirits
Risen from the bones
Of the Clan Mothers.
I listened.
I heard.
The talking drums and chants
Were riding on the wind.
It was time.
I donned my shawl,
Stole into the night
To dance,
To celebrate,
For the buffalo had returned.

JAMIE SAMS
MARCH 26, 1992

THE MEDICINE WHEEL OF THE THIRTEEN CLAN MOTHERS
The Gifts, Talents, and Abilities of the Feminine Principle

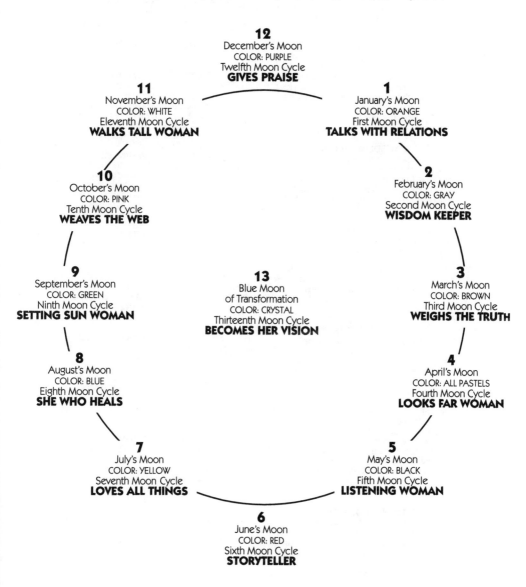

12
December's Moon
COLOR: PURPLE
Twelfth Moon Cycle
GIVES PRAISE

11
November's Moon
COLOR: WHITE
Eleventh Moon Cycle
WALKS TALL WOMAN

1
January's Moon
COLOR: ORANGE
First Moon Cycle
TALKS WITH RELATIONS

10
October's Moon
COLOR: PINK
Tenth Moon Cycle
WEAVES THE WEB

2
February's Moon
COLOR: GRAY
Second Moon Cycle
WISDOM KEEPER

9
September's Moon
COLOR: GREEN
Ninth Moon Cycle
SETTING SUN WOMAN

13
Blue Moon
of Transformation
COLOR: CRYSTAL
Thirteenth Moon Cycle
BECOMES HER VISION

3
March's Moon
COLOR: BROWN
Third Moon Cycle
WEIGHS THE TRUTH

8
August's Moon
COLOR: BLUE
Eighth Moon Cycle
SHE WHO HEALS

4
April's Moon
COLOR: ALL PASTELS
Fourth Moon Cycle
LOOKS FAR WOMAN

7
July's Moon
COLOR: YELLOW
Seventh Moon Cycle
LOVES ALL THINGS

5
May's Moon
COLOR: BLACK
Fifth Moon Cycle
LISTENING WOMAN

6
June's Moon
COLOR: RED
Sixth Moon Cycle
STORYTELLER

1 TALKS WITH RELATIONS

The Mother of Nature
Keeper of Rhythm, Weather, and the Seasons
Guardian of the Languages of the Trees, Stones,
and Creatures ▲ The Maker of Relatives /
Keeper of Earth's Needs/ Mother of the
Planetary Family
SHE TEACHES US . . .
How to understand unspoken the Languages
of Nature ▲ Kinship with all life forms and
how to enter the Sacred Spaces of others with
respect ▲ How to honor cycles, rhythms, and
changes of the seasons and weather ▲ How
to meld with the life force and rhythms in all
dimensions, learning the truths of each
How to LEARN THE TRUTH

2 WISDOM KEEPER

The Protectress of Sacred Traditions
The Keeper of the Stone Libraries and Earth
History ▲ The Guardian of "the Remembering"
and the Art of Memory ▲ The Mother
of Friendship, Planetary Unity, and Mutual
Understanding
SHE TEACHES US . . .
The Arts of Self-development and Expansion
How to access Planetary Memory, personal
recall, and ancient wisdom and knowledge
How to understand the wisdom that every life
form holds and its missions ▲ How to be
a friend and to restore friendship by honoring
the viewpoints of all life forms
How to HONOR THE TRUTH

3 WEIGHS THE TRUTH

The Keeper of Equality and the
Guardian of Justice
The Fair Judge of Divine Law and the Destroyer
of Deception ▲ The Mother of Truth and
Protectress of the Underdog ▲ The Mother
of Self-determination and Responsibility
SHE TEACHES US . . .
How to find the ability to respond and how to
be self-determined ▲ How to feed the
positive, not the negative, by using Divine Law
How to use equality with justice, being
accountable for our actions and words ▲
How to use personal integrity, ethics,
and values to find healing solutions
How to ACCEPT THE TRUTH

4 LOOKS FAR WOMAN

The Seer / Oracle / Dreamer / Prophet
Keeper of the Golden Door and the Crack in
the Universe ▲ The Mother of Visions, Dreams,
and Psychic Impressions ▲ The Guardian
of the Dreamtime and the Keeper of
Inner Potential
SHE TEACHES US . . .
How to understand our visions, dreams, feelings, and impressions ▲ How to enter the
Dreamtime, go into other realms, and
through the Crack in the Universe ▲ How to
properly use our psychic abilities and gifts
of prophecy for humanity ▲ How to use
spiritual boundaries, psychic self-defense,
and respect those boundaries in others ▲
How to use our inner potential to become
healed healers
How to SEE THE TRUTH

5 LISTENING WOMAN

The Mother of Tiyoweh, the Stillness,
and Inner Knowing
The Keeper of Discernment and Guardian of
Introspection ▲ The Interpreter of Messages
from the Spirit World ▲ The Counselor and
Advisor / the Keeper of Hearing
SHE TEACHES US . . .
How to enter the Stillness and hear our heart's
small, still voice within ▲ How to find and
understand the Inner Knowing we carry in our
Spiritual Essences ▲ How to listen to the
viewpoints and opinions of others and the
voices of the Ancestors ▲ How to understand
body language and unspoken thoughts / hearing with the heart
How to HEAR THE TRUTH

6 STORYTELLER

The Guardian of the Medicine Stories
The Keeper of Heyokah Medicine and Humor
The Teacher Who Teaches Without Pointing a
Finger ▲ The Preserver of Speaking from
Personal Experience and Truth
SHE TEACHES US . . .
How to teach through telling stories that con-
tain lessons ▲ How to balance the sacredness
with irreverence / using humor creatively ▲
How to speak from our experience without
judging others or being self-righteous ▲ How
to be a student in life as well as the teacher,
preserving the wisdom gained
How to SPEAK THE TRUTH

7 LOVES ALL THINGS

The Mother of Unconditional Love and
All Acts of Pleasure
The Keeper of Sexual Wisdom and
Self-respect ▲ The Sensual Lover / the Mother-
Nurturer / the Warmth of the Feminine ▲ The
Guardian of the Needs of the Family
SHE TEACHES US . . .
How to use respect, trust, and intimacy in all
relationships ▲ How to love all aspects of
our lives, lessons, sexuality, and physical
beings ▲ How to be a loving woman,
nurturing mother, sensual lover, and trusted
friend ▲ How to forgive ourselves and others,
developing acceptance and shunning
criticalness
How to LOVE THE TRUTH

8 SHE WHO HEALS

The Intuitive Healer / Midwife / Herbalist/
Keeper of the Healing Arts
The Singer of the Death Song and Keeper of
the Life and Death Mysteries ▲ The Guardian of
the Medicine Roots and Healing Herbs and
the Servant of Humankind ▲ The Mother of
Intuition / All Rites of Passage / Cycles of
Birth, Death, and Rebirth
SHE TEACHES US . . .
How to serve others with a happy heart, using
our healing abilities ▲ How to understand and
honor the life cycles of birth, death, and re-
birth ▲ How to believe in the miracles of life
through our connections to our Spiritual
Essences ▲ How to understand the Plant
Kingdom and the healing uses of all
parts of plants
How to SERVE THE TRUTH

9 SETTING SUN WOMAN

The Keeper of Tomorrow's Dreams and Goals
The Guardian of the Needs of the Next Seven
Generations ▲ The Mother of the Proper Use of
Will / Will to live / Will to survive / Will power
▲ The Keeper of Mother Earth's Resources and
the Guardian of Preservation
SHE TEACHES US . . .
How to preserve and use our resources without wasting anything ▲ How to prepare for
tomorrow by planning today / Making and
meeting goals ▲ How to show concern,
dependability, and compassion through the
ways we live ▲ How to properly use our wills,
using our intents to provide for future
generations
How to LIVE THE TRUTH

10 WEAVES THE WEB

The Mother of Creativity / the Muse /
the Artist / the Creatress
The Manifester of Dreams, Who Brings Visions
into Reality ▲ The Guardian of Life Force,
Who Teaches Women to Give Birth to Their
Dreams ▲ The Keeper of Survival Instinct and
the Mother of the Creative / Destructive
SHE TEACHES US . . .
How to use our desire to create and bring our
dreams into tangible forms ▲ How to tap
life force; using energy to build, change, or
manifest our needs ▲ How to manifest our
visions and give them life through our actions
and artistic talents ▲ How to create new
from old and how to destroy the limitations to
creativity
How to WORK WITH TRUTH

11 WALKS TALL WOMAN

The Guardian of Leadership and the
Keeper of New Paths
The Mother of Beauty and Grace and the
Keeper of Innovation and Persistence ▲ The
Role Model of Health, Physical Fitness, Stamina,
and Letting the Heart's Desire Take the Lead ▲
The Keeper of Personal Impeccability and the
Guardian of All Forms of Inner Strength
SHE TEACHES US . . .
How to be our personal best and still be
vulnerable and human ▲ How to keep our
bodies and minds flexible and in good health
through advancing and retreating ▲ How to
seek and find new paths to growing and
learning, leading through example ▲ How to
develop inner strength / How to attract and
release
How to WALK THE TRUTH

12 GIVES PRAISE

The Mother of All Acts of Thanksgiving and
Keeper of Abundance
The Guardian of Ceremony and Ritual / the
Keeper of Magic ▲ The Mother of Encouragement and the Guardian of Celebration ▲
The Wisdom Keeper of the Art of
Giving and Receiving
SHE TEACHES US . . .
How to return thanks for the abundance we
need before it arrives, making space to receive
it ▲ How to celebrate every victory in life
with joy—ours as well as the accomplishments
of others ▲ How to use right attitudes to
create magical changes in the Self ▲ How to
create abundance through praise,
giving, and receiving
How to be GRATEFUL FOR THE TRUTH

13 BECOMES HER VISION

The Guardian of Transformation and
Transmutation
The Keeper of the Emergence of Spirit into
Physical Form ▲ The Mother of Alchemical
Changes and Rites of Passage into Wholeness
▲ The Guardian of Personal History,
Becoming, and Myth
SHE TEACHES US . . .
How to become our visions and own our
wholeness ▲ How to release the old Self
and step into the realized dream ▲ How to
honor the process that brought us through the
changes and transformation ▲ How to mark
the Rite of Passage into Wholeness and
celebrate the Vision we have become
How to BE THE TRUTH

Introduction

The story of the Thirteen Original Clan Mothers was passed to me through the two Kiowa Grandmothers who were my teachers in the early 1970s. Cisi Laughing Crow and Berta Broken Bow gave me a legacy, upon which I was to build my life. As near as we could figure, Cisi was 120 and Berta was 127 years old when I was a young woman of 22. Both of these Grandmothers were born shortly after the Trail of Tears in the mid- to late 1840s when their families, along with many others who refused to be enrolled and to live on reservations, traveled south to the freedom afforded in the mountains of Mexico. In the past twenty years or so, the Bureau of Indian Affairs of the United States government has tried unsuccessfully to reclaim these families by offering to enroll them and bring them back to reservations in the United States.

The Traditions that were allowed to live because of the refusal of these people to give up their connection to the Earth Mother are the basis of these stories. I am truly grateful for the wisdom of this Woman's Medicine and for the strength it took those Native American families to carve out new lives in a strange land. Because of their persistence, these Ancient Teachings are still alive today.

I am very grateful that my first teacher in Mexico, Joaquin Muriel Espinosa, took me to Cisi and Berta, realizing that I needed to learn Woman's Medicine instead of insisting that I follow the male Warrior way. His insight has opened my life and path in ways I did not understand at the time. I honor the greatness of his humility and his desire for my best interests every time I see women following a male Medicine way, becoming confused and sometimes taken advantage of because they have not been trained to respect the feminine principle in themselves.

Many other female Elders have spoken to me of the Clan Mother stories of Woman's Medicine but were saddened that much of the history has been lost during the preceding generations. I have found great joy in being able to revive the history, which would otherwise be lost, and to share our Woman's Legacy with the world. As it was then, and shall be until we change ourselves from within, the Legacy of Woman and the Earth Mother is at risk. Our female and male roles in humankind stem from the Thirteen Original Clan Mothers who emerged as aspects of the Earth Mother and Grandmother Moon, because all things are born of the feminine.

To become a fully grown woman, which in Native American Tradition happens around the age of fifty-two, I was instructed to work on my personal journey by developing my personal talents and gifts, using the Thirteen Original Clan Mothers as role models. I was taught how to understand the Medicine of each of these ancient Grandmothers and how to relate to each as my teacher. Although

I have many years to go before attaining my majority, I have come to love these Clan Mothers who have been my Spirit Teachers and I trust how they speak to my heart. The Clan Mothers were the Spirit Teachers of the female Elders who were my physical teachers in Mexico and have taught many spiritual lessons to the Medicine Lodges of Women for centuries. The Thirteen Original Clan Mothers represent the aspects of what I have come to find most beautiful in woman and in the feminine principle.

These Clan Mothers have taught me to see the beauty in my sisters and brothers of all races and creeds. They have comforted me when I was weary or in pain and have taught me how to heal myself. Grandmothers Cisi and Berta passed the gift of knowing the Original Thirteen to me, and now it is time for me to pass this gift to the Sisterhood of Humankind. This is not to say that the men of our Earth will not benefit from these Grandmothers, for the men are also the children who were born of woman and have a female side. Now, however, it is necessary for all women to know the legacy they have been given in order to heal themselves before they reclaim their roles of healing and nurturing others. In this manner, the wounded feminine aspect in women will no longer need to be hostile, angry, separatist-oriented, or manipulative in order to cover old pain. From this vantage point, women can then present the healed role models they represent, leading others through example, instead of through male conquest or competition, allowing our world to reclaim a new point of balance between male and female.

It was many years after receiving these stories of the Thirteen Original Clan Mothers that I realized that these Teachings were common to many Tribes and that bits and pieces of this legacy had been passed from the Black Lodges or Women's Medicine Circles for hundreds of years. The Beloved Women of the Cherokee, the Clan Mothers of the Iroquois, the Grandmothers or Wisdom Keepers of the Kiowa, Choctaw, and many others have heard parts of this legacy. I began to more fully understand how the Dreaming Circles of Women kept this legacy alive through the sharing of their visions and dreams.

Although this legacy is not from one particular Tribe or Nation but rather came to me from my two Kiowa Grandmother teachers, it belongs to all of the Children of Earth. I was first told these stories in Spanish since I did not speak Kiowa. I was told by Cisi and Berta that as I learned the lessons of the thirteen steps of the Woman Wheel, more understanding would come to me. In truth, the spirits of the Thirteen Clan Mothers have guided and shaped my personal progress as a woman for the last eighteen years and continue to teach me as I grow.

I have added some references to one or two of the stories that have been told to me by other Tribal Grandmothers over the years, having discovered that all the histories of the Earth have been very similar. The overall view of the story of the Thirteen Original Clan Mothers has been shared in the Black Lodges of Women all across Native America, but the Indian language words that I have used in this text are of the Seneca language because it is most familiar to me.

I asked the Thirteen Original Clan Mothers how I could best present their Medicine Stories. I was told that the Seneca Medicine Wheel with the Pathways to Peace and the Twelve Cycles of Truth could give me a blueprint or structure that would allow people to see the whole picture. I discovered that truth is found in every Tradition, and sometimes, the blending of those truths brings further clarity. So I have taken the liberty of placing the stories of each of the Original Thirteen Clan Mothers on the Seneca Wheel to show the importance of truth and peace in Woman's Medicine among every Tribe and Medicine Lodge.

The *Twelve Cycles of Truth* in our Seneca Teachings have been assigned to months for simplicity's sake. I have added a thirteenth Cycle of Truth—*Be the Truth*—in order to complete the Medicine Wheel of the Thirteen Clan Mothers. Because of the difference between moon cycles and the calendar months used in our modern world, I have referred to a moon cycle falling in a certain month. As we all recognize, moon cycles fall in more than one month, but I have chosen to adapt the simplest way of conveying each Clan Mother's essence to our present way of thinking. I prefer that those who follow the lunar calendar look to those cycles and dates for the correct moon cycle that each Clan Mother holds.

The shell of Turtle shows us that the Earth Mother gave us the first lunar calendar. The circle framed in the center of the shell has thirteen parts and is representative of the Thirteen Original Clan Mothers and their guardianship of the thirteen lunar cycles. The Sacred Turtle is the embodiment of the Earth Mother and as Turtle's shell protects her body, the Thirteen Clan Mothers and their lunar cycles, depicted on her shell, protect the Mother Planet and all living things. It is through connecting to these rhythms and cycles that this story cannot be considered a traditional legend particular to one Tribe, but I can assure you that it is Woman's Medicine gathered from all of the places *the Remembering* was held by Grandmother Wisdom Keepers.

The basic story has been unchanged. The only additions on my part are the descriptive passages and some names of the Totems of each Clan Mother. Cisi and Berta described some animals with physical characteristics but did not use the modern names we know them by. The animals' modern names came to me via the Thirteen Original Clan Mother Spirits speaking to my heart and showing me their Medicines.

I have supposed that when an animal became extinct in one area of the world and was only physically recorded in petroglyphs, like the camels and mammoths depicted in North and South America, the oral legends of those creatures continued, but the actual animal became a mythical beast to those who had never seen one. I believe that this is one reason that Cisi and Berta would call the camel "the humpbacked four-legged of the desert who needs no water." Another example of this is found in the Paiute Tribe, which holds the Big-horned Sheep as sacred, even though most of these creatures were killed, like the buffalo, with the coming of European settlers. Petroglyphs of Buffalo and Big-horned Sheep still speak to our Tribes by carrying the sacredness of our Ancestors' Medicines.

The Thirteen Crystal Skulls are part of the original story and Tradition and were also spoken of by four other Grandmothers of different Tribes. To my knowledge, nothing has been written about the history of these Crystal Skulls based on Indian oral Tradition or history. I have put the information on the Crystal Skulls that I received from Cisi, Berta, and Joaquin's teachings in the part of this book's Conclusion, called "Entering the Council House of the Thirteen Original Clan Mothers."

For eighteen years my connection to the Medicine of the Thirteen Original Clan Mothers has grown inside me. Each new lesson presented by the Thirteen Clan Mothers has added to my understanding and has forged the trails to my personal growth. I have chosen to open these teachings and my personal vision in order to share the map of healing I have received. These Medicine Stories and Traditions are my Give-away to human beings everywhere, so that we may continue to dream the dream, and to dance the Dance of Creation, bringing inner peace and, therefore, world peace.

My Healing Quest Vision of the Thirteen Clan Mothers' Shields

The Medicine Shields of the Thirteen Original Clan Mothers are a part of the ancient legend that surrounds the life lessons and the gifts each Clan Mother gives to humankind. In the Americas, the lodges, palaces, and temples that carry emblems of Turtle are reminders to our modern world that the legacy of the Sisterhood is still alive. Whether carved in stone like the Turtle Temples of the Mayans in the Yucatan, or painted on frescoes in the Toltec and Inca places of worship, or carved in petroglyphs across North America, these emblems of Turtle represent our connections to the Earth Mother and her thirteen different aspects, the Original Clan Mothers.

Oral history tells us that each Clan Mother made a Medicine Shield that represented her talents, strengths, and abilities. These traits could be called on by anyone who chose to develop those same gifts within the *Orenda* of the Self. Orenda, in the Seneca language, is the Spiritual Essence that contains the Eternal Flame of Love where the Great Mystery lives inside all things. The Orenda houses the guiding light and the inner voice that teaches us our potential and our greatest capacity to love and to be loving.

In ancient times, to call on the spirit of one of the Thirteen Wisdom Keepers, a person needed to focus on the identity and abilities of that particular Clan Mother. To connect to the spiritual identity of a Clan Mother's Medicine, we need to Enter *Tiyoweh*. This discipline is the Indian way of calming the mind and sitting in the Stillness, to listen or receive. The ceremony of Entering Tiyoweh is always done alone, away from the bustle of daily activity. Then, the person uses focus to invite a particular Clan Mother into the fertile silence of her or his Sacred Space, allowing the purity of her or his heart to send the unspoken invitation. Since the Clan Mothers were never physically described, their Medicine Shields were often used as the focal point, held gently in the mind's eye. The person seeking the wisdom held by a Clan Mother was then able to allow the receptive side of her or his nature to be visited. This visitation was not from the Spirit World as with an Ancestor's Spirit but rather was an inward journey that rekindled the flame of the thirteen aspects of feminine transformation from within the female side of human nature.

Grandmothers Cisi and Berta were fine teachers and always told me that the Thirteen Clan Mothers never appear in the same manner or form to anyone seeking their counsel. By using the ability to appear as all of the faces of womankind, the Clan Mothers can touch and teach each individual in a unique way. This flexibility of form is important since equality is one of the foundations of their teachings. If they appeared in the same form to everyone, it would be too easy for us, as human beings with human limitations, to brag that some of the Clan Mothers' talents belonged only to a particular race or genetic line.

The Thirteen Original Clan Mothers came to walk the Earth in adult human bodies that did not age. I was never told why the Earth Mother chose to have her spiritual aspects embody the forms of fully grown women, but I suppose that the fragility and mortality rate of children during the Ice Age could have had some bearing on the decision. The ability of the Clan Mothers to possess bodies that did not become ill or age could be legend or could be fact—it is not for me to say. I was taught that when the Clan Mothers' missions were completed and they disappeared from the face of the Mother Planet, the Thirteen Crystal Skulls were left in their places. I have sought to understand their Medicines with my heart, not with my mind. I have been in the presence of a few of the Crystal Skulls and I know in the deepest part of my being that they hold the mind-set of the Earth Mother and the feminine principle on our planet.

In my personal eighteen-year process of living with the Clan Mothers' Medicines, I focused on developing my own abilities as I related to each one individually. For me, the culmination of this learning process has been in sharing these teachings through this book and in using my own intuition and creativity to make the Medicine Shields of the Thirteen Clan Mothers.

These Medicine Shields are actually tiny drums that represent the heartbeat of the Earth Mother. Coming out of each drum/shield is the mask each Clan Mother wears for me to see. Each Medicine Shield has three feathers at the bottom, representing the way I see the Spirit World and the Red Road of the Natural World come together in the heart of each living thing. Three feathers also represent the balance of our male and female sides with the center feather holding the Great Mystery's love.

In September of 1991 on the Autumn Equinox, I went on my seventeenth Vision Quest with the purpose of completing some personal healing. Since 17 is my personal sacred number, I knew that my intent to *reclaim the love* would be honored. I had worked hard, prepared well, and earned the right to move forward. The rust that had gathered on my spirit from too much work and overextending myself had left me depleted and the magic of life had faded a bit. I had committed my love, time, and energy to helping everyone else and letting myself always be last. Consequently, I contracted cholera in April of 1991 and then double pneumonia in May. My body screamed, "No more!" I knew then that it was time to start reclaiming the love by committing to taking my Moontimes and days of silence that had been forgotten in my flurry of activity.

The messages I received from the Thirteen Clan Mothers during my rest and preparation time made it clear that I would be given the vision of each of the Clan Mothers' Shields and that I was to share my entire process of reclaiming the love with others. In order for me to do that, I must explain the way I have been taught Woman's Medicine before I discuss the making of the Medicine Shields of the Thirteen Clan Mothers.

Traditionally, in ancient times, women did not go on Vision Quests. However, the women of the Black Lodges did go on Healing Quests that were a part of the function of the Medicine Lodges of Woman. This type of quest is different, however, from the Warrior Way of doing a Vision Quest because women hold their visions inside of themselves in the womb space. On the other hand, men, having demonstrative natures, must seek their visions through stopping all activity, food and water, or anything else that would keep their intellects in the way. To go beyond any limitation, the active male principle must be forced to be still. Through reaching the female side of his nature, the man is then ready to receive his vision.

My Elders taught me that women suffer enough during Moontime cycles, pregnancy, labor, and birth. There is no reason for a woman to suffer further, to prove her ability to compete with men, or to place the living treasure she represents in peril. Women would not place their children or the Earth Mother at risk, nor would they insist that a child should suffer to prove that he or she is worthy of love. The Great Mystery does not ask further suffering or pain of any woman. Womankind is already doing her part by giving birth to children, as well as giving birth to the dreams of humankind, holding the vision of abundance for the next seven generations.

For women in our White Buffalo Tradition, a Healing Quest supports and protects the role of women as Mothers of the Creative Force and takes a year of preparation. For the year prior to going on her Healing Quest, a woman takes a minimum of three days of silence a month, every month without fail. These three days of silence and retreat are during her Moontime but are not necessarily the full Moontime; her flow may last longer. If she is past her time of bleeding or has had a hysterectomy, she can choose to take this retreat time during full or new moon, depending on which moon cycle is most appropriate for her rhythms or feelings.

During the monthly retreats, the woman visualizes opening her womb to receive the fertilization of the Great Mystery's love, giving life force to the seeds of her dreams. She opens herself to receive the Earth Mother's strength and nurturing to replenish her body. She opens her heart and mind to receive visions and creativity. Everyone's experience is different, but these times of retreat are often as powerful as any Vision Quest. The only activities are of one's own making during the Moontime retreat. No reading, no television, no recorded music with words, and no artificial input should intrude. It is fine to sing, drum, dance, return thanks, create poetry, art, and such, but to fill oneself up with anything but self-expression, thanksgiving, and/or receiving can be counterproductive.

Food and water are very important during this time of cleansing and retreat. Eating lightly and naturally so that the body has no attention on nourishment is of utmost importance. Hunger and thirst can really block a woman's ability to cleanse the womb and stay focused so that her mind is also cleansed of unneeded chatter. The Moontime is a time to be filled, fed, replenished, and nurtured. It is not a time to create any kind of stress for the body, mind, heart, or spirit. We go into retreat to receive, and anything that keeps us from receiving is a waste of energy and time.

After a year of taking this special time for the Self, it is clear to a woman that she can trust herself, commit to herself, open her receptive side, and be comfortable being alone. The rewards of this preparation are in finding the joy of connection to her Orenda (Spiritual Essence), her body's rhythms, the Great Mystery, her Totems, the Spirit World, Grandmother Moon, and the Earth Mother.

The way I was taught to conduct a Vision Quest or Healing Quest for a woman, since women are naturally receptive, is to never disconnect a woman from the female elements of water and earth. Woman's role is to nurture, receive, and give birth. Therefore, on a Healing Quest, we must nurture all parts of the Self, receive the visions, and give birth to those dreams. A hut, lean-to, or single-person wigwam is made to sit on the outer edge of the woman's circle of stones that will represent her Sacred Space for three days. In the center of her circle is a smaller circle of stones that she will use for her campfire. This smaller circle for fire represents the Eternal Flame of Love the Great Mystery placed inside her Orenda. She will stay up every night and feed that fire, feeding the fire of Creation inside herself, and then sleep and dream during the day inside her hut.

A woman on a Healing Quest is given distilled or fresh natural spring water to keep the tides of her feelings high. The high tides of feelings bring forth the conductive nature of her intuition and a watery womb to receive her visions, giving them life. Just like a woman's fertility cycle, when the womb has gathered tissue and water in order to make the right environment for impregnation, the whole body is supported by the water she drinks. Lack of water in a woman's body can keep her disconnected from the natural female elements. Dehydration can also create hallucinations that do not serve the internal seeds of her visions, causing them to be dry-birthed. All seeds need water and earth to sprout, just as the seed dreams of humankind need these elements inside a woman's body in order to come to fullness.

Cisi and Berta also insisted on corn cakes being eaten during the three-day period. Two flat corn cakes, three to four inches around, were eaten per day because the corn kept the body heat stored during the night and represented the element of earth in the body. If corn cakes are not available, cornbread, corn nuts, or small, fat, homemade corn tortillas will do. The water and corn do not distract a woman from the intent of the Healing Quest but rather support her system so that all four of the Clan Chiefs of Air, Earth, Water, and Fire are inside her Sacred Space. In her circle of stones, to assist her in her quest, the woman breathes the air, feeds the fire, blesses her body with the water, sits on the earth and eats the corn to feed her fertility—the kernels or seeds of the future.

After three days and three nights of giving thanks, singing, dreaming, and receiving her vision, the questing woman completes her journey by opening the East stone of her circle, saying final prayers of thanksgiving, and returning to camp. It is an honor for those in camp who have prayed for her success to return to their friend's sacred circle and retrieve her bedroll, drum, and other items from her hut. The Medicine Person who held the energy for the woman who was on the hill now welcomes her by smudging or smoking her body with sage and cedar, while the others are traveling back to retrieve her things. The rest of the completion process of the Healing Quest is individual, depending upon the attending Medicine Person's preference, training, and Tradition.

The entire process of taking a monthly Moontime in silence for a year and completing a Healing Quest is a major commitment to the Self that enables any woman to receive from the Earth Mother the same quality of healing and nurturance she gives to others. Needless to say, this type of

Woman's Medicine teaches women to honor and love themselves and their roles in life, and how to reclaim the magic of the feminine. After one Warrior Way Vision Quest, followed by sixteen Healing Quests, I can attest to the validity of the nurturing Woman's Way and the changes it has made in my life. I feel it is time for women to stop suffering needlessly and to reconnect with the Earth Mother, who is the source of all acts of pleasure.

Due to the nurturing way I was treating myself during my preparation time, to receive the joyous visions of the Medicine Shields of the Thirteen Clan Mothers was effortless. I was reclaiming the love of living, of being human, of being a woman; and I was rediscovering the magic and the joy that life had never stopped offering me. The shift in my perceptions brought me back to the ways of the Grandmothers, allowing me to feel them again.

"We come from the bones of our Ancestors," Grandmother Cisi's voice said inside my memory. Then I remembered Grandmother Berta telling me that any animal's bones give us the structure we need in order to learn the Medicine that particular Creature offers us.

I use animal bones to make spirit dolls that are my own Kachina-like sculptures of the Ancestors who come to me in visions. In ancient times, the toys of Indian children were horses and buffalos made from bones left over from dinner. That was the reason I decided to revive this traditional art form. I realized that I could take my own artistic endeavor further by making bone dolls of the Thirteen Clan Mothers. It was comforting to think that I would have the Clan Mother dolls near me during my healing process. The Thirteen Clan Mothers came to me one by one, while I gave them a form by making a doll. As I walked the mountains and valleys in northern New Mexico, I found many of the bones I needed, and I traded for some of the others I would use. Each vertebra bone gave me the forms I needed for the masks of the Clan Mothers so that no labels could be placed on their identities. After six or seven dolls had been made, the spirits of the Clan Mothers instructed me to make bone masks and to affix each individual mask to the shields. Each shield represents the Medicine of a particular Clan Mother as she showed me the face or the mask holding the mystery of her Medicine. These Medicine Shields have become my personal map for reconnecting with the Thirteen Original Clan Mothers and the focal point I use to hear them with my heart. Every time Grandmother Nisa (Moon) came full, I was gifted with another piece of the beauty of Womankind that guided my personal journey in healing.

When we learn about the beauty inside us and complete the lessons of the feminine, we will have owned those Thirteen Shields of the Sisterhood as our personal protection and strengths. At that point, we will have become our visions. After completing these thirteen cycles of transformation, our next step will be to create new life maps for humanity, teaching how to use our creativity as healed healers, without wasting the Creative Force inside us on old limitations. We will not only be creating from the joy within us, but we will also be exercising our right to create effortlessly. When the human struggle, suffering, and pain are transmuted into the wholeness of planetary healing, the unified intentions and missions of the Thirteen Original Clan Mothers will be a reality.

The Beginning of the Legacy of Woman

After the destruction by fire that ended the First World of Love, the Thirteen Original Clan Mothers were created as the healing aspects of Grandmother Moon and Mother Earth, representing all that is beautiful in Woman. As parts of the Original Dream, the Thirteen Original Clan Mothers came to walk the Earth, forming the Sisterhood that bound all women together as dreaming counterparts in order to manifest the Original Dream of Wholeness on the physical plane. These seeds of inner peace were planted in the hearts of every human's female side. Today, this Original Dream of Wholeness is being nurtured in the hearts of women worldwide and is being birthed through their shared visions as they open their dreams to the light of love and build those dreams in tangible form.

During the making of this Legacy of Woman Dream, the feelings that would need to be shared among women in order for the Human Tribe to heal were sealed in the Earth Mother's tears. These tears were the Medicine that would transform the pain created when the First World of Love was destroyed by greed. The hearts of the Human Tribe had been wounded, and from those deep and jagged wounds, fear and separation were born. The Two-legged Children of Earth no longer trusted one another and feared that they had been abandoned by the Great Mystery and the Earth Mother. It was for this reason that the love and compassion of woman was born.

It was then necessary for the Earth Mother's feminine aspects to be taken from the Dreamtime and allowed to walk the physical plane in order for human women to take their places as nurturers and Mothers of the Creative Source. The wholeness of woman that had its roots in the Spirit World and was connected to Earth through the Dreaming Circles of women, was birthed into the physical world in order to fulfill the promise of healing. This healing of the Earth Tribe's wounds will continue until the Original Dream of the Earth Mother is restored in the tangible world. Perfect peace and harmony, respect for all living things, love without conditions, truth as the ultimate guideline, and equality for all are but a few of the parts of the Original Dream of Wholeness.

Healing begins to take place on our Mother Planet through this original Council of Women, creating the Legacy of Woman, and allowing all women to find their roles in the Children of Earth's healing process. It was through these Thirteen Clan Mothers that the truth of healing was discovered: *When we heal ourselves, others are healed. When we nurture our dreams, we give birth to the dreams of humankind. When we walk as loving aspects of the Earth Mother, we become the fertile, life-giving Mothers of the Creative Force. When we honor our bodies, our health, and our emotional needs, we make space for our dreams to come into being. When we speak the truth from our healed hearts, we allow life abundant to continue on our Mother Planet.*

Thirteen Moons pass every time the Earth Mother completes one rotation around Grandfather Sun. Thirteen is the number for transformation (although it has been maligned by many fear-ridden philosophies). As every year is completed, a cycle of transformation in the growth and healing process of the Earth Mother's children takes place. These cycles of healing and enlightenment bring forth the powerful aspects of the female principle every time Grandmother Moon comes full.

From the beginning, as life forms came to inhabit Earth, there was but one great land mass. This land mass was originally called Turtle Island because Turtle was, and is, the most fertile creature on Earth. The Two-leggeds were given the mission of preserving the fertility of the Earth Mother, who would provide for all of their needs if they honored the Sacred Space of all living things in the physical world. When this mission was neglected, with greed causing the humans of the First World to rape women and to pillage gold from the Earth Mother's body, the feminine was defiled. The Thirteen Original Clan Mothers had not yet manifested but were the Spirit World Guardians of preserving the fertility of the Earth Mother.

It was during that time of great pain that the Clan Mothers passed the legacy of honoring woman and preserving the Earth Mother to humankind. As these Clan Mothers came to walk the physical plane, they built a Council House in the shape of Turtle to be a reminder to all women that in order for the Children of Earth to survive, the women must honor themselves and their true Mother, the Earth. These Spirit Ancestors of womankind came to walk the Earth in order to understand their Medicines, developing the strengths they needed to meet and overcome the challenges of being human.

The Thirteen Original Clan Mothers decided to forge the bonds of Sisterhood that would unite all women as one. This Sisterhood was based on a bond of blood that marked the cycles of fertility in women. These cycles of fertility are based on moon cycles of twenty-eight days between bleeding. To this day, women who live, dream, or pray together will have their Moontimes or menstrual cycles at the same time so that their wombs are open simultaneously, allowing the dreams of humankind to be planted inside and then nurtured as a group.

Every woman has the potential to birth the dreams of the Sisterhood whether she can birth babies or not. The womb space is the balance point of gravity in the human form and the power place of the physical realm found inside the body. Women who have had their wombs removed can give birth to their dreams and projects without having the physical organs. The Sisterhood welcomes every woman who accepts the roles that will honor all women equally and who will contribute her talents to the whole. Little girls become women, and a part of this Sisterhood, with the flow of their first Moontime. These young women mark their Rites of Passage into the Sisterhood by becoming Mothers of the Creative Source. In other words, as young women are educated as to their roles in womankind, they also contribute to the birthing cycle of the dreams that will shape the future of our planet. The Sisterhood is responsible for teaching Woman's Medicine to young women before they mate and give birth to children of their own.

Through Rites of Passage and the education of young women, the Legacy of Woman is then firmly established in the hearts and minds of the future generations. Then, the old patterns of family and planetary dysfunction can be healed. These were the original aims of the Sisterhood brought to womankind during the Ice Age that followed the First World's destruction by fire. From that first Turtle Council House, all circles, wheels, societies, and clans of women were given birth. The Medicine Lodges, Dreaming Circles, Totem Clans, Sisterhoods, and all aspects of honoring the Mother Earth came from these Thirteen Original Clan Mothers. These Clan Mothers were not of any particular race, nor did they possess any particular belief systems that could limit womankind. They were the Mothers of all races and the healing aspects of womankind who then birthed the healing potential now present on our planet. The Knowing Systems that they represent are the Foundations of Truth that allow all women to be the Guardians of humankind's dream of achieving wholeness.

When these truths were passed to me in my twenty-second year of life by my two Kiowa Grandmother teachers, I asked Grandmother Cisi why the red race had been given the history of the Thirteen Original Clan Mothers. She told me that the red race was given the Guardianship of Earth Medicine and the mysteries of the Earth Mother. Grandmother Berta explained that many pieces to the puzzle of the Sisterhood were held by wise women of all races, but how those truths came into being had almost been forgotten as Traditions changed and eons passed. The blueprint of the first Medicine Wheel of the Sisterhood was passed orally through the Black Lodges, Moon Lodges, and Medicine Societies of Women in Native America in order for the Legacy of Woman to survive. The original wheel of the Clan Mothers was based on the thirteen moons of the year and had twelve positions around the wheel, with the thirteenth in the center.

The Medicine Wheel of the Thirteen Original Clan Mothers is based on the creed of "Life, Unity, and Equality for Eternity." Life is in the East of the Medicine Wheel where the day is born with the rising of Grandfather Sun. Life in the East teaches us that each new Sun announces a new beginning when life abundant is available, asking us to participate by using all our abilities. Unity is in the South where faith, trust, innocence, and humility begin the Earth Walk of physical life and where we all see as children. In the South, Unity teaches us that unless everyone wins, nobody wins. Equality is in the West of the Wheel where all our dreams are born and all our promises of tomorrow live. Equality in the West teaches us that our dreams will only manifest in the future if we honor the equality of every life form. Eternity sits in the North of the Medicine Wheel, the place of wisdom, and teaches us that all cycles of change and all lessons in truth will continue throughout time. Every lesson of growth brings us closer to wholeness, teaching that our spirits are forever a part of the Great Mystery throughout eternity.

Each one of the Thirteen Original Clan Mothers holds a part of the foundation of truth within the Legacy of Woman. These talents and abilities are woven from the hidden mysteries of Grandmother Moon and are reflected through

Mother Earth in the physical embodiment of woman. Each aspect of the Thirteen Clan Mothers carries a part of the truth and corresponds to the thirteen moons of the year. The first moon birthed the ability of *learning the truth* and applied that talent to all Relations, all worlds, and all mysteries. The second moon brought the gift of *honoring the truth* and applied that talent to self-development. The third moon birthed the ability of *accepting the truth* and tempered these lessons with taking on the additional responsibilities of justice, self-determination, and balance. The fourth moon created the ability of *seeing the truth* in all realms through dreams, impressions, and prophecy. The fifth moon gave birth to the talent of *hearing the truth* in the physical and spiritual realms, understanding harmony through listening. The sixth moon brought the talent of *speaking the truth* and with it came the lessons of faith and speaking with humility. The seventh moon birthed the ability of *loving the truth* in all things, therefore, loving all things for the truth held inside. The eighth moon spun the talent of *serving the truth* by being of service to others in all of the healing arts. The ninth moon brought the gift of *living the truth* into being, teaching dependability through living the truth today in order to preserve tomorrow for the unborn generations. The tenth moon gave birth to the talent of *working with the truth,* using all aspects of creativity in order to bring the truth into physical manifestation in a creative way. The eleventh moon wove the ability of *walking the truth,* showing how to lead through example, how to stand tall and "Walk Your Talk." The twelfth moon birthed the talent of *giving thanks for the truth,* being based in returning thanks for all that is received. Expressing our gratitude created all ceremonies connected to giving or receiving the abundant lessons and bounty of life. The thirteenth moon came forward to give the gift of *becoming the truth* that is the cycle of transformation; the regenerative nature of completion that then moves to a new beginning place, in order to enter the next cycle of growth. From these cycles of truth the Thirteen Original Clan Mothers forged the Sisterhood and the Legacy of Woman.

Every Clan Mother came to walk the Earth in order to honor the Legacy of Woman and to make the Sisterhood strong. As each one of these ancient Grandmothers took her place in the Sisterhood's Council, she was given a mission. Each was to develop all aspects of her gifts and abilities in order to discover her own Medicine. This Medicine would then be opened to all of womankind through the making of that Grandmother's Medicine Shield. Every woman who sought the truth of these Medicines could understand because each Medicine Shield spoke to her seeking heart through color, form, and concept. The mystery of each Clan Mother's Medicine Shield would have to be felt deep inside each female Two-legged before the Medicine could be called upon for strength during each woman's personal journey of self-discovery.

Like the Ancient Grandmothers who had walked those paths of discovering the Self before them, the ensuing generations of women were never given the answers but merely given a map, a guideline, allowing them to express their own uniqueness and to learn their own lessons in their own ways. The original Medicine Shields of these Grandmothers have long since vanished, but the Medicine still stands in unity. As the guiding light of the Sisterhood, the spirits of these ancient Grandmothers still sit in Council inside the inner Earth with the light of their Whirling Rainbow Dream coming forth as the Aurora Borealis.

The gifts that each moon and each Clan Mother represent contain the abilities of each, as well as how she learned the lessons of physical life, using her gifts in order to be in balance while meeting the challenges she faced. The lesson that still stands before the women of today is one that was understood in the hearts of every Ancient Grandmother. That lesson is exemplified through *"Life, Unity, and Equality for Eternity."* The Sisterhood was formed in order for womankind to be able to see all aspects of the Self as equal, all talents, male and female, as contributing to the whole. We are being asked to honor the gifts of womankind and to call on the strength of our sisters in order to discover ourselves. The circle will come full when every human can see the beauty within the Self, as well as in all others. The transmutation of competition, separateness, hierarchy, jealousy, envy, manipulation, control, selfishness, greed, dependency, old wounds, and self-righteousness must be accomplished before we will come to wholeness. These attitudes are the enemies of humankind and are found within the Shadow-self, rather than outside ourselves.

As more women take their roles in the modern world of corporations and business, they often find themselves losing touch with the feminine. This is almost expected since the corporate work force is dominated by men. The role models of the ancient Clan Mothers can assist these modern women in maintaining their sense of Self and enable them to become leaders through example rather than through competition, backstabbing, or conquest, but the challenge to accomplish these goals depends upon the strength of the Sisterhood. Women must support other women in a way that allows those who chose difficult paths to learn to call upon their sisters, maintaining the understanding of who they are and what they can become. In this manner we can also support the development of the female aspect in our male counterparts, and then pass the legacy of wholeness to all of our children.

The timelessness of the Medicine that each Original Clan Mother holds will apply to our world no matter how many generations pass, because these truths are eternal. We are the Mothers of the Creative Source. The fertile aspect of our nature comes through being able to nurture the truth found in our dreams and to feed our dreams, giving them life, and then to build dreams in the physical world. After those dreams are birthed, we then are able to share the skills necessary for others to do the same. This is a part of the timeless wisdom that our wisewoman Grandmothers of the Turtle Council House offer us.

In each aspect of the Original Thirteen, we find a part of the Legacy of Woman that will fuel the fire of our personal and unified creations. To share that wisdom with our peers and our daughters is to honor the ceremony called the Give-away. The Give-away teaches us to share the wisdom that was shared with us, passing it on so that for eternity, the Teachings, Traditions, and Medicine will live.

The Legacy of Woman and the bonds of the Sisterhood will never be broken even though some human beings insist on standing outside of that circle of love and compassion. Those who stand outside are not to be hated or shunned. They are the Children of Sorrow who have never known their true Mother. They are the product of families torn apart, riddled with dysfunction, unable to break the chains that bind them to their pain. Their hearts, which seem hardened, have never known the safety of transformative tears or loving arms and gentle healing. These children of pain and sorrow come from such profound woundedness that the only life they know is one in which they must defend their viewpoints because they fear that they are unworthy of love.

The Earth Mother loves the wounded, even as they rape her body and claim material possessions in order to assert their right to be. She offers them love and rest. Then, she offers to heal their eyes that cannot see, their ears that cannot hear, and their hearts that cannot understand. The Earth Mother's waters offer to wash away the memories of anguish and personal grief held in human hearts. We hear the voice of our Earth Mother through our female side. Women are being offered an opportunity to become living extensions of her love, by healing themselves. As healed humans, we may become pockets of safety where others, still wounded, can seek the tools to use in finding their own paths to healing themselves.

As women, we are continually writing the history of the Legacy of Woman. We cannot point a finger at men or each other without owning the pain of past generations who forgot how to give or teach human compassion. Our own family trees are filled with teaching situations and with tragic examples that may have blinded our own Ancestors to the value of truth as it is found in love. Now, the destiny of wholeness of the human race falls to the Sisterhood because all things are born of woman.

The Thirteen Original Clan Mothers are here to teach us how to become our visions and how to heal each other as well as our world. The women who have completed all the lessons on this Medicine Wheel of life have been called wisewomen, holy women, saints, or goddesses and have been given a thousand different names. These fully realized females have appeared in a million or more roles throughout time, and yet, every living woman is a potential role model for humanity. The women who have been recognized as role models were all born of the Earth Mother and learned the lessons of her thirteen aspects, the Thirteen Original Clan Mothers. They are all ancient Grandmothers who spun the webs of our present world to deliver their children from the dark night of the soul. They are eternal and they offer their strength to each of us, female and male, in the spirit of truth and in the name of love.

All of us, as Two-legged humans of Earth, are being asked to return to the Ancient Turtle Lodge that exists inside the shell of the Self in order to discover and rediscover the talents we hold. The fertility of our Earth Mother and All Our Relations depends upon how we heal ourselves. After we are healed, it is our task to create new maps of how to use the energy we used to waste on worry, hurry, pain, grief, and conflict, in order to create a unified world of peace. We discover the essence of our true Mother's desire for peace when the *h* is moved from the end of the word *Earth* to the front, spelling *Heart*.

TALKS
WITH
RELATIONS

Mother of Nature talks with her kin,
Stone Person,
   Wild Flower,
     and Wolf are her friend.

Weaving the rhythms of the seasons,
She rides the Winds of Change,
Opening her heart with gladness,
A shelter from hunger and pain.

Guardian of the needs of the Earth,
Making relatives great and small,
Mother, I see you in the dewdrop,
I hear you in the Eagle's call.

Clan Mother
of the
First Moon Cycle

TALKS WITH RELATIONS is the Clan Mother of the first moon cycle and is the Keeper of *learning the truth*. This Cycle of Truth falls in January and is understood through finding kinship with all life. Talks with Relations' teachers are the Allies of nature: the Four Winds of Change, the Cloud People, the Thunder-beings, the Creature-beings, the Tree People, the Plant People, the Little People (Devas/Fairies), the Stone People, the Clan Chiefs of Air, Earth, Water, and Fire, as well as all other life forms. These relatives of our Planetary Family are our teachers as well.

Through Talks with Relations, the Mother of Nature, we learn that we are all relatives in the Planetary Family. The Tree People, Creature-teachers, Stone People, Cloud People, and all other life forms are our Sisters and Brothers. Our Aunts and Uncles are the Four Clan Chiefs of Air, Earth, Water, and Fire. Our Mother is the Earth, our Father is the Sky, and our Grandparents are Grandmother Moon and Grandfather Sun.

To *learn the truth* we must open ourselves to the vast worlds within worlds that make up all of the Great Mystery's Creation. Talks with Relations is the aspect of the

Earth Mother that contains a seeking mind, a willingness to learn, and an understanding of the rhythm of each life form or area of Earth being viewed. This first Clan Mother's cycle is protected by the color orange. Orange carries the Medicine of kinship with all life because it is the color of the Eternal Flame of Love that the Great Mystery placed in the hearts of every part of Creation. Anytime we find a feather, a stone, a flower, or a shell with the color orange in it, the lessons that Sister or Brother can teach us are the lessons of making relatives, right relationship, respect and/or kinship with all life. Through learning the truths found in every life form within the Planetary Family, we are given the opportunity to see the similarities between us. We may find that a flower or a brook can be one of our greatest teachers. When we accept that everything in our world is alive, we are able to access the parts of ourselves that have become numbed or deadened, in order to heal and revive our own aliveness.

Kinship speaks of having right relationships with the Creative Force, with the Self, with our Orendas or Spiritual Essences, with our bodies, with family, friends, worthy opponents, and with All Our Relations in every part of the natural world. These relationships can become loving, productive situations that offer us opportunities to exchange ideas and to learn the lessons of sharing, with unity, in order to grow in truth.

Talks with Relations is the Mother of Nature who welcomes all life forms into her Clan. She sees the beauty of each and honors the talents each holds. She is the Keeper of

Rhythm who teaches us how to find our own rhythm, as well as teaching us how to respect the rhythms of all other things. In learning the truth, we find that every life form has a Sacred Space and a rhythm. To enter those Sacred Spaces, we are forced to learn the rhythm of the life form in question. If we learn that rhythm and ask permission, with respect, we can enter the world of those Sisters and Brothers without disturbing the natural order. Talks with Relations teaches us those rhythms and how wild creatures are willing to accept some humans without fear and why they run from others. The acceptance or nonacceptance results from the human's intent, willingness to respect the rhythm and Sacred Space of the Creature-being, and/or willingness to learn the truth about that life form.

Talks with Relations is the Guardian of Weather and the Seasons, who sees to the needs of Earth. This Clan Mother understands how to use the Clan Chiefs of Air, Earth, Water, and Fire to produce the climatic balance necessary for global survival. She teaches human beings that messing with the forces or the elements is a tricky thing because every action contains a reaction. The results may not be readily apparent but they will surely affect the balance of the Earth Mother's intricate ecology. If a human being is going to call for water as a Rain Medicine Person, that human had best be mindful of the amount the soil can handle and how the rain will affect the life forms downstream. Talks with Relations is the Keeper of these mysteries and always urges caution so that the rhythms of all life can be maintained.

ⵣ ⵣ

The Making
of Relatives

Talks with Relations marveled at the luxurious green of the Earth Mother's verdant forests and valleys. The Great Ice Mountains had not yet traveled this far south and so parts of the only land mass, Turtle Island, were given a short reprieve. Life was teeming amid the nooks and crannies of every inch of the sunlit soil and plant growth that spread before her. She stretched and raised her arms to the light of Grandfather Sun. "Oh, what a pleasure it is to be alive," she whispered to herself.

Just then a movement, sly and barely perceptible, caught her attention. She slowed her breathing and squatted low in the sprawling bunch of wild irises and tall cattails at her feet. Not daring to make a sound, she stilled herself until her body gave off no perceivable rhythm of its own. She did not want to disturb the natural occupants of this forest glen or to keep them from their daily routines, which would eventually bring them to the brook that ran far to the left of her hiding place. She was content to wait and see if the creature that had created the rustle in the undergrowth would show itself.

It was not long until a tiny red fox peeked around a boulder resting at the side of the bubbling brook and dashed for the water's edge, took a quick drink, and then dashed back to safety. After deciding it must be safe, despite the strange smell that wafted in and out with the changing breeze, the fox returned. As the little fellow drank from the stream, he occasionally peered around to assure himself that his senses were not fooling him into complacency. Suddenly, he was so startled that he became paralyzed when he found himself looking into the kindest eyes he had ever seen. The eyes seemed to be attached to a Two-legged human.

"Greetings, Brother Fox," Talks with Relations said gently. "I trust that I did not frighten you."

Fox forgot himself and replied spontaneously, "I thought I was the one who was so expert at the art of camouflage. You ought to be a fox, not a Two-legged! How did you do it? Oh, you don't have to answer that, I already know how because I do it myself."

"Well, Fox, it may surprise you to know that I have walked the Earth for many Suns and many Sleeps getting to know All My Relations," she replied. "It is important for me to learn the ways of all my children because I am the Mother of Nature and I must learn the needs of every Creature-teacher, Plant Person, and Stone Person so I may serve my family in a good way."

Fox looked at Talks with Relations and saw that she was telling the truth. He began to wonder how this beautiful and generous Two-legged had happened to choose him to talk to, but he was afraid to ask. He was taken aback when her laughter filled the glen with the most melodic, songlike sounds he had ever heard.

"Oh, Fox," she said, "you are a master of invisibility but you have forgotten to mask your thoughts. Don't you know that I have learned the truth held in the hearts and minds of every living thing? You need not be afraid to ask me anything. Grouse taught me how to enter the Sacred

Spiral of rhythm in order to be in harmony with all of my children. In learning the truth about rhythms, I have been able to weave our thoughts and hearts together so there is no separation between us."

At that moment, Centipede came scampering down a log that had fallen across the brook in the last big rain. Her multitude of legs, rhythmically moving in time, suddenly seemed to trip upon one another as she tried valiantly to come to a halt in front of Talks with Relations. Her long back arched as she pulled up to stop, with her rear end curling up like a dry autumn leaf before finally coming to a halt. "My goodness," she whispered, nearly out of breath, "I thought I heard your sweet laughter, Mother. I'd know that musical sound anywhere. What a pleasant surprise!"

Fox looked from Talks with Relations to Centipede, wondering how they knew one another. Then he decided he had better sit down on the boulder by the brook to sun himself. It appeared that this reunion would probably take a while and his feet had been getting cold while he was standing in the water, listening to Talks with Relations.

"Centipede, it has been many long moons since we have spoken. I must thank you for teaching me how to find my body's center and stride. The long walks to the sea and to the plains took many Suns and Sleeps, but my arms and legs were working in harmony. It felt wonderful with every body part working in rhythm with the other. We can both remember when I was a mess of arms and legs, tripping over every pebble and scraping every bush, can't we?" Talks with Relations said.

Centipede giggled and replied, "Well, I was so happy to see you again, I nearly rolled down this cottonwood log. I forget my own Medicine too, when I get excited. I keep on growing extra legs in my old age and I seem to have to teach the new ones how to work in unison with the old ones over and over again."

Talks with Relations smiled and said, "I certainly understand how you feel, Many Legs. Setting up the rhythms of the seasons has been a task as well. The Earth Mother is still changing her path in the Sky Nation and the Green Moons of new sprouting grasses are growing shorter while the White Moons seem to grow longer with more snow and ice."

Fox spoke up and asked, "Is that why so many of the Creature-beings of the steppes are coming our way?"

Centipede nodded and Talks with Relations agreed. "You see, Fox, the Earth Mother has given me the task of learning about the needs of all the Earth Tribe so I may assist her in finding the correct path across the Sky Nation. Eventually, there will be Four Seasons and Four Winds of Change that will assist all of us in finding the rhythms of harmony. The three White Moons will give us a time of rest when the Ice-beings will cover the soil. Then the Green Moons will begin, for three cycles, bringing new life to the Plant People. Then the three Yellow Moons will bring a time of ripening and fullness. The three Red Moons will follow bringing the time of harvest. The Thirteenth Moon is the Blue Moon when all the Children of Earth will find their natural ability to change or transform."

Centipede sighed and smiled, "It will be a good thing to see, Mother, and all of us will give thanks for the work you are doing in our behalf."

Talks with Relations was pleased that she was learning the truth of how to fulfill the needs of all the Children of

Earth and how to understand their Medicines. Life was good and each new day brought new lessons to be learned, new truths to explore, and new rhythms to add to the whole. She was discovering that she made every living thing her relative when she entered the flow of each relation's rhythms and listened to the inner drum of the heartbeats of each. Her mind flew to the memory of how she had first learned that lesson. As Grandfather Sun's light sent warm orange beams through her closed eyelids, she drifted to that long-ago moon and saw Swan drifting across a high mountain lake.

That Sun had been unusually warm. Talks with Relations had been speaking with Bluejay, who was teaching her the Medicines and talents of the Standing People. Bluejay was not talking *for* the trees, because the Standing People could talk. Talks with Relations had asked Bluejay to come with her because his Medicine was *using intuition to speak the truth* and in those early days, she was just learning how to use her human body to sense things. Being a little unsure of her new skills, she had asked Bluejay to accompany her. For hours the two friends had sat with the Standing People, listening as the Wind Chief gently blew through the limbs of the trees, bringing their voices to life.

Talks with Relations had first experienced human frustration during that Sun. She was able to understand the Medicine of Aspen, who was the seer and carried *observer* Medicine, because her own eyes could see the eye-like forms in Aspen's trunk every place a branch had disconnected and fallen. She was able to feel the Medicine of *inner peace* when she sat with her back against Pine's sturdy trunk. She felt Dogwood's Medicine of *balance* when she saw the blossoms, which formed the Four Directions of the Sacred Hoop. But her intuition was failing her in hearing and understanding the languages of these Standing Relations.

Bluejay was very kind to Talks with Relations and called for a break in the lessons. He could see that her frustration was bringing her close to tears.

"How very human she is, and yet, how very inhuman in her willingness to treat all things with such respect," he thought to himself. *"I am not afraid to speak the truth to her because she wants to learn the truth more than anything else. My intuition tells me she must also learn the importance of resting when her body's rhythms are being pushed beyond their capacity to endure. It must be difficult for her, no longer being in Spirit-form, and having to limit herself to the perceptions of a human body."*

Bluejay took Talks with Relations down the hill to the lake and had her sit in the sand along the shoreline, where clumps of soft green grass stood like hillocks meant for napping. While she settled her body on a grass-covered rise, Bluejay told her that he was going to bring a friend to join them and that she should relax while he was gone.

Talks with Relations was so caught up in her own frustration that she did not hear Bluejay's message, and so her mind kept on whirling with thoughts of how she could learn the language of the Standing People. She did not even notice when Bluejay returned with his friend Swan. Swan had glided effortlessly across the lake and was floating gently near the water's edge, patiently waiting. Bluejay finally started squawking a long tirade of admonitions in order to get Talks with Relations' attention.

"Well, Swan, we could push her in the lake to wash the frustration out of her head, or we could call Ostrich to dig a hole in this sand and then the three of us could bury her head," he screeched, but still there was no reaction from Talks with Relations. Bluejay saw Ostrich down the shoreline and called to her. While she was trotting over, he continued his mocking monologue.

"Well, here comes Ostrich. You will be shown how to bury your head in the sand instead of burying it in needless frustrations," Bluejay said loud enough for Ostrich to hear.

Talks with Relations was still lost in her turbulent thoughts when Ostrich sauntered up and shrugged her shoulders, wondering what to make of this young, troubled woman. Swan waited patiently while Ostrich and Bluejay decided to get the woman's attention. After a conspiratorial giggle, Bluejay went to rest on a nearby piece of driftwood and Ostrich bent over and tweaked Talks with Relations' nose. Talks with Relations was so startled she cried out—not from pain, for Ostrich had been very gentle, but from the shock of suddenly seeing two of the largest heavy-lidded eyes she had ever encountered at close range.

Everyone was laughing uncontrollably except for Talks with Relations, who was stunned into silence. Bluejay commented that she must have been tied up by her own machinations. Swan replied that Ostrich, whose Medicine was *how to interact with others through communication*, could lend a helping wing now that they had Talks with Relations' attention. Each comment brought further peels of laughter until the young woman saw the ridiculousness of the situation and joined in herself.

In between rolling waves of guffaws, Ostrich explained to Talks with Relations that when others were not communicating clearly or interacting in a way that would include everyone, Ostrich also had the tendency to bury her head. When even one person was excluded from a group, Ostrich would imitate those refusing to listen to everyone's ideas by burying her head in the sand until someone noticed. They usually noticed when they were confronted with Ostrich's rear end sticking in the air, giving them an idea of what she thought of them. In the present situation, Ostrich had not needed to bury her head because Talks with Relations had already buried her own head in her frustrations.

The laughter had definitely changed the mood of the afternoon, and Talks with Relations was now refreshed and paying attention instead of wondering why human limitations seemed to curtail her natural abilities to simply know. She was learning the lessons of how to use human senses, and the laughter felt good as it rolled from her lips and made her belly jiggle. Her heart was feeling the warmth of friendship and her skin was tingling from the spray of water Swan's wings had stirred up during the excitement. She decided that it was good to feel the pleasures of a body and was happy to be alive.

Ostrich and Bluejay watched silently as Swan spoke to Talks with Relations in a soothing way, gently sliding across the glassy water creating another change in mood. "You see how my body curves and my neck slopes and undulates when I move across the water?" she asked. Talks with Relations nodded in agreement as Swan continued. "The Water Spirits do not resist the movement of my body.

They assist me in feeling the flow of their currents as well as my own. Watch me glide into the lake and watch the gracefulness of my neck as I show you the Water Dance."

Talks with Relations' body began to be lulled into the same rhythm as Swan's as she watched. It seemed as if a small breeze had brought the lapping waves of the Water Spirits into Talks with Relations' body. She began to drift and dream as the hypnotic movements of Swan's body taught her to surrender.

When she awoke, she understood how she could learn the languages of all living things. She could do more than observe and feel from her own viewpoint. She had learned how to surrender her own Sacred Space and Sacred Point of View, how to ask permission and when it was received, how to enter the Sacred Space of another and to learn their language.

She was excited as she relayed her Dreamtime experiences to Swan, Bluejay, and Ostrich. In her dream, she had flown with Falcon and learned his Medicine of *hunting for solutions*. Falcon had taken her deep into the jungles of Turtle Island and had shown her the steaming green realms of dense vegetation. There, the Earth Mother mirrored the steam of smoky human confusions and frustrations. Together they had flown through the foggy confusion of the dream until they could see clearly. The snow sparkled on far-away peaks as they had viewed the mountaintops of the jungle below, where the great apes lived among the highlands of dense growth.

Gorilla was the wordless storyteller who acted out and mimicked until the observer could see the solution or point of the story for himself or herself. In the dream, Talks with

Relations had watched Gorilla while she circled with Falcon, seeing the mime from all directions. It was not long before Gorilla's strong Medicine of *communication and teaching through actions* had brought understanding to Talks with Relations' heart. His movements had been funny at first until she had understood how he was teaching the others of his Tribe to accomplish a given task. It was then that she noticed that he had imitated a younger ape in order to get its attention, then made a game of it so that the youngster would imitate him.

It became clear to her that Falcon had showed her a solution to her problem. She did not need to feel that she was separated from other life forms because she had a human body; she could imitate their habits and see how it felt to be them. Through imitating the actions of her Creature-teachers, she could then surrender to the feelings she had when becoming like them. It did not matter that her teachers were plants, stones, animals, clouds, or Wind and Water Spirits. Understanding their languages would take time, but the more like them she became and the more she could understand how and why their lives were similar to her own, the easier it would become for her to know how each species chose to communicate.

Ostrich, Bluejay, and Swan were very happy that Talks with Relations had broken through the frustration and into understanding. The foursome retreated to the soft shadows of the forest with Talks with Relations leading the way. She was determined to use her newly found understanding to communicate with her Tree Relations. Until now, she had merely observed and tried to listen as the Wind Spirits moved gently through the emerald and jade boughs of the

Standing People. Now it was time to practice and develop her communication skills.

With all her friends settled around her she began to announce her intention. "I have learned how to surrender to the rhythms of the Sacred Space around me, and now, with permission, I would like to become like a Standing Person," she said.

The ancient Pine Tree Person dropped a pinecone that rolled to her feet as an offering of friendship. She accepted the Give-away with pleasure. Talks with Relations knelt and dug a hole in the soft soil and needles, burying her feet up to the ankles. Then she stood tall and proud and lifted her arms like branches to the rays of sunlight filtering through the dense green of the forest. Silence enveloped all of those gathered as she closed her eyes and became a human tree. It was then that she heard the voices of the Standing People come from their wooden hearts and speak to hers.

"Our language is *heard through the heart*, not the ears. We speak of all we see in a place, for we are the silent observers of the Earth. Our roots draw deeply from the well of love found in our Earth Mother's soil and our limbs reach higher every day to seek the light of Grandfather Sun. We are the living balance between Mother Earth and Father Sky, female and male, receiving and giving. Of all life forms, we are the closest in makeup to the human beings because we show them how to honor the balance of heaven and earth within themselves. We show them, through example, how to be the silent observers of life, how to stand tall, and how to give and receive."

Though nothing stirred in the forest, no breeze blew through the boughs of these Tree People, Talks with Relations heard the voice of ancient Redwood. It pointed out to her that with her arms arched upward, her body created two circles. The circles formed a figure eight. The upper circle met the lower circle in her heart, with the upper one encircling the Sky Nation and the lower one connecting her to the center of the Earth Mother. It was as if she were standing on top of one circle and holding the other one above her, using her body as the cross-connection between the two.

"These are the two Medicine Wheels of life," Redwood said. "The human beings, like the Tree People, have the ability to be the balance between the earth and sky. When the Two-leggeds reach for the most they can be, the Sky Wheel brings the messages of the Spirit World to them through their human hearts. The Earth Wheel allows the plants, stones, animals, and elements of nature to be the Earth Mother's teachers and interpreters of those spiritual messages. Human beings feel and understand the messages that the Great Mystery sends by observing the actions of the teachers that these planetary counterparts represent. Meeting in the heart, both Medicine Wheels show that heaven and earth, the spiritual and the tangible, are equal and are one. You see, Talks with Relations, the only true limitation of being human comes when the heart is closed. When the heart is open, all of Creation can be accessed and understood. You have become that balance now and it will serve you well."

The memory of that time and the lessons learned filled the Mother of Nature's body with a warm feeling, gently bringing her back to the moment. The orange glow that had reflected Grandfather Sun's light on her eyelids had changed to a deeper salmon color, signaling that this Sun was nearly at its end. She could hear the trout jumping for flies in the melodious brook. She could smell the first wafts of night-blooming jasmine and she tasted the moisture that was collecting on the stones at the water's edge. Inside her mind, pictures of these changes were dancing with hundreds of other perceptions. She could hear the faint snore of Fox, who had fallen asleep, and the scratching of Centipede's many legs against the cottonwood trunk.

"Yes," she thought, "I have learned well. Truth speaks to me now, in hundreds of ways, through all the senses of body, heart, mind, and spirit. I can feel the rhythms of the animals' feet through the soil as they approach the water for their evening drink. I can feel the light of stars even before they poke holes in the purple blanket of the early evening sky. Life sends me flutters of feelings deep in my belly with every rhythmic change around me and I feel those changes inside of me, for I am an extension of it all."

With her eyes still closed, Talks with Relations gently and quietly reached for the Stone Person she had hanging around her neck by a thong. The rock had a natural hole in it that had been created by the constant dripping of water over hundreds of passing Suns and Sleeps. The Stone Person's name was *Oneo* or Song. This special Medicine Stone still sang to her and recorded all her heart felt and all she experienced, reminding her of the history she was creating by being alive. The natural hole in Oneo's body was a sign that the rock was a protection stone. Because the hole was created by water, the Stone helped Talks with Relations to stay in touch with her feelings and to be aware if danger was present. Talks with Relations' body was made of the same minerals as the rock and therefore helped her stay in tune with the heartbeat of the Earth Mother.

The Stone People, being the libraries of Earth history, had been very helpful when she had learned their language. Through her journeys she had come to understand the markings on their bodies in much the same manner she had learned the languages of the Standing People. Through the Stone People, she had come to understand that all forces in nature have cycles and that these cycles are present in the growth of all things. She had been able to review the history of all that had happened on Earth and she was shown the natural evolution of all life forms as the stones had recorded it.

The Shell Cousins from the seas had taught her to listen to the rhythms of the tides and to her own body's cycles. The Cloud People had shown her the faces and forms of all things in the natural world. When one of the various Children of Earth was in danger, the face of the one who called for help would take form in the clouds. The Clan Chiefs of Air, Earth, Water, and Fire had blended and separated in her presence to teach her the spontaneous forces of creation found in nature. With this Knowing System firmly rooted in her heart, Talks with Relations was able to command the weather, bringing life-giving rains or new lava flows to maintain the balance needed on the planet.

"*Learning the truth is a continuous adventure and brings with it a constant source of fulfillment,*" she mused. "*I have been blessed with the hunger to learn, the joy of discovery, and the desire to serve my kin. I have learned the languages of every part of the Earth Tribe. Each day, I discover the caring and compassion that allows me to learn more. Life creates more life, and so I will continue to celebrate the lessons I have learned, in order to share them with all my children forever."*

Talks with Relations opened her eyes and saw that Day had quietly passed the Pipe to Night. The Starry Medicine Bowl of the night sky had produced a quarter moon and the nocturnal animals were stirring. Centipede and Fox had faithfully waited for Talks with Relations to return from Entering the Silence, not moving an inch from their former places. Grandmother Moon's blue-silver light played on the crests of the water that flowed across the rounded stones of the creek bed while the water spirits murmured their evening traveling song.

When Talks with Relations spoke to her friends, she whispered, "I am pleased that you waited for me, children. During my silence, I remembered how much I have learned about the truths present in every part of Creation and how much more I can learn as our world continues to evolve."

Centipede curled herself into a ball and rolled down the log to be closer to Talks with Relations. "Mother, maybe your gathering wisdom is similar to my growing legs," she whispered. "I may be growing extra legs because I am becoming older and wiser. I suppose that each of our Relations has some way to measure the distance they travel on this Good Red Road of life."

Talks with Relations replied, "Yes, Many Legs, we all have our unique ways to gather wisdom, but the way we share our languages and our understanding is the key to our common growth as a Planetary Family."

Fox laughed and wiggled his whiskers before he interjected, "I understand that key, Mother. Fox is the protector of the Planetary Family because no one can learn the Medicines and languages of nature if they can't see what is right in front of them. All wisdom is camouflaged, like me, unless people believe in the invisible world, which only becomes visible when they open their hearts to understanding and learning the truth."

The Clan Mother of the first moon cycle smiled. Being the Mother of Nature meant that she would follow whatever came to her naturally. At this moment, her heart was so full that it was natural to allow the love in her heart to spill over into the world, allowing all of the Children of Earth to know they were not forgotten and that their needs would always be taken care of.

Talks with Relations had learned the truth about being in a human body and now it was up to her human children to discover it for themselves. When each individual Twolegged opened his or her heart to learning the truths of the Planetary Family, she would be there to teach them. When the Human Tribe opened their hearts with respect for all living things, she would be there to nurture them into respecting themselves and each other in kind. When the cycles and seasons brought pain to the human race, she would be the healing unguent found in the natural world around them.

The intangible world of spirit, found in the tangible world, was awaiting discovery. Her human children would be the last to learn these truths. She found joy in the knowledge that human arrogance would one day melt away. That Sun would rise when the cycles and seasons brought those who were willing to give up their pain, home to their hearts.

"Yes, life is good," she whispered into the star-filled night, just loud enough for those with open hearts to hear.

WISDOM KEEPER

Oh keeper of ancient knowing,
Whisper your wisdom to me,
That I may always remember
Life's sacred mystery.

The stories of the Grandmothers,
Brave deeds, great and small,
The progress of the Faithful,
Who answer our Mother 's call.

The cycles and the seasons
That mark our every change,
The rebirth of our visions,
The spirit we have reclaimed.

Here truth is the victor
Of the war that dwells within,
Bringing every human heart
To celebration in the end.

Clan Mother
of the
Second Moon Cycle

WISDOM KEEPER is the Clan Mother of the Second
Moon Cycle and is the Historian of all Earth Records. She
is the Keeper of the Stone Libraries, the Protectress of Sacred Traditions, and the Guardian of the Remembering
and/or planetary memory. She teaches us how to develop
the Self through *honoring the truth* in all things. February is
her month and gray is the color that connects us to Wisdom
Keeper's moon cycle and her Medicine.

Wisdom Keeper reminds us that all history is kept in
the libraries of the Stone People and that to access that history, we must hear the voices of the Rock Tribe who record
the Remembering for the Earth Mother. To honor the truth
of all that has been, we must tap more than human, cultural
traditions or stories. The history of all that has happened on
our planet is forged in stone so that the body of the Earth
Mother can offer tangible records to those willing to learn
the Language of the Stone People who hold her memory.

Wisdom Keeper also *honors the truth* as it is seen from
each person's Sacred Point of View because all individuals
experience life's events in a different manner. In her wisdom, this Clan Mother understands that there is truth in
every life form's journey. In our arrogance, human beings

▲▲

are the only part of the Earth Tribe to insist that their particular religion, philosophy, or Tradition holds the only truth or path to wisdom and understanding. For this reason, she is also the Mother of Friendship, showing us how to be a friend and how to have friends.

Wisdom Keeper teaches us that knowledge of the expansive view of the Planetary Family is the key to Self-development. She shows us how to honor the truth in every race, creed, culture, life form, Tribe, and Tradition through seeing the similarities in all. The color gray is nonthreatening or neutral and represents friendship. Through the color gray, Wisdom Keeper teaches us how to interact with others, always honoring their Sacred Spaces and Sacred Points of View, without feeling as if we must defend our own viewpoints. As we honor our own truths, we develop our sense of Self and allow others to do the same. Every new understanding of the truths that others carry adds to our personal wisdom and knowledge, creating further development of right relationship to All Our Relations as it is experienced within the Self.

We can call on the Medicine of Wisdom Keeper to restore friendship, to help us to honor the truth in all things, to tap the history of Earth, to assist us in developing the Self, or to increase our memory potential. Some people born during the second moon cycle/month suffer from short-term memory loss because they have not tapped the gifts or talents they were given through their natural connection to Wisdom Keeper. Her Medicine can help the Children of Earth to heal that loss of memory.

By assisting us in reclaiming the gifts of personal recall, Wisdom Keeper shows us how to return to a memory and be able to use any feeling, wisdom, tactile sense, spoken word, or idea in the memory for our growth. This Clan Mother teaches us that anything we have ever experienced can be pulled from our memory banks, at any time in the future, to support or assist us in our life lessons. Wisdom Keeper pays attention to detail and shows us how those remembered details can be used as guidelines to hone our awareness skills into the Medicine of being totally present in any given moment. When we are paying attention to the details of the here and now, we are not lost in worrying about the past or the future. From the talent of being fully present, we are able to learn the Art of Expansion through Self-development.

▲ ▲
Following the Wisdom Trail

Wisdom Keeper was walking through the dazzling, sunlit mesas, watching Grandfather Sun's light dance across the snow-covered monoliths that surrounded the enchanting desert that lay before her. The Earth Mother wore a patchwork blanket of red with oranges and yellows, created by the giant rock formations. The deep shadows, outlined by the canyons and arroyos, wove pale blues and lilacs into the whiteness of the Ice-beings, blending with the greens of Juniper, Cedar, and Pine. The Tree People of the high desert were content to be the standing connections between the Earth Mother's many-colored cloak and the brilliant blue canopy of Father Sky. Wisdom Keeper was feeling that same connection of serenity during her morning trek as she followed the trail that led to a series of secret caves. These openings in Mother Earth's body were nestled in the recesses of one of the desert's sacred places called the Canyon of Time.

When she reached the fork in the trail that would take her up the rising path to the caves, she spied a flat Stone Person sitting in the frosty purple shadows of a towering tree giant named Ponderosa Pine. Wisdom Keeper moved closer to inspect the surface of the tablelike stone that had caught her attention. She rounded the trunk of Ponderosa and patted his enormous form in greeting, carefully stepping across an icy mound of melted and refrozen snow. On the Rock Person's surface was a perfectly frozen snowflake. The intricate pattern of the snowflake seemed to float above the blue-gray of the stone's surface.

Wisdom Keeper bent closer, being careful that the warmth of her breath did not melt the frozen web suspended in the early morning frost. "Oh Snowflake," she whispered to herself, "what a genuinely rare gift of winter you are."

The snowflake surprised Wisdom Keeper by answering her whispered thoughts, causing the Clan Mother's heartbeat to quicken. "You may call me Ice Web, Mother. When Grandmother Spider wove the web of Creation, she created Snowflakes to represent the webs of dreams that would travel from the Dreamtime to Earth, becoming living, physical experiences."

Wisdom Keeper had never encountered a talking snowflake before. In her curiosity, the Keeper of Earth's

Records felt impelled to ask Ice Web further questions in order to fully understand the roles that the Great Mystery gave the Ice-beings of winter. "What an extraordinary mission you have, Ice Web. Will you tell me more about how your Medicine assists our Planetary Family so that I may hold that understanding for the Two-leggeds?"

"Of course I will, Wisdom Keeper. I was preserved in frost so that my passage through your life would not go unnoticed. You must record the purpose of my role in nature so that every Child of Earth will know how her or his dreams and visions aid the spiritual growth of the whole Planetary Family.

"Mother, every one of the Children of Earth has feelings and dreams according to his or her place in the scheme and balance of nature. When combined, all of those dreams and feelings make up the needs of the Children of Earth. The snowflakes are the messengers of those needs because our bodies hold the patterns of each individual dream. When Grandfather Sun's warmth melts our bodies into water, the feelings of the collected dreams are poured into the Earth Mother's soil, giving her the understanding of her children's deepest desires."

Wisdom Keeper was impressed with Ice Web's understanding and the simplicity of the Great Mystery's plan to keep the Earth Mother advised of the needs of her children, which brought up another question. "Since the streams and rivers of the Earth Mother's body are the vessels that carry her feelings in the form of water, are you saying that her feelings are made up of the combined desires and emotions of all her children?"

"Exactly! Now you understand why the Snowflake Tribe's patterns are so important. Due to life's changing experiences, all of the Children of Earth have new feelings daily. What each Child of Earth wants in his or her life is translated into an individual Snowflake Medicine Wheel that reaches the Earth Mother's heart upon melting," Ice Web replied. "During the Green and Yellow Moons, those same feelings come as Raindrops because the seasons are ripe for the growing of dreams. We are the messengers of the White Moons because those dreams must be held in crystallized form until the season of rest and reflection is over. Then, during the Warming Moons, our frozen patterns of dreams and visions may thaw, being released into the Earth.

"Each snowflake holds the web of life's lessons as it is woven by one of the Children of Earth. Every member of our Clan reflects an individual view of the Web of Life as it is dreamed by someone who lives on our planet. Each life form in Creation is a part of the whole, but individually, each one sees life from her or his Sacred Point of View. The dreams that teach each individual to live life, through making choices, comes from the Sacred Space and Point of View of that person."

Wisdom Keeper smiled because she caught a glimmer of understanding about her own choice to make the trek to the secret caves on this frosty morning. The Clan Mother felt that her encounter with Ice Web was not by chance. She decided to ask a question that could affirm her inner knowing.

"Ice Web, you hold the patterns of my dreams and my heart's greatest desire, don't you?"

Ice Web answered Wisdom Keeper by complimenting the Clan Mother on her astuteness and then allowed her to continue sharing her thoughts.

"To fulfill my mission of being the Guardian of Earth History, I must travel up this pathway and visit the secret caves far above us in the Canyon of Time. Inside those caves the Earth Mother will take me on a journey that will complete my understanding. I will be challenged and will go through the final Rite of Passage of my training. I must be willing to test the talents I have worked hard to develop. If the Earth Mother feels I have successfully completed my lessons and have the skills to be a Wisewoman, I will take my role as the Guardian of Sacred Traditions by honoring the truths I hold. After this Rite of Passage, I will hold the Medicine of the Remembering of our Planetary Family. The Medicine of Planetary Memory is the honored truths found in the Sacred Points of View of every living thing on the Earth Mother throughout all worlds of time."

Wisdom Keeper understood that Ice Web's designs were mirroring the dreams, aspirations, and collected Knowing Systems that the Clan Mother had accumulated during the earlier parts of her Earth Walk. Now the time was approaching to open her vision and understanding to others, sharing her wisdom with the Children of Earth. Ice Web was set in her path to remind the Clan Mother of the circles within circles of life forms who would depend upon the wisdom she carried and how well she had developed her skills.

Ice Web held Wisdom Keeper's innermost desires in frozen patterns, so it was not surprising that the snowflake could tap the Clan Mother's thoughts. Ice Web felt Wisdom

Keeper's anticipation and replied to the Clan Mother's unspoken words.

"Mother, the steps you are taking that will complete your training with this Rite of Passage are very important. My frozen patterns hold your former dreams, and will melt, returning to the Earth Mother. You might want to release those same patterns within yourself before you enter the caves above the Canyon of Time. In reviewing the steps and lessons that brought you to this point in your path, you will free yourself to face the future. The Remembering carries a Medicine of its own that will allow you to access all of the places, insights, and situations that have influenced the woman you have become. In recalling all that has gone before, you may then place yourself in the here and now, owning the reality of all that you are."

Wisdom Keeper agreed with Ice Web and decided to take the time she needed to prepare herself before entering the caves. The Remembering represented more than holding the Earth Mother's history. It was a vital part of her own Medicine that could allow her to pass into her next set of lessons without being caught in past accomplishments or old patterns. Wisdom Keeper could see the value of allowing herself to savor each former step of her own passage, feeling and recording the sense of well-being each had bestowed. Then she would be able to move forward, claiming her right to the wholeness she had achieved.

The Clan Mother came from her thoughts, looked to the sky, and then spoke, "Grandfather Sun's rays are touching the patterns in your body. The Earth Mother will soon gather my innermost feelings to her heart as your frozen form changes to liquid and sinks into the heart of this

Stone Person and then to the soil below. Ice Web, I want to thank you for being my teacher and sharing your talents with me. I will leave you here and continue my trek, but know that my heart will always sing your praises with thanksgiving."

Wisdom Keeper began walking up the trail to the Canyon of Time, bidding Ice Web farewell. Soon she was traversing the craggy path surrounded by jutting boulders of rust and amber. Here and there, she greeted the Standing People who grew on the sheer cliffs of the Canyon of Time. It was past midday when she reached what appeared to be the end of the boxed canyon and rounded an outcropping of rocks that most people would not have noticed. There behind the rocks, a chalky cliffside framed the entrance to the secret caves. Wisdom Keeper offered a pinch of corn pollen to the soil at her feet, reverently asking the Spirit Keepers of the Sacred Caves if she could enter the area. She was given a sign that her presence was welcomed when a gentle breeze caressed her face.

She stood silently on the shelflike floor of the upper canyon looking toward the entrance to the series of seven caverns, then approached the opening. The seven caves represented the Seven Sacred Directions of East, South, West, North, Above, Below, and Within. Wisdom Keeper turned and knelt before the entrance to the caves and bent, kissing the Earth. She straightened her spine, remaining on her knees, and raised her arms to Father Sky, singing a song of thanksgiving for the opportunity she was being given to complete her final Rite of Passage. When she had finished her song of gratitude, she sat in silence in front of the entrance to the first cave.

■■■

Wisdom Keeper began her process of remembering by recalling her first experiences of taking a human body and followed each memory to completion. The Creature-teachers who had aided her during those Suns and Sleeps floated into her mind, allowing her to review the lessons each had imparted.

Pig had taught her the Medicine of *using intellect and reasoning ability*. Mouse had taught her *how to pay attention to detail through scrutiny and how to keep herself from becoming overwhelmed by completing only one task at a time*. Chipmunk had given her the understanding of his Medicine of *respecting the smallest parts of nature through interrelationship and equality*. Chipmunk had taught her how to see parallels in the natural world and in people's ideas, showing her the validity in all points of view. Turtle Dove had taught her how to *nurture the dreams of peace* and how to find that peace inside herself. Each of her Totems had offered her the wisdom they carried in order to teach her how to make the most of her abilities. She silently thanked each one and continued recounting the lessons she had learned.

When Wisdom Keeper had finished taking in all of the goodness of each event in her life and had released the past with joy, she called to the Earth Mother, asking permission to enter the first cave. A gentle wind carried a dry leaf from the tree above into the cave's entrance, beckoning her to enter. Wisdom Keeper grabbed a handful of soil, touched that hand to her heart, then tossed the soil over her shoulder to signal that she was leaving the outer world and her earlier earthly experiences behind her. Taking a breath to fill herself with life manna and to find her inner balance, she silently slipped into the cave.

The Earth Mother's voice immediately filled her ears. "Wisdom Keeper, you are now in the cave of the East. The seeking, male side of your nature that searches for enlightenment and clarity lives here and in your human body. Through these lessons of the East you have gained the ability to be the Protectress of Sacred Traditions. What have you learned?"

"Mother, I have sought truth and have learned that all living things create new Traditions when they honor the sacredness found in the individual as well as in the whole of Creation. I have experienced the clarity of their knowing when they desire understanding as much as they desire the breath of life. Now I know that all Sacred Traditions are created when the individual seeks and finds a way to reconnect to the Great Mystery's love. I understand that my role of protecting these Sacred Traditions comes through teaching our human children how to allow every individual to rediscover her or his connection to the Great Mystery for herself or himself. I must protect the Great Mystery's Sacred Tradition of free will by showing humankind that every individual has the right to reconnect to the Maker in her or his own way. The Orenda of each human should be the guiding light for that person. The truth of illumination is found through honoring every person's right to have personal truths, following the voice of his or her own Spiritual Essence. I have learned that the Sacred Traditions may be preserved by ignoring the rigid human rules that evolve when one human wants others to follow the leader instead of the voice of truth inside her or his own Orenda."

The passageway from the first to the second cave was illuminated, indicating that Wisdom Keeper could continue.

As she stepped into the second cave, the Earth Mother's voice said, "Daughter of my spirit, this is the cave of the South. What have you learned that you could trust?"

Wisdom Keeper replied, "I have learned to trust the truth inside me, Mother. I have learned to trust the innocence of the young and the young at heart. I have learned that all wisdom, teachings, and history come from the truth presented in the Sacred Points of View of all life in the natural world.

"I have discovered that in innocence and humility there is a great power that transcends self-importance, which is the mask that humans use to hide their insecurities and their pain. I have found that faith and trust are the gifts of forgiveness and that through forgiveness the Human Tribe can reclaim the wisdom of childlike wonder."

The entrance to the third cave was illuminated and Wisdom Keeper stepped forward once again. As she approached the center of the third cave, the Earth Mother's voice asked, "What have you discovered about the West Cave's lessons as they apply to being human, my child?"

Wisdom Keeper answered by saying, "I have realized that the future depends upon the feminine principle in all things because all things are born of woman. I have come to know the beauty of nurturing and compassion through giving birth to those qualities within myself. I have learned how to hold the seeds of knowing in my womb until they are ready to be shared. I have honored my female body by only sharing sexual pleasure with those who would treat my total being with utmost respect. I have learned that the place of all tomorrows, the West, is a place of darkness where there is no fear of the unknown because it is like returning to the Medicine Bowl—womb of the Mother of all things. I have found the strength of retreat and silence that taps the feminine power of introspection and receiving answers. It has been good to understand the art of self-exploration, because through the feminine principle, I have learned the wisdom of loving myself."

The passageway to the fourth cave was illuminated and Wisdom Keeper took a deep breath as she walked through. In the Cave of the North, the Earth Mother spoke. "Tell me what wisdom you have gathered from the North, little one."

"In the place of healing and gratitude I have discovered the wisdom of those who have fully experienced human life. The lessons of their Earth Walks have served them well. I have learned to be grateful for all opportunities to grow. Some have been difficult, some joyous, but all have taught me wisdom because I have learned to seize every opportunity, adding understanding to my Knowing Systems and compassion to our world. I have learned that healing comes to those who do not blame life's experiences but rather give thanks for the growth potential being offered. I have gathered the wisdom that can be gained from personal experience. I have accepted the healing that has come from right attitude and I have learned to be deeply grateful for it all."

The passageway to the fifth cave was illuminated and Wisdom Keeper entered. There she found a petroglyph of Whale covering the far wall. The Earth Mother spoke to her and said, "This is the cave of the Above direction, daughter. What have you discovered about the wisdom held above?"

Wisdom Keeper did not pause, but replied instantly, "Mother, I have discovered that our spirits come to Earth from the Sky Nation, traveling from the Spirit World like shooting stars. The fire in our hearts is the Eternal Flame of Love and that fiery essence will one day return to the Starry Medicine Bowl of the night sky. I have come to understand the idea of destiny. Every human being has the opportunity to thank the Great Mystery for the beautiful creation that he or she individually represents by being his or her personal best. If we honor the talents and abilities we have been given, developing those gifts to the fullest, that is fulfilling destiny. The song of Whale is the Medicine Song from the Dog Star in the night sky that teaches human beings how to remember their talents, using them to rediscover the destiny of wholeness that their spirit holds."

In the silence, the passageway to the sixth cave was lighted and Wisdom Keeper entered. The Earth Mother's voice softly echoed, "This is the cave of the Below direction, daughter. What wisdom have you gathered from this direction?"

Wisdom Keeper noticed the ivory tusk of a great woolly mammoth filling the right side of the cave and smiled inwardly as she answered. "The wisdom of the Below direction is applying all that has been learned to one's Earth Walk. Like Mammoth, the art of *remembering* is strong Medicine. Nothing is ever lost if human beings consider the information they gather and the life lessons that they experience sacred enough to commit to memory. Repeating that wisdom to the generations that follow ensures that the Teachings will live forever. I have learned that Knowing Systems are founded in experience, not beliefs. Two-leggeds must bring the remembering and the wisdom of spirit to the Below direction and walk it for themselves."

The final passageway was illuminated and Wisdom Keeper stepped inside the seventh cave. The spirit of her Totem filled the cave and she sensed the presence of Lynx as the Earth Mother's voice spoke once again. "This is the final cave of the Within direction. What have you learned about the life that lives inside you, my child?"

Wisdom Keeper spoke, "Mother, I have learned that every living thing has a heart filled with love, desires, dreams, plans, and great Medicine. For myself, I have learned that the unspoken wisdom of my heart is like a rare jewel that allows me to glory in being alive. I have learned only to share that wisdom when it is asked for. I have learned that there are no secrets in the universe because all answers dwell within. Those seeking wisdom can access those secrets at any time, if they go inside and seek the light of the Eternal Flame of Love. Like Lynx, Knower of Secrets, who guards the silence of inner knowing, the twinkle reflected in the eyes of any Child of Earth mirrors the hidden fire of wisdom that dwells within. The mysteries of all worlds can be accessed through the heart when the seeker is willing to open and receive."

The Earth Mother spoke once again, "You have learned many things, my daughter. I am pleased that you have developed these ways to honor the truth. You have followed the Wisdom Trail and you have found that the voice of your Orenda is your constant guide. You have discovered that the Wisdom Trail always leads to the Within direction—your heart. The completion of the Seven Sacred Directions of Wisdom is your final Rite of Passage in understanding human life. Have you also discovered why these caves exist above the Canyon of Time?"

"Yes, Mother, I realized that all human beings must accumulate wisdom over time to mark the cycles and seasons of growth and change in the tangible world. The experiences of the Earth Walk allow every Two-legged to stand on all of the spokes of the Wheel of Life. In time, when they are ready to hear the voice of their Orendas, they feel the tug of their own spirits urging them to grow. Without experiences, which need time to digest and be fully understood, the lessons of each direction or spoke would become murky. The Great Mystery has given us the gift of time so that our passages and our growth can be fully experienced. The wisdom gained, like this cave, is above the Canyon of Time for it is eternal wisdom that will forever be recorded in the person's Orenda."

The Earth Mother blessed the part of herself represented in this Clan Mother of the Second Moon Cycle by surrounding Wisdom Keeper with love. The feeling of completion and wholeness entered Wisdom Keeper's heart, filling her with visions of the Whirling Rainbow. A sense of inner peace flowed through Wisdom Keeper's veins and she was ready to move from the caves and step into Grandfather Sun's light, continuing her journey among the Two-leggeds who she came to serve.

As Wisdom Keeper stepped from the cave, she realized that one Sleep had passed and that dawn had broken. Grandfather Sun was filling the world with the colors of a newborn morning. She raised her arms to the rays of Grandfather's fiery light and sang her song of greeting and thanksgiving. Then she knelt and kissed the soil of the Earth Mother's body. The road had been long, the trials many, but now she

understood why the Great Mystery never tested human beings on their strengths but only on their weaknesses. The
Wisdom Road could only be traveled through experience—
trial and error. She had earned the right to be the Protectress
of the Wisdom Road because she had walked it by honoring
the truth in herself.

WEIGHS THE TRUTH

The Protectress of the meek
Weighs the truth for all to see,
Divine Law, seeking balance,
Setting the spirit free.

And here, amid the chaos
Of earthly trials she stands,
Ready to issue justice,
Compassion in her hands.

She answers when deception
Shows the destructive face
Of human greed and hatred,
Dividing every creed and race.

Keeper of Great Mystery's laws,
Whose guiding ways we seek,
May we accept the oneness of
The truths we hear you speak.

Clan Mother
of the
Third Moon Cycle

WEIGHS THE TRUTH is the Clan Mother of the Third Moon Cycle, who teaches Divine Law. She is the fair judge of human rights, the Keeper of Equality and the Guardian of Justice. She does not judge our actions by bestowing punishment but rather teaches us the principles of Divine Law. The actions we take are based on our decisions. If we decide to hurt another consciously, we have also made the decision unconsciously to receive the lessons connected to harming another. Weighs the Truth teaches us that we are the ones who in finding and accepting the truth of our actions, must decide what we will learn in order to make amends for following that crooked trail.

This Keeper of Justice sees all sides of every situation with clarity and cannot be fooled by half-truths or lies. As the Guardian of the Underdog, she is not swayed by personal opinion and obliterates the illusion of class distinction, hierarchy, wealth, supposed power, or popularity. She demands that justice and equality be applied to every life form in Creation. By observing the obvious in every situation, this Clan Mother levels the ideas of self-importance that keep human egos out of balance. She instructs us by showing us her own humility, allowing us to see our arrogance.

▲▲

Weighs the Truth teaches us that taking on additional responsibilities is important in developing our self-determination. This Clan Mother understands the idea of weighing all sides of any situation in order to determine the truth. Self-determination can be seen as our ability to respond to all sides of life, and to all our talents, and accept the truths found even if we do not like what we have discovered. The Destroyer of Deception role in our lives shows us that when we are self-determined, we have accepted the truth of what gives us joy and are not confused or influenced by what others want us to be. We can then respond to our heart's greatest desire and find happiness through the determination found in the Self's sense of well-being.

This Clan Mother's moon cycle falls in March and is connected to the color brown. The rich soil of the Earth Mother reflects this color and represents the Earth Mother's connection to Divine Law. The Cycle of Truth that corresponds to the third moon is *accepting the truth*. Weighs the Truth teaches us to accept the truth inside us, as well as accepting the truth of the experiences we encounter in life. If we look at ourselves with a cold eye, accepting what we find, the truth of our strengths and our weaknesses can destroy the illusions that limit our potential.

Weighs the Truth teaches us that we do not need to focus on what is weak or wrong with us but rather on what is strong and right with us. Divine Law shows us that cause and effect do rule our universe of polarity. If we feed the negative by being critical, the shadow side of our nature is fed. When we praise right action and work to develop the skills of our talents, our Orendas or Spiritual Essences expand.

••

▲▲

Bearer of the
Burden Basket

Weighs the Truth sat in her wigwam, staring at the earthen walls made of mud and leaves. The supporting branches of her circular lodge were made of Birch. Here and there, a stray piece of white bark caught the reflection of Grandmother Moon's full face as the light filtered through the smoke hole in the center of the wigwam's domed roof.

On this warm night, she had no need for a fire and was content to sit in *Tiyoweh*, the stillness. It was comforting to know that she could call on Birch's Medicine of *discovering truth*, here in the stillness of her seeking heart. Snowy Owl's spirit was with her on this night while she had to make a decision regarding justice. One of the ghostly white pieces of birch bark seemed to reflect Owl's image across the circular space of her hut. Weighs the Truth was comforted by Snowy Owl's Medicine of *eliminating lies and deception*. Owl was a Wisdom Keeper. His spirit had accompanied her since the early days of her Earth Walk, earning her trust and friendship through the trials, challenges, and tribulations they had shared.

On this summer's Sleep, during the full moon, Weighs the Truth was confronted with a situation that would test all of her abilities in order for justice to be found. Two women from the Tribe had come to Weighs the Truth five Suns past to ask for a judgment. Running Water had accused Blue Goose of taking more than her share of the communal food stores. Blue Goose had accused Running Water of being nosy, passing rumors, and not keeping her eyes and ears out of the Sacred Space of others. Weighs the Truth had passed the four Suns and Sleeps required for her to smoke the situation. On the rising of Grandfather Sun, the Clan Mother would issue her decision in front of the Tribal Council.

To see beyond the smoke-filled illusions of this difficult situation, Weighs the Truth had approached the East Direction on the dawning of the first Sun of her decision-making process. She had offered her Pipe to Grandfather Sun and had asked for clarity and spiritual enlightenment. Then she had returned her thanks for the gift of clear seeing and feeling that the East Wind would send her, doing so before the actual message arrived, thereby making the space for that message in her heart. Next, she had loaded her Pipe and sat in Tiyoweh, the stillness, to smoke the spirits of each Relation that had been asked to come into the tobacco. With each puff, she felt the Medicine and strengths of the spirits of the East come into her body. The smoke from the Pipe wafted toward the Sky Nation, creating a stir in the East Wind, bringing the clarity she sought. The East Wind reminded her that when clarity was sought with unconditional love, the light of Grandfather Sun would illuminate the seeker's ability to embrace the expansive view without preconceptions.

When the purple sage-blossom blanket of the night sky settled itself across the Sky Nation on that first Sleep, Weighs the Truth was given further illumination as she watched the Starry Medicine Bowl. Later, during her sleeptime, her dreams were filled with more visions and enlightening facts regarding Blue Goose and Running Water.

During the dawning of the next Sun, she repeated her ritual, inviting the spirits of the South to show her what she could trust about the situation and the women involved. That evening, again, she watched the night sky for portents and signs. Her dreams spoke to her of the lessons of innocence and humility that needed to be learned in this matter.

When dawn broke on the third Sun, Weighs the Truth took her Pipe to the ridge of Sacred Mountain, repeating her Spirit-calling Ceremony. This time she called to the West Wind, asking for the strength to go within and seek the answers that would bring a fuller understanding of the omens she had seen and the messages she had received. The West Wind was asked to show Weighs the Truth how her decision would affect the future of the two women, their Tribe, and the unborn generations yet to come. In the evening that followed, Weighs the Truth was again given the answers she sought during her observance of the night sky and her sleep-time dreams.

The fourth dawn brought the North Wind's Spirit-calling Ceremony and Weighs the Truth stood on the edge of the ridge of Sacred Mountain, asking for wisdom. The gratitude she felt for the answers already received was sent to the Great Mystery, as she added her thanks for the wisdom yet to come. Weighs the Truth asked for healing to come to all concerned and that the goodness of Divine Law found in this lesson would enrich the lives of all observers. Then she gave thanks for the opportunity that this situation had afforded her to further develop her own skills of accepting the truth in herself and in others.

Weighs the Truth sat in her wigwam reflecting on the signs she had found in the Starry Medicine Bowl of the night sky this evening and all of the messages of the past four Suns and Sleeps. She called on the Spirit of Snowy Owl, who guarded the Above Direction of her Sacred Space, and asked for his spirit to manifest in the lodge. Then she called upon Weasel, who guarded the Below Direction of her Sacred Space. Last, she called upon Crow, the Guardian of Divine Law who was the protector of the Within Direction of her heart. In the stillness, with the night vision she found by sitting in darkness with her eyes wide open, she waited.

She saw a spirit come forth to perch on the branch that stuck out from the mud walls. Several branches were built into the wigwam's earthen walls, creating hooks for hanging household items, leggings, pouches of dried food, and Medicine Bundles. Owl picked an empty branch, hooted a greeting, and then waited for the other Totem Spirits to arrive.

Weasel took his place on top of a stump that the Clan Mother used as a table and silently greeted her with a nod. Crow's spirit entered the smoke hole at the top of the wigwam, perching on a branch across the lodge from Snowy Owl. Crow cawed a greeting, signaling that the four friends were all present and ready to begin their Powwow.

Weighs the Truth was grateful for the Totem Spirits who had come to assist her in making her final decision regarding Running Water and Blue Goose. She showed her Totems the respect she held for their wisdom by offering each one her outstretched palms, signaling through sign language that she was grateful and willing to receive their counsel.

Crow began by reminding all present that Divine Law was the balance found in every natural part of the Great Mystery's Creation and not in the laws made by humankind.

Together, these four friends would have to find the answers that would preserve the justice of Divine Law, as well as the fairness that would bring balance to the lives of all concerned. Crow asked Weasel to ferret out the truth. Since he was the detective of the creature kingdom, Weasel could use his Medicine of *guile, stealth, ingenuity, and observing the obvious* to bring the truth to light.

Crow asked Owl to use his Medicine of *wisdom, discernment, and destroying deception* to aid the group in seeing the whole truth. Owl's natural call in the wild was always asking "who," but he invariably discovered the answers to where, when, how, why, and what as well. Snowy Owl was able to find answers to all of those questions because he could easily spot the difference among a truth, a half-truth, and a lie. Time passed as the four friends considered the puzzling question of how justice would best be served.

Weighs the Truth's Totem Spirits stole into the darkness when all of the facts had been reviewed, allowing her to once again sit in the stillness. She then positioned her body like the great lizard, called Crocodile, in order to tap his Medicine of *digesting and assimilating the truth*. Like the great lizard of the rivers, she took her meal of thoughts below the waters of her personal feelings and ingested each morsel of truth in order to integrate all she had learned. As the Clan Mother rested on her belly in her sleeping robes, she sent her spiritual umbilical cord from her navel deep into the Earth Mother's body. The fibers of light that comprised the umbilical cord sent streams of warmth into her body from deep within the earth while she dreamed of various solutions.

In her dream, she rode the back of the black-and-white striped pony called Zebra. Zebra reminded her of his Medicine that *nothing was final or absolute in the natural world, nothing was just light or dark, black or white.* As she rode through the dream, she passed through plains of windswept golden grasses and mushroom-shaped trees whose branches formed domed silhouettes against the horizon. Faster and faster she rode through the dreamscape until the stripes on Zebra's body blurred into a mass of radiant light, melding with her own hair, which blew freely in the wind, and her body, which had become a living extension of the galloping form of her Four-legged companion. Suddenly, the dreamscape changed and the two found themselves in another setting.

Zebra came to a halt in front of a fern-filled grotto where clean, pure water tumbled over a limestone shelf into a clear pool below. Weighs the Truth dismounted, listening to the waterfall. The grotto was sprinkled with tiny blue flowers and orange Indian Paintbrush. She noticed something moving behind the stream of water. Raccoon emerged, eyes sparkling inside of her black bandit's mask, smiling as if she had expected the Clan Mother's arrival.

"Hello, Mother. It has been a long time since we have looked into each other's eyes. I can see that you have fared well," Raccoon said.

Weighs the Truth felt the warmth of Raccoon's greeting deep inside her belly, as she moved forward to greet her old friend. "My heart is full, Little Bandit," replied the Clan Mother. "It is good to look into your eyes again. What words of wisdom do you have for me now?"

"Well, Mother, I am still *the protector of the underdog, the weak, frail, and elderly.* My Medicine becomes stronger every day while greed and inequality continue to capture the hearts of the Human Tribe. I have come to tell you that when you make your decision with the rising of Grandfather Sun, you may want to consider the rights of those who were depending upon the communal food stores but were not taking their share, in order to leave more for the others. These members of your Tribe have been planting, gathering, and storing as much as the others, but in their meekness and humility, they have chosen to provide for others in need by taking less than their share."

Raccoon had revealed the missing piece to the confrontation between Blue Goose and Running Water—the rights of those who were inadvertently affected by the actions of both women would have to be considered. In her dream, Weighs the Truth could see Zebra snorting and pawing the ground, catching her attention. Zebra whinnied and then spoke up, "Nothing is ever black and white, is it, Mother?"

The dream faded, causing Weighs the Truth to move her body, disengaging herself from the dreamscape, returning her thoughts to the warmth in her belly that was being fed to her by the Earth Mother. The umbilical cord of light fibers blended all the feelings she had encountered during the four preceding Suns and Sleeps with the wisdom gathered from her Spirit Totems as well as the reminders collected in her dream. Together, the mass of feelings, impressions, facts, and wisdom whirled inside of the Clan Mother's belly, giving her a great deal to digest before the rising of Grandfather Sun.

Weighs the Truth reviewed Running Water's accusation in detail. Running Water had said that Blue Goose had taken more than her share of the food that had been planted, tended, gathered, and stored by all members of the Tribe. If Blue Goose had hoarded more food for her family than was her rightful share, the Clan Mother was concerned with the deeper issue of why Blue Goose would have done such a thing. Weasel had shown Weighs the Truth the pain that Blue Goose held in her heart, having lost her child to starvation two winters before. Owl had seen through the deception that Blue Goose had tried to employ when she accused Running Water of being nosy in an effort to hide her fears of being caught and of losing another child to starvation. Blue Goose had been wounded and had not been able to heal the loss of her child, because she blamed herself for not having gathered enough food for her family.

Running Water was another matter. True to her name, her laughter was like the melodies made by running streams and brooks, but her weakness was in running to tell on others, no matter how small the assumed offense. It was true that Running Water did not keep her own counsel or her eyes and ears to herself. Sacred Space was maintained in tribal living conditions by observing a certain amount of politeness. This rule for happy living was a good one that required every member of the Tribe to avert their eyes when the personal lives of others could be viewed. Anything that was inadvertently overheard in passing was considered privileged information, not to be repeated, out of respect for the Sacred Space of another.

Running Water was certainly a busybody in most instances and out of her need to be noticed and acknowledged had created several problems in the past. Her behavior stemmed from never having been recognized as a child, living among a family of many children, with parents too busy trying to provide for the physical necessities, to nurture the emotional needs of the youngsters. During her childhood, Running Water had developed a tattletale personality, finding that she could get attention if she behaved herself and used a self-righteous attitude to point out the offenses of others. But the kind of attention Running Water received was avoidance and mistrust. In her own confusion about whether or not she was getting noticed, Running Water had effectively cut herself off from true friendships.

Blue Goose was acting from old pain and fear; Running Water was acting from woundedness and a need to be loved or recognized. Each woman sat on one side of the Great Smoking Mirror, projecting what each supposed was the truth into the smoke-filled illusion that could confound the most astute observer. Weighs the Truth took the nurturance she needed from the spiritual umbilical cord she had sent from her navel into the Earth Mother's body and let go of the problem, sleeping until dawn.

Just before midday, Weighs the Truth changed her buckskins and donned her regalia. The doeskin of her regalia had been tanned and then worked with charcoal and tallow, producing the blackened hides from which she had fashioned the dress, leggings, and moccasins. The Clan Mother reached behind the mud-fashioned shelf in her wigwam and brought forth a special bundle. Carefully, she unwrapped the Crow mask that she had carved so long ago and looked into its face. Each black feather on the Crow mask had been affixed with a glue that Weighs the Truth had made from the hooves of Buffalo, slivered and boiled in water. She had spent two moons in the creative process and was pleased with the results even now, so many winters later. The bill on the mask was yellow, symbolizing that Divine Law was dispensed with unconditional love, like the yellow of Grandfather Sun. The eyes on the mask were red, representing the faith held by the Keeper of Divine Law, who knew that accepting the truth was an act of humility.

When Grandfather Sun was at the zenith of his journey across the blue Sky Nation, Weighs the Truth sat down in full regalia in the midst of the Tribal Council. Running Water and Blue Goose sat in front of the Clan Mother, encircled by the Elders who composed the Wisdom Keepers of the Tribe. Beyond this circle were all of the other members of the Tribe, silently waiting for the proceedings to begin. The words of thanksgiving were spoken by Weighs the Truth, giving gratitude for the opportunity of sharing and healing presented in the situation at hand; then burning sweetgrass was passed, so the smoke would cleanse any bitterness or negativity the group might hold against the two women asking for justice.

Weighs the Truth began by saying, "I have reached a decision in this matter after the four Suns and Sleeps required by Tribal Law to accomplish my task in a good way. I have consulted the Totem Spirits, the Starry Medicine Bowl of the night sky, the Four Winds of Change, the Ancestors, the Four Clan Chiefs of Air, Earth, Water, and Fire, and Swennio, the Great Mystery. I have been fed by the Earth Mother and blessed by the Sky Father. I have seen the hearts of these two women and found the solution I feel is necessary to bring healing and balance back to our Tribe."

"Blue Goose took more than her share of our food stores because she was afraid of losing another child to starvation. She carries the self-blame of a mother who felt helpless when death took her baby. Although she was driven by shame and fear, this was selfish behavior that did not consider the rights of those who worked equally hard to create the winter stores that we all depend on. For Blue Goose to walk the Beauty Way again, she must return the extra portion she took. Then she must go to the woods to gather double the amount she secretly pilfered from our Tribal stores. The berries, wild tubers, nuts, and greens that she gathers are to be equally distributed to every family who lost a loved one to hunger in the last Starving Moon. When this task is completed, Blue Goose will spend one Sun with each family, sharing the story of her loss and hearing the story of the loss that each family experienced. During the next thirteen moons, Blue Goose will care for different children who lost their parents to starvation. During each moon cycle, she must treat as her own each child that she tends.

"Running Water spoke out of turn when she tattled on Blue Goose, not respecting the natural right of every Tribal Member to determine for himself or herself what is correct behavior based on his or her Sacred Point of View. Running Water is to accompany Blue Goose as a silent companion, assisting her in gathering and when she visits each grieving family. Running Water is not allowed to speak during the time she assists Blue Goose, nor is she ever to speak of what she heard or saw, at any time in the future. For the next thirteen moons, Running Water will not speak at all; she will listen. She will assist Medicine Woman and me during healing and counseling sessions, but she is forbidden to speak of anything she sees or hears, at any time in the future. Both women will reappear before this Council in thirteen moons. *Da naho*, it is decreed."

The thirteen moons passed quickly and the Tribal Council convened again. Weighs the Truth sat in her Crow regalia in the center of the circle, asking Blue Goose to speak of what she had learned on her healing journey.

"I have learned that every member of this Tribe has suffered losses, Mother. I have shared my grief and theirs equally and I have come to realize that we work together for a reason. Unity, sharing, and caring for one another is the strength that binds us together as one. I have given away my fear of scarcity and have discovered the faith that once eluded me. I am no longer afraid of growing old alone if my children die, traveling to the Spirit World. I have made peace with myself and no longer carry the blame or shame that clouded my understanding. I have extended my family beyond the boundaries of blood kin and have loved every child who needed me. Through their loss of relatives, each grieving adult and child has shared with me a common bond that was created by setting aside our sorrows, finding the joy, comfort, and understanding of each other's company."

Weighs the Truth thanked Blue Goose and asked Running Water to speak of the lessons she had learned during the past thirteen moons. Running Water had not spoken since the last time she faced this Tribal Council and her discomfort was apparent. She struggled to get a rasping word to escape her throat in vain. A few moments passed as she tried again, finally finding her voice.

"These thirteen moons have changed my attitude, my path, my understanding, and my sense of self. I want to express my gratitude to you, Mother. Through listening to the stories of others, I have seen and heard the story of my own passage from woundedness into healing. I have learned gentleness and compassion for myself by being caring and nurturing toward others. I now understand the folly of my former need to be recognized as a worthwhile person. I felt worthless because I had never seen my own potential or talents, I had only experienced the critical voice in my head that told me I was never good enough. Because I believed I was not worthy of being loved, I harmed others by insisting they follow a path made of the same painful rules that I had imposed on myself. I learned compassion from Blue Goose and the others who shared the pain in their hearts. I learned how to move past my resentment of the judgment you pronounced thirteen moons ago. I have been privileged to share in Medicine Woman's healing arts and in your fairness, common sense, counseling ability, and compassionate wisdom. For these gifts and the healing of my heart, I am truly grateful."

Weighs the Truth's heart was filled. Trills of celebration and keening cries of victory filled the morning air, expressing the rejoicing of the Tribal Members. Everyone had seen the changes in the two women and had waited expectantly for this day. The Beauty Way had been restored to the Tribe without unjust punishments or decisions that could have split them apart. The balance of Divine Law had been served. Each woman had accepted the truth of her actions, finding ways to support and heal the old pain that had created those crooked trails. Life was good and the abundance found in this caring Tribal family was in balance again.

Weighs the Truth saw that Running Water and Blue Goose had learned the value of Sisterhood by coming together in diversity. Both women had been forced by their own actions to rely on the other, to see their similarities, and to go beyond their judgments to find a common bond. From that understanding, a friendship had sprung, making sisters of the former enemies. Running Water had discovered the first true friendship of her life and Blue Goose had healed her fear of abandonment.

Weighs the Truth sent gratitude to Swennio, the Great Mystery, for the lessons she had learned about being the Bearer of the Burden Basket. The Clan Mother no longer felt burdened by her role of dispensing justice. She realized that every Two-legged carries the burden of being responsible for her or his own actions. To grow, every human being picks the lessons he or she needs to learn, adding the experiences to the Burden Basket he or she carries on his or her Earth Walk. The responsibility of accepting the truth of those lessons is left to the individual, determining whether that person feels encumbered or freed by the experiences.

From that Sun, Weighs the Truth would always be reminded that Crow holds the *caw* that rides the winds to all nations. "Divine Law will bring life abundant to All Our Relations if we feed our goodness and starve the shadow that is fed by old pain. Only then will humankind accept the truth, understanding that the Great Mystery created all Two-leggeds to *Walk in Beauty* as living vessels of love."

LOOKS
FAR
WOMAN

Mother, teach me how to see
The shining lights of stars,
The faces of the Ancestors,
In worlds both near and far.

Show me how to welcome
The visions appearing to me,
Seeing the truth in detail,
Unraveling each mystery.

Walk me through the Dreamtime
Of altered time and space,
That I may share those visions
With every creed and race.

Doorkeeper of all dimensions,
I seek your Medicine ways
Of how to earth my visions,
Seeing truth, inside me, today.

Clan Mother of the Fourth Moon Cycle

LOOKS FAR WOMAN is the Clan Mother who is the Guardian of the Fourth Moon Cycle, which falls in April. The full spectrum of pastel colors is connected to this Clan Mother's cycle because she carries the Medicine of Prophecy, *seeing the truth in all colors.* She is the Doorkeeper of the Crack in the Universe and the Golden Door of Illumination that leads to all other dimensions of awareness. She stands at the Crack in the Universe and safely guides all human spirits taking Dreamtime journeys into the other realms and then, back home, being present and fully conscious of their bodies.

This Clan Mother is a Seer, an Oracle, a Dreamer, and a visionary. She teaches us the validity of our impressions, dreams, visions, and feelings as they exist within our inner potential. Looks Far Woman instructs humankind on how to unravel the symbols found in psychic impressions. She shows us how to see the truth in every vision we receive in the tangible and intangible worlds. In her wisdom, Looks Far Woman assists every seeker in finding the seeds of personal and planetary prophecy that the Great Mystery planted inside all human beings. She knows that all Two-leggeds can access the ability to see the truth in all dimensions, if they

▲▲

seek the light of the Eternal Flame of Love and if they are willing to receive the visions that come when the heart is open.

Looks Far Woman understands that all possibilities and probabilities exist in the future. She teaches us that tangible events are only manifested through each individual's freely made decisions. Every human being has the ability to use the information found in sleeptime dreams and/or Dreamtime waking visions to change the course of her or his personal experiences. Looks Far Woman sees all potential truths, as well as how an individual will ignore or take heed when omens or portents appear. Looks Far Woman is willing to teach humankind how to see those truths by using their own abilities, but she will not give pat answers on what the future holds for any individual.

Looks Far Woman shows us how to observe everything around us and how to remember every detail. This Clan Mother enjoys teaching us how to recall anything we have seen in order to reconstruct useful information. Looks Far Woman instructs us how to distinguish between the tangible and intangible parts of what we see when we have developed second sight or the ability to see in both worlds at once. When we fine-tune this talent of second sight, she teaches us how to know which vision is true prophecy and which vision is just a probability. In the final development of this Clan Mother's lessons, human beings are able to fully understand any signs, portents, omens, or symbols presented to their awareness.

Looks Far Woman presents the lesson of respecting boundaries by showing us that it is not okay to look into another person's Sacred Space unless we are asked by that individual to do so. She shows us the pitfalls of looking too far, too soon, by reminding us that we can destroy the beauty of the moment. When we forget our ability to use free will, by forecasting what a future outcome will be, we can trap ourselves into projections, expectations, and a loss of potential opportunity. The lessons we refuse to experience will usually catch up with us later, in another form. Looks Far Woman shows us how to observe each opportunity, knowing when to follow that path and when to choose another road. Our personal clarity depends upon our ability to observe the obvious, allowing us to then make personal choices in order to alter our Sacred Paths and grow. This Clan Mother tells us how to see the truth in all of life's situations.

▲ ▲

Doorkeeper of the Crack in the Universe

Looks Far Woman sat in the darkness of the cave, gazing into the inky water of her blackened Medicine Bowl. The firelight flickered, sending waves of light across the water's surface. She felt herself being drawn into her own reflection, as her eyes mirrored bottomless wells and the water seemed to part, revealing another level of unfathomable space. Stars appeared in the indigo vastness that emerged from the silent water, allowing her to send her spirit traveling into the universe that was appearing before her eyes.

She sailed inside her Orenda, cloaked in the Spiritual Essence, moving into the world within worlds being opened for her to view. The passing of planets, stars, comets, swirling energy, and other heavenly bodies made her feel at one with Creation. She could see the movement of the Great Mystery's breath as new worlds were exhaled into the void of deep space. She traveled on, taking in every marvel of the Starry Medicine Bowl of the night sky.

She passed millions of campfires nestled together, forming an arch across the Sky Nation. She watched the spirit forms of the Ancestors, holding council around the campfires of stars. She watched as they saluted her passing by raising their hands in greeting. Some Spirit Warriors rode with her on their ghostly white horses as far as the next camp, others followed, running on the winds.

Looks Far Woman absorbed every new vista that crossed her line of vision. The light of a thousand suns lit the surfaces of passing planets. Radiant colors and hues bounced back from the planetary bodies, creating a feast for her eyes. In the far distance, the Clan Mother could see what appeared to be a lightning storm. Fire Sticks crashed upon one another, battling in the mulberry-colored void, drawing her ever closer to the erratic, silent explosion of zigzag dancing forms.

In the middle of the circle of Fire Dancers, she saw an emerging vision. The appearance of a crack, motionless amid the dancing lightning bolts, brought her focus to the center of the raw, creative forces displaying their dance before her. She heard the voice of the Earth Mother: "Looks Far, you are seeing the Sacred Fire of Creation. Trust, follow the flow, see, and know. The Crack in the Universe holds

the Golden Door of Illumination that leads to all other levels of awareness. You have traveled into the vastness of the
worlds within your own Spiritual Essence, your Orenda.
The worlds within worlds that comprise the Sacred Space of
your own being are awaiting your discovery. You will be the
Keeper of the Door that leads through the Crack in the Universe of opposites. Through exploring the Orenda, each
member of the Human Tribe will discover and reclaim their
ability to see the truth of oneness."

The voice faded and Looks Far Woman journeyed further into the crackling, explosive dance of the Sacred Fire
before her. She felt no burns as her spirit form moved
through the fiery lights, reaching the timeless abyss inside
the Crack in the Universe. The emerging form of the Golden
Door reflected its blinding golden light, sending rays of light
through her spirit form, lighting the darkness of the deepest
part of the crack's inner chasm. She waited as the Golden
Door moved forward, coming to rest in front of her.

The voice of the Earth Mother gently spoke to her
heart. "Daughter of my spirit, here you will stand for all
time, showing others how to see the truth within themselves and within all things. To grow beyond human limitation, all Children of Earth must face their limitations and
hesitations. They will come to you and see the truth within
themselves through your limitless eyes. If they are willing
to give away their illusions, they will pass through the
Golden Door into their next level of understanding. If they
fear their own potential, they will return to the place within
themselves that gives them comfort, until they are ready to
grow. The art of seeing the total truth of the vastness of the
Orenda, and seeing the truth of all of the worlds that exist

within the creative force of that Spiritual Essence, can be overwhelming. Many cycles of the Wheel of Life are required before that level of seeing the truth is attained. Many will come, many will turn back, many will falter and then move through the Golden Door, but you must hold the door open for all who have the courage to see."

Looks Far Woman understood the words spoken by the Earth Mother and cherished the role she was given. The blinding light of total truth illuminated every part of her Spiritual Essence as she moved through the Golden Door, seeing all of the potential in Creation, allowing it to be indelibly written in her heart.

When the Clan Mother returned her consciousness to her body, the timelessness of her journey ended. Hundreds of moon cycles had passed during Looks Far Woman's final Rite of Passage, discovering the truth inside the worlds within worlds. The water in her Medicine Bowl had evaporated, the ashes of her fire had returned to the earth of the cave's floor, the dripping of lime water had grown new rock formations, but her ever-young body was the same. She had returned from the Crack in the Universe, ready to serve her human children by teaching them how to see the truth.

Looks Far Woman realized that her ability to see the truth would need to be honed into tiny glimpses to match the capacities of her individual human children. She was grateful that she had learned how to see the truth through the eyes of others. This talent of seeing through another's eyes gave her the ability to duplicate each individual's level of seeing truth without overwhelming her or him. She had learned how to show her human children the illusions present in their paths, gently leading them through every cycle of growth and change.

Looks Far Woman understood the value of never missing a step on the Great Medicine Wheel of Life. Some would try to move too fast and burn up their human bodies, others would allow fear to keep them from their natural progress, but Looks Far saw the truth in compassion and was willing to nurture every Two-legged through the process of spiritual evolution. The Great Mystery was not to be solved, and that same mystery existed in every part of Creation, allowing the beauty of each life form to manifest in its own time.

Looks Far Woman intended to help others observe the obvious lessons found in the natural world and apply those truths to themselves. The Creatures could show the Two-leggeds how to use their physical bodies and personality traits to survive and earn longevity. Then it would be possible to show the Two-leggeds how to master the life force in those bodies, by showing them the truth of discovering the creative forces of natural elements that made up their human forms. Through seeing these truths, humankind could then grasp the expansive picture presented by their spirits. They would come to understand that all things, including themselves, contain living spiritual forms.

After the lessons of life force were learned, the Human Tribe could learn to Enter the Stillness in order to discover the secrets of the spirit and the potentials found in exploring the nontangible worlds. Every lesson of the realms of spirit could be accessed through nature. The spirits of every life form in the natural world were ready and willing to become teachers for the Two-leggeds who sought their guidance. The worlds of truth represented in every circle of Relations would lead to new Medicine Wheels of experience in the worlds within worlds.

Looks Far Woman could see the patterns of spiritual evolution as they spiraled out before her, creating the probable future of the Human Tribe. It made her heart glad to feel how her role in the Earth Tribe's evolution could assist the growth potential of her human children and all life forms. *Seeing the truth* was an ever-evolving talent that brought further understanding of the Great Mystery and how all things were constantly growing and changing inside the Original Source.

Looks Far Woman passed many winters rediscovering the miracles of life on the Mother Planet. She showed her human children how to observe the changes in the weather, how to divine through the natural elements, how to read the faces of the Cloud People, and how to understand the messages that were presented in their lives. She taught her human children how to read the gifts of life force found in every part of nature as signposts to guide them on their individual Sacred Paths.

Learning how to see was not an easy task for some humans. These stubborn Two-leggeds insisted that if they could not see the whole truth in a glance, the truth was not there. Looks Far Woman was not concerned that some humans were willing to look and others were not. Fear of the unknown troubled the Human Tribe because they had not developed the ability of seeing the truth in all lessons. In her deep compassion, Looks Far Woman nurtured the fearful and gently guided them through a multitude of healing steps that allowed them to release their fears by only looking as far as they were ready to see.

One Sun, while Looks Far Woman was spending some time in solitude, a young boy came stumbling up the rugged path that led from the hot springs to her cave. Carrying his sister's bruised, limp body in his weary arms, he explained that his sister had been raped, beaten, and left to die by traveling hunters. He laid the girl's body at Looks Far Woman's feet. He wanted to know if his little sister would ever return from Eternal Land. Her unseeing eyes were wide open and the grimace of terror still locked her jaws as if she had been frozen in time. The girl had passed fourteen winters, but it was doubtful she would last another Sun. She had not spoken, eaten, taken a drink, or moved since he found her. He had traveled for three Suns and Sleeps, bringing the girl to Looks Far Woman, who was his last hope.

Looks Far Woman hid her feelings as she examined the girl. The Clan Mother looked past her own feelings of anger and heartbreak to see if the girl's spirit had been broken forever. The light of the Eternal Flame was weak inside the child's Orenda but it flickered and sputtered each time the boy spoke to her.

Looks Far Woman worked to keep the girl, who was named Star Fire, from losing touch with life. She was afraid that Star Fire's spirit would slip through the Crack in the Universe, and she would forget who she was, wandering into Eternal Land without a hope of ever returning. Star Fire's brother, Little Eagle, followed the Clan Mother's instructions. He gathered the cupped lava rocks that served as lamps, filled each with dried grasses dipped in melted pine sap, and then placed the bowls around the edge of the hot springs that bubbled at the rear of the caves that Looks Far Woman called her home. Little Eagle worked quickly, starting a fire and lighting the lamps. Together, they lifted Star Fire into the water, supporting her body so that it would float in their arms.

Looks Far Woman sang to Star Fire's spirit, the girl's body being relieved of any stress while it floated in the warm mineral waters that simulated the safety of the womb. Although Looks Far Woman was present and aware of what she was singing, the child in her arms, and the presence of Little Eagle, she was also aware of the part of herself that was standing at the Crack in the Universe, making sure that Star Fire's spirit did not wander away. At times like this one, the Seer was grateful that she could easily master seeing the many levels of awareness in the tangible and intangible worlds simultaneously.

Many moons passed while Little Eagle and Looks Far Woman worked with Star Fire, slowly bringing the girl's spirit back from the edge of Eternal Land. The Clan Mother insisted that Little Eagle stay by his sister's side during the healing process because his voice offered Star Fire a way to grasp something familiar, giving her a pathway through the void that was created by the violation. The brutality of Star Fire's trauma had shattered her sense of being, tearing a hole in her Sacred Space, allowing fragments of her spirit to explode, abandoning the girl's senses inside the vastness of the void. In darkness, without her Spiritual Essence intact, Star Fire's connections to the tangible world, her recovering body and broken mind, were minimal.

Looks Far Woman traveled into the void regularly, collecting shattered fragments of Star Fire's spirit. Every Sun and Sleep, the Oracle guided the shards of spirit back into the girl's Orenda. Looks Far Woman placed a Medicine Wheel of Stone People and Medicine Bundles around Star Fire's body to contain the portions of the child's spirit in a constructed Sacred Space until enough of the girl's essence was collected to bring her back from the void. Little Eagle and Looks Far Woman waited and watched, spoke and sang to Star Fire; then they returned thanks, sending love to the Great Mystery every time a tiny bit of progress was made.

The Sun finally dawned when Star Fire's eyes lost their glazed stare and flickered with recognition when her big brother greeted her. She had been eating and drinking for some time but had had no awareness of herself or those who attended to her needs. Looks Far Woman realized that the healing process would continue for many moons, but the crisis of losing Star Fire's spirit was now over.

Slowly, Star Fire began to trust Looks Far Woman, as the Clan Mother took the girl through a multitude of small healing steps on the path back to wholeness. Through learning to take care of her personal hygiene, feeding herself, talking about her feelings, walking in nature, and learning to feel safe, Star Fire firmly rooted herself in the tangible world of family life. Laughter would come to the girl's lips when she shared in Little Eagle's antics, making fun of the standoff he had seen in the glen between the Bear and the Honey Bee. The passage of moons had worked its Medicine, allowing Star Fire to share in the happy routine of Looks Far Woman's life. Little Eagle and Star Fire, having lost their parents, stayed with Looks Far Woman for many seasons.

From time to time, other humans would seek the Clan Mother's wisdom, traveling far distances to hear what Looks Far Woman had to say. The day came when it was time for Little Eagle to move on, having found a mate among a band of visiting Two-leggeds. Star Fire was saddened by Little Eagle's departure, but she had adopted Looks Far as her mother, feeling that the caves and springs were now her home. Little Eagle and his mate promised that they would return to visit the two women who were part of their kin. Star Fire, having no desire to live with a mate or have children, had decided to train with Looks Far Woman in order to develop her natural abilities as a Seer and a Dreamer.

Upon Little Eagle's departure, Star Fire began her training in earnest. Looks Far Woman tested her adopted daughter when they went on Medicine Walks, telling the girl to shut her eyes from time to time and to describe in detail everything she had seen during the preceding moments. When visitors came to the two women's fire, Star Fire would be tested on the observations she had made during the visitors' stay. Through seeing these obvious truths in the tangible world and being able to recount every detail, Star Fire honed her ability to see. After completing these lessons, the Clan Mother began instructing Star Fire in how to use the blackened Medicine Bowl filled with water, gazing into the inky pool to see beyond the tangible.

Looks Far Woman understood the keen abilities that Star Fire possessed. Every Two-legged who had survived the shattering of the luminous egg that held their Sacred Points of View could access other realms, because fragments of their spirits had journeyed into the Void of Creation. The process of becoming a Seer or a Dreamer would test Star Fire's strength to confront and to go through the memories of trauma that would be encountered in the visions that appeared. This part of any abused human's healing process was a delicate one that could be very frightening, but Star Fire was strong now. Many moons passed as the young woman challenged and bested the nightmares of the past, moving beyond the shadowy remnants of her former pain, clearing the feelings that could inhibit her ability to see clearly.

Looks Far was proud of her adopted daughter's progress. The girl had passed twenty winters and was becoming a talented Seer. Often, when visitors would arrive, asking for help in finding a lost child or for some clue to a mysterious illness, Looks Far Woman would instruct Star Fire to look for answers. The girl's clarity was a rare gift and reflected the caring Looks Far Woman had taken in training the young Seer.

From time to time, Looks Far Woman would recall the early lessons that had led her to become the Doorkeeper of the Crack in the Universe. The Earth Mother had taught Looks Far Woman to read the faces of the Cloud People and see the source of an illness buried deep in a patient's body or mind. As a young Dreamer, she had learned to travel on the winds with Dragonfly, using Dragonfly's Medicine, *breaking through the illusions of the tangible world*, to retrieve information. When Looks Far Woman had learned to use the blackened Medicine Bowl, she had called upon Swan's Medicine to *surrender to the flow* of the Dreamtime, entering the parallel worlds of reality. Lizard's Medicine of *dreaming solutions and visioning* taught her the way to access the expansive dream of worlds within worlds. She called upon Mole's Medicine of *seeing in the dark and being able to travel under the earth* when she was looking for items that may have been buried. When Looks Far Woman felt the presence of evil, she called on the Medicine of Flicker the Woodpecker. Flicker carried *the strongest protection against the shadow and evil.* The young Oracle would allow her spirit to ride the back of Panther when she sought the truth of future events, because Panther carried the Medicine of *leaping fearlessly into the Void of the Unknown.* Panther's yellow eyes saw with clarity, being the color of Grandfather Sun, even in the nothingness of empty space. These Spirit Totems were Looks Far Woman's teachers and Allies in the natural world, assisting her in her continuing quest to see the truth in all realms.

With Eagle's help, Star Fire had retrieved the passion that illuminated her ability to see. Eagle's lofty ideals allowed the girl to know that she carried the ability to reclaim the wholeness she had once felt before her violation. Each time Star Fire brought a part of herself home to her Sacred Space, Eagle gifted her with new spiritual clarity, bringing her to the place where Looks Far Woman could finally take her through the Crack in the Universe safely.

Looks Far Woman entered the cave when the fading light of Grandfather Sun was painting the outside world in brilliant hues of vermillion. She looked at Star Fire, tending a small twig fire, and broke the silence. "Daughter, the time has come for you to travel beyond the realms you have journeyed through. Go and purify yourself in the bubbling water of the hot springs, then meet me in the cavern where we use the Medicine Bowl to seek vision."

Star Fire nodded, then unhurriedly made her way out of the cave. Having total trust in her teacher and adopted mother had instilled a sense of safety in the girl. Looks Far Woman marveled at the young Dreamer's balanced attitude of acceptance. Star Fire had maintained her relationship to the Earth Mother and tangible reality as well as her understanding of the intangible by using Dolphin's Medicine of *how to use the breath in order to tap the available energy, life force, or manna.* Like Looks Far Woman, the young Oracle could journey beyond the physical realms and, upon returning, properly use the breath to bring her body functions into balance again.

While Star Fire prepared herself for the journey, Looks Far Woman sat with her memories. The Clan Mother recalled every step on her own path that had honed the skills she now possessed. She reviewed the hours she had spent learning to focus her mind on one location so that she could propel her spirit to that place within the Dreamtime. She looked at the lessons she had mastered by stilling her thoughts and following glimpses of vision until they revealed whole pictures of truth. She remembered her frustrations and her triumphs along the arduous path of becoming a Seer until she felt complete within her being. She would also achieve a wholeness of her own during Star Fire's passage.

Looks Far Woman recalled the Earth Mother's words of encouragement when she had learned how to master the gifts she had been given. The Earth Mother had blessed Looks Far Woman by passing her this Medicine of seeing the truth. Now, Looks Far Woman was responsible for giving those same skills to all of the Human Tribe. If Star Fire was successful and made it through the Crack in the Universe, Looks Far Woman's final Rite of Passage would be complete. The Clan Mother would know that she had impeccably trained another woman, who would then be responsible for passing the Medicine to others. The caring, patience, and tender guidance Looks Far Woman had shown in helping Star Fire develop her gifts would bring luster to the whole Human Tribe. Star Fire's success would signal that Looks Far Woman's circle of experience was complete and that Seer and Dreamer Medicine would be available to humankind throughout time.

Looks Far Woman was ready to face the future, having reviewed the past and released it in order to see the truth of the here and now. She stood up and walked with silent determination to the place in the giant cavern where the next turn in her Sacred Path would be revealed.

The two women sat in the vision cavern, peering into the blackened Medicine Bowl. The surface of the water was lit by the flames of their twig fire. Star Fire would be journeying alone, but Looks Far Woman would observe the girl's effort by using her talents as a Seer.

Star Fire melded her consciousness with the water and fire seen in the Medicine Bowl by focusing without blinking. Gently, she surrendered her mind to the flow of the life forces of the elements of fire and water, using the fire to burn away her random thoughts and water to cleanse her total being of the need to control the journey. She continued by bringing the Earth Mother's magnetism from the soil beneath her into her body's center of gravity, her womb. With the breath, she brought the element of air into her lungs and used the life manna to stabilize her bodily functions. Finally, she opened her heart and gave over, surrendering to the love of the Great Mystery. The connection was now complete, combining the Clan Chiefs of Air, Earth, Water, and Fire with the raw Creative Potential of the Great Mystery, melding these natural forces with Divine Love inside her Orenda.

Through limitless space, Star Fire traveled on a beam of love, beholding the dreamscapes of earlier journeys as she crossed the vast expanse of the Void. Much time passed as she sailed through the Dreamtime, finally reaching unfamiliar territory. The Bow of Beauty stood before her, glittering in the light of stars. The golden bow was inlaid with pearls, representing pearls of wisdom, and with rubies, glistening in the reflected golden light. The Bow of Beauty spoke to Star Fire: "Child of Looks Far Woman, the arrow of your spirit form can be mounted upon my bowstring and shot into the Void if you possess the faith reflected in the red of these precious stones inlaid in the arc of my bow. Like yourself, through living with the grit of human life, the Oyster produces the pearls of wisdom that have brought you this far on your healing path. Are you ready to travel farther?"

Star Fire agreed and her spirit form was shot by the Bow of Beauty into the Void of the Unknown. Blazing colors flew past her, blurring the dreamscape, as she traveled far and fast into the new realms of the Dreamtime. When her vision cleared, she saw the erratic dance of lightning bolts far in the distance. The silent storm of raw creative force drew her forever forward, drifting easily, seemingly being pulled by her own fascination. Suddenly, as she drew very close to the Fire Stick Beings crackling silently before her, she spied an apricot light that reminded her of the rising of Grandfather

Sun. The radiant apricot color lightened into shades of buttercup and sunflower yellows, revealing a large chasm as space seemingly split in the center of the burnished golden orb. A figure appeared in front of the enormous crack in space, faintly outlined in purest gold. As the figure took on more substance, Star Fire was drawn closer until she could see the face of the spirit form.

The welcoming arms of Looks Far Woman encircled the girl's spirit form as she felt all the love in the universe course through her being. Together they watched the Golden Door of Illumination appear, rising from the Crack in the Universe. Looks Far Woman stood aside and questioned her daughter with eyes filled with compassion. A blinding light appeared inside Star Fire's spirit form in the place where her heart resided in her human body. The Eternal Flame of Love blazed with a passion for living inside the girl's dreaming body, signaling that she had forgiven those who had wounded her and had *seen the truth* of how that pain had served her by opening her to the gifts she now held. She had become a healed healer who had passed through the dark night of the soul to reclaim the love. Her connection to the Creator and to all life was complete. Star Fire nodded to her mother and allowed the light of love, beaming from her heart, to draw her through the Crack in the Universe.

The visions that every human encounters on the other side of the Golden Door, through the Crack in the Universe, are the reflections of joy that exist beyond the illusions of physical sorrows. In that other world, we are shown how to use the energy that we once used to heal ourselves, to experience the joy of human life. The worlds within worlds are opened to every Two-legged who chooses to travel beyond the pain that limits our ability to see the truth.

Looks Far Woman will always stand at the Crack in the Universe, holding the Golden Door of Illumination open for those who have the ears to hear, the eyes to see, and the hearts to understand.

LISTENING WOMAN

Echoes of the Ancestors
Ride the Winds of Change,
Voices of the Creatures
Calling out my name.
Singing spirits on the breeze,
The crashing of waves to shore,
The pounding of Earth Mother's heart
Teach me what to listen for.
In stillness, before dusk and dawn,
Hidden messages are set free.
Like the chants of my people,
Their rhythms speak to me.
My ears can hear this music,
And my heart can understand.
Clan Mother of Tiyoweh,
I am yours to command.
I listen for your whispers
On a course you will chart,
Searching for the still voice
That lives within my heart.

Clan Mother
of the
Fifth Moon Cycle

LISTENING WOMAN is the Clan Mother of Tiyoweh, the Stillness, whose moon cycle falls in the month of May. The color connected to her moon is black and represents seeking an answer. Her Cycle of Truth is *hearing the truth*. This Clan Mother teaches us how to enter the Silence and how to listen to the ever-present messages of nature, our hearts, the Spirit World, the viewpoints of other humans, the Creature-teachers, and the Great Mystery. In Seneca Tradition, Entering the Silence is called *Tiyoweh* (Tie-yo-whey), which is translated as the Stillness. Once a person can access the Stillness and can hear the small, still voice within, that person has the potential to realize personal wholeness because she has accessed the voice of inner truth.

Listening Woman teaches us to listen to all of the viewpoints represented in our world in order to learn the harmony that can be found through allowing each life form to have its Sacred Point of View. This Clan Mother teaches us that we will never learn or expand if we do not listen to what is being said. She shows us the crooked trail of having to talk all the time; when we are talking, we are not listening. When we ignore or cut off the voice of another person

▲▲

who is telling us something we don't want to hear, we may be stopping our own growth. Many wounded people in our world do not want to hear the truth because they feel that it hurts them. The willingness to listen to the truth about oneself when it is delivered with loving compassion is a great talent and can heal old wounds.

Listening Woman has the ability to hear more than the words of her human children, even when they are afraid to speak the truth of how they feel. This Clan Mother listens to others with her heart, as well as with her ears. She can hear the unspoken heart's desires of her human children, as well as their unspoken fears. She can hear the nonverbal languages of the animals, plants, and stones as well as the voices of the Ancestors, coming from the Spirit World. Listening Woman's talents are derived from her ability to be totally still, to take in all the impressions she can gather, and then to formulate a concept of the whole.

Listening Woman teaches us how to discern whether people are speaking the truth by listening to the inflections and feelings contained in their words. She shows us that many humans do not know how to express their personal truths because they deny their true feelings. Some humans may lie to cover their fear of retribution or punishment; some people tell lies to feel included or important. But all people who speak untruths are detectable if we develop the art of listening. Showing compassion for those who feel they must lie is a sign of spiritual maturity. The person who lies is wounded. The untruthful people of our world are only lying to themselves, because they have not heard the voice of their Orendas or Spiritual Essences. To live in total truth is to know the light of the Eternal Flame of Love.

Listening Woman hears every thought, senses every feeling, and receives every impression in Tiyoweh, the Stillness. She uses her gift of prophesy based on the information she collects. The Clan Mother of Tiyoweh can foretell the probable future, showing us our potentials to follow the Beauty Way or the crooked trail. She sends us warnings when we are off balance and encouragement when we are walking with grace. The omens, portents, signs, and guideposts of life come to us because Listening Woman has heard our hearts, our spoken intent, our unspoken desires, or our needs. The messengers she sends our way are the Allies of Nature, the Ancestor Spirits, the Creature-teachers, and/or the voices of our Orendas.

▲▲
Entering the Stillness

Listening Woman remembered the first human experience she went through when she came from the spirit world to walk the Earth. Many, many moons had passed since then, and yet the sweetness of that first moment was alive in her memory, giving her comfort amidst the all-consuming tasks she faced being an adviser and counselor to her human children. Her senses drank in the smells and sensations of that long-ago time, allowing her to float back into the precious memory of her first awakening.

Listening Woman came into her human form in a giant cavern where the blackness was complete. Even with her eyes open, she was surrounded by total darkness and vast nothingness. She did not know that her human eyes could encompass the beauty of the natural world. She was enveloped in the scent of damp earth, a faint, acrid smell of growing rock formations, and the clean, sweet perfume of her own body. In the darkness, she felt her human flesh for the first time, reveling in the sensations of smooth skin and pliant, well-formed muscles. She touched her head and was surprised at how her hair softly covered her shoulders, falling below her hips like a mantle to protect her from the chill of the cavern.

With each movement of her body, she felt other textures. Tiny grains of pebblelike sand covered the surface beneath her, gently rubbing her legs. She heard moisture dripping from the ceiling above, giving delight, as a drop or two hit her skin, sending new sensations through her body. The soft roundness of her belly and breasts was very different from the strong muscular legs that curled beneath her torso while she sat on the cavern's floor. Her fingertips traced the line of her lips and she noticed that they were full and soft, the texture of the skin being different from the chin beneath or the cheekbones above.

As she fingered the curve of her eyes, she gave a start when she realized that the eyelids were coverings used to protect the sensitive round orbs beneath them. One eye watered, cleansing itself from her unknowing touch, sending a tear coursing down her cheek. She noted the unfamiliar sensations of discomfort and wetness as a part of her discovery. She made a mental note that some parts of this human form were very sensitive and would need to be handled with care.

As Listening Woman continued her discovery by touching her neck, she felt the strong, lean curve of the graceful pedestal that held her head above her body, noticing that there were solid structural protrusions just beneath the skin in the back. The skeletal forms of her spine that gave her flesh a frame felt angular in comparison to the firm smoothness of the muscles that covered them. Her fingertips moved up the side of her neck and she felt the shell-like appendages of her ears.

In the deep darkness of the cavern, the Guardian of Inner Knowing could hear the slightest movement of her hands, the gentle rasp of her breath, the dripping of water droplets, and the rustle of her legs against the cave's floor when she shifted her body's position. She drank in every sound as she moved and touched her feet, toes, ankles, and shins, marveling in the magnificence of the human form she had inherited. As Listening Woman stretched her body and found the ways in which she could position her form, she discovered gurgles coming from the organs within her torso. A slight ache in the middle of her belly resounded with a rumble that echoed through the cavern. She was concerned with the new development and silently sent her thoughts to the Earth Mother.

"Mother, I do not understand this sound and the ache in my middle. I feel like something is missing, and yet I know that the Great Mystery created these beautiful human forms in wholeness. What do I need to learn?"

The Earth Mother's voice filled the mind and heart of Listening Woman as she answered her daughter. "These sounds are a part of the human body, child. Sometimes these gurgling noises mean that the body is digesting the fuel that is needed to give the body strength. At other times, the rumbles mean that the body needs sustenance to maintain its stamina. You are feeling the ache because there is a hunger for the food your body needs."

Listening Woman sat in the Stillness, feeling the ache deep in her belly, and listened to the accompanying sounds to become familiar with the language of her body's needs. She asked the Earth Mother how she could feed the form that housed her spirit. The Earth Mother spoke to her daughter, explaining that a basket of food had been placed in the cavern very close to the Clan Mother and that by using her sense of touch, Listening Woman could find it and feed herself.

The Keeper of Introspection began to grope the space around herself in a circular motion, encountering the basket of food a short distance away. She felt the textures of each of the food substances while the Earth Mother told her how to taste and chew and swallow. The sounds of eating were very different, depending upon the choice of foods she made. Some sounds were softer, allowing her to hear the swirl of her tongue over the juicy flesh of a ripe peach. When she bit into a carrot, the loud crunch of her teeth against the firmness of the vegetable echoed in her ears and filled the emptiness of the cavern with waves of startling sounds. Listening Woman was amazed by the volume of the noises and paused, afraid to continue or swallow.

The gentle laughter of the Earth Mother filled the Clan Mother's sense of inner knowing, relieving her trepidation. The Earth Mother's joyous assurance that all was as it should be gave the Clan Mother a desire to crunch louder.

The Keeper of Discernment found the feelings inside of herself that told her it was all right to continue; so she crunched down on the bite of carrot and made the loud echoes again and again, filling the cavern with the sounds of enjoyment that came from relishing the sweet taste of the carrot.

Listening Woman noticed that her body was no longer groaning and that the feeling of something being missing was gone. A new feeling of fulfillment had replaced the emptiness, and she noticed the contentment and sense of well-being that flooded her body. She kept the basket near her in case the rumbles started again, because she had no idea how often her new body would need food. She returned her attention to the sounds and sensations found in the obsidian blackness of the cavern.

The stillness was interrupted by the reverberating sound of liquid dripping from the ceiling of the cavern and hitting a large pool of water behind her. The Earth Mother urged her to find her sense of direction by noting where the sounds came from and to follow the splashes until she reached their origin. The Clan Mother crawled toward the drip and splash noises until she felt the same kind of wetness she had discovered when the tear had rolled down her cheek. The Earth Mother explained that the liquid was water and did not taste salty like the tear from Listening Woman's eye. This sweet water was used to quench thirst, a dryness, and was essential to her human body.

Listening Woman learned how to cup her hands and take the water to her lips and drink. The accompanying sounds were not unlike the gurgles she had heard coming from hunger. The Clan Mother discovered that she could make different noises when she lapped the water, slurped, or swallowed. The echoes of each sound filled the pregnant void with a myriad of resounding waves of vibrations, giving Listening Woman a multitude of new noises to experience. At one point in her process of reaching into the water, the Clan Mother encountered a small stone. She pulled the Stone Person from the pool and felt the solid form, noticing that it was much harder than the bones of her body and larger than the pebbles that covered the floor of the cavern. When the Stone Person spoke to her in the same way that the Earth Mother had spoken to her inner knowing, Listening Woman was so startled that she dropped the Stone Person into the pool of water with a resounding splash.

The Stone Person continued to speak to her, explaining that he was a friend. Groping in front of her to retrieve the rock, Listening Woman found herself making all sorts of strange noises. Her breath started to come in harder gusts and she could hear the pounding of her heart as she frantically felt below the water's surface for the friend she had dropped in her moment of surprise. The Stone Person guided her hands to his resting place and then began to explain how he could aid her in the further discovery of her gifts, talents, and abilities.

"I am a Rock Person who holds the libraries of all that has passed on the Earth Mother. Together, we can approach the outside world, learning what you need to experience in order to fulfill your mission. You have already begun that journey by learning the language of your body's needs, how to hear the Earth Mother's voice, and how to listen to my words. Here in the darkness, you are beginning to develop the skills of understanding that make up the many levels of sound without sight, taste and touch without visual contact, and feelings without outside confusing influences. These first encounters with your abilities of perception will allow you to hear the truth in every situation you encounter in physical life. The darkness of the Void of the Unknown will be comforting to you and the answers you seek will come through your ability to hear them."

Listening Woman's breath came in soft, even rhythms as she held her new friend to her heart. The Keeper of Discernment felt a kinship and a trust between herself and the Stone Person, who called himself *Hagehjih*, Old Man. In his ancient form Listening Woman found the comfort of a kindred spirit, because her own Spiritual Essence was as old as the Earth Mother and Grandmother Moon, who were created in the Spirit World by the Great Mystery. Old Man understood the Clan Mother's desire to find out all that she could about her humanness and the things she needed to master on her path to wholeness.

That friendship had been the beginning of her journey. The long-ago memory and how much she had grown with Old Man's assistance, created a chain of pictures and sensations that flooded Listening Woman's mind and senses. She recalled her first experience with light and the gentle steps that Old Man had insisted that she take when they emerged from the cavern. Old Man had introduced her to Ant, who had taught her the Medicine of *patience*. Ant had spoken of the wisdom of taking the time needed for her eyes to adjust to the light that filtered into the cavern. The brightness of the outside world grew as the Clan Mother and Old Man spent one Sun and Sleep closer to the entrance of the cave, allowing Listening Woman to keep her hearing abilities intact while she blended her talent of listening with the new experience of sight. Her excitement at seeing new colors and forms nearly got the best of her in those first sighted moments. The urge to rush into discovery had to be curtailed for her to maintain physical, emotional, and spiritual balance.

Now, many moons later, Listening Woman was happy that she had honored the wisdom and harmony that had allowed her to emerge from the cavern into the outside world in a balanced way. Her mind returned to another memory of the progress she had made during the winters she had learned about the other Two-legged humans she would share the world with during her journey on the Red Road of life.

In those early times when she encountered other human beings, Listening Woman was able to develop her gifts of inner knowing because humans had not yet developed speech. The Human Tribe spoke *Hail-oh-way-an*, the Language of Love. This nonverbal language expressed the heart of any matter a Two-legged needed to communicate. In silence, the observer had to watch and note the expressions, movements, and feelings being shared by the one who was communicating. To receive the wholeness of any message, the listener had to focus on the person communicating without interjecting or interrupting. Listening Woman had mastered the art of hearing the Language of Love and oftentimes heard the thoughts of others through her ability to access their inner knowing as well as her own.

The Clan Mother remembered how she had been able to teach others the same talent of understanding the voice of another's heart and how the Human Tribe had benefited in those early times. Since then, the Earth Mother had completed many rotations around Grandfather Sun and the Children of Earth had grown and changed—some for the better, some for the worse. The progression of human spiritual evolution was a concern to Listening Woman because she had witnessed the truth and she had witnessed the crookedness that some verbal language had brought forth in those who wanted to hide the misaligned truths of their intentions. Greed and desire for control had given birth to forked tongues and double meanings in the spoken word. Her talents had naturally been honed into precision during the course of her encounters with individuals who spoke with the seeming sincerity that masked their hidden agendas.

Listening Woman had developed the gift of being a true observer by entering the Stillness of her own being and having no preconceptions while she listened to others, observing every movement of their bodies and every crescendo or cadence of their voices. The Clan Mother could easily see if the speaker was nervous, hiding something, or merely shy. Over the passing of seasons, Listening Woman earned her role of being the Keeper of Discernment. Every feeling of warning that issued forth from her navel, the feeling center of the body, sent shock waves through her sense of well-being and allowed her to discern who to trust and with whom she needed to exercise caution. Many of her lessons had been hard earned; she had been forced by circumstances to pay attention to actions rather than words. This form of observing took a deeper concentration and focus, as the Clan Mother delved farther into listening to her heart's impressions of the speaker in front of her. It had been during one of those particularly difficult situations that Listening Woman had been blessed with hearing the voice of her Orenda, her Spiritual Essence.

The bitter cold of that winter Sun had made it almost impossible to relax into Tiyoweh, the Stillness. Listening Woman had nearly decided that the time was not right for her to hear the stories of the two men who had asked for her advice. The winter winds pressed through any tiny opening in the hides that covered the entrance to the cavern of the Tribe she was with, creating unwelcome wafts of cold that sent every muscle into tense knots. The Clan Mother knew that she risked becoming short tempered with the men and that she might have a difficult time discerning their shivers from the telltale signs that usually allowed her to perceive hidden meanings or untruths. She knew that in meeting with these two men, she would have to stretch her capacity to hear the truth, listening to their inner thoughts and unspoken intentions.

During the time that the three spent together, the Clan Mother listened with her whole being, sensing the urgency of the situation as well as the impatience of one of the men. The viewpoints of the men differed greatly, making each certain that the other was incapable of understanding. The Guardian of Introspection took the time she needed before saying anything and told the men that they would meet again during the following Sun.

After the men left her fire, Listening Woman felt confused by all she had heard, the gestures of each man, and the way the bitter cold had robbed part of her focus. As she sat gazing into the flames of her twig fire, she closed her eyes and felt deep inside her own being. A feeling of warmth roused itself from the stillness and poured though her like golden honey, sweet and rich. The Clan Mother felt herself expanding beyond the limits of her human form and then beyond the walls of the cavern the Tribe called home. In the stillness, she heard a faint whisper, a voice she did not recognize. The orange flames flickered with light and shadow against her closed eyelids as she followed the whisper into the grayness that bordered her senses. The journey took her into the blackness of the Void of the Unknown, beyond the boundaries of her perceptions. The voice grew clearer and more animated the closer she traveled to the sound.

A light began to emerge in the darkness of the Void, leading Listening Woman to a brilliance she had never encountered before. The light was made of multicolored bursts of flame that changed with the cadence of the voice that spoke from the center of the fire. Listening Woman felt a lump rise in her throat and tears sting her human eyes as she discovered the voice of her Orenda. She had ventured beyond her human form, yet she could feel every emotion and subtle change in her body. She heard the sound of her throat trying to swallow, the crackling of the twig fire, the almost imperceptible sob caused by her joyous tears, and the voice of her Spiritual Essence.

In her state of heightened awareness, the Clan Mother understood all of the steps of her passage and how each and every lesson had brought her to this moment of personally realized wholeness. The voice of her Orenda was the welcoming voice that signaled that she had come home to the true Self. An overwhelming rush of emotions rocked her body with feelings of gratitude, satisfaction, permanence, humility, wonder, nurturance, belonging, achievement, and the desire to know more. She was taken aback by the beauty of the Eternal Flame of Love that held the Orenda's voice, dancing in her mind's eye.

In a heartbeat, she was aware of the Earth Mother's nurturance of her physical form and the Great Mystery's loving protection of her Spiritual Essence. The two worlds of spirit and of tangible substance had become one inside her Orenda. She heard the harmony of Creation issue forth from the center of her being, singing the music found in all spheres of life. Every life form had a melody intricately harmonizing with all of the others.

There was no room for discord in the symphony of sounds that flowed through her perceptions. Her heart, body, mind, and spirit had a new sense of wholeness. Nothing seemed too far or too great to encompass, as her ability to hear every voice in Creation grew stronger inside her being.

The desire to have every human being share in her experience was interrupted by the voice of her Orenda. "Self of myself, you are expressing the Creator's desire of unlimited joy. You are blessed with the generosity of spirit that wants all others to find this inner knowing. Until each human being has walked the paths to wholeness that you have walked, they cannot fully understand the ecstasy and bliss of your experience. Every being must be given the opportunities that they need in order to find their individual paths home, to the true Self. Listen to their hearts and guide them in ways that allow them to know that they may accomplish the tasks of homecoming for themselves."

Listening Woman asked the voice of her Orenda if there were some way that she should direct her human children, and the voice of her Orenda replied. "Teach them how to listen to the voices of the natural world. Call upon Hawk, who is *the messenger* that carries those words of wisdom, to assist you in showing the Two-leggeds how to listen. Teach them the compassion of Ant, whose Medicine is *patience* and the wisdom of Armadillo whose Medicine shows them *how to keep the feelings and troubles of others out of their Sacred Spaces by using boundaries.* Show the human beings the listening abilities of Rabbit and how he teaches his Medicine of *not listening to unrealistic fears.* Point out the Medicine of Mockingbird, who teaches Two-leggeds *the gift of recalling and repeating all they have heard.* Call upon Ferret to use his Medicine of *ferreting out the answers by using deduction and reason.* Porcupine can assist your children by teaching them the Medicine of *faith and innocence.* They will need to have faith in their paths, their abilities, and their connections to the Great Mystery, as well as the kind of innocence and humility that keeps the limitations of skepticism and arrogance from daunting their progress."

Deep inside her heart, Listening Woman recorded all that the voice of her Orenda had shared with her. The Guardian of Introspection understood that she had completed her final Rite of Passage, which reflected her personal realization of wholeness. Her next step on the Great Medicine Wheel of Life would be teaching her human children how to hear and interpret the messages they received. The roar of the Sea Lion resounded in her memory, reminding her that she could call on the abilities of the Seals and Sea Lions to teach her human children the Medicine of *riding the waves of their emotions and feelings in order to discover all facets of themselves.* Through trusting their feelings, her human children could learn the many levels of discernment necessary for hearing the truth.

Listening Woman had learned many lessons during that Sun of bitter cold and fiery feelings of wholeness. Then she had applied the new understanding to the two men who had asked for her counsel. She had taught the two men how to see the harmony of the other's viewpoint by making them stand in the position of the other, pretending to voice the opposite viewpoint until they respected the other's opinion.

Those earlier events seemed so very long ago. During the generations that followed, Listening Woman had grown and continued to develop her skills. As if they were rare Medicine Objects, she quietly put away her precious memories, wrapping them in Tiyoweh, using the Stillness like a Medicine Bundle to hold the sacred remembrances of her passage.

Now, it was time for the Clan Mother to enter Tiyoweh and listen to the words of a young woman who was struggling to understand her dreams and the messages she had received. As Grandfather Sun rode low in the Sky Nation, Listening Woman helped the young dreamer to interpret the symbols and spoken wisdom she had gathered from her visions. Listening Woman showed the younger woman how to ask herself leading questions that would enable her to find her own answers. The tools that the Clan Mother used sparked understanding, always asking the young woman to think, to remember, to feel, and to honor the still, inner voice that insisted that the dreamer hear the truth inside her own heart.

Listening Woman would listen to the girl and then ask, "How did that make you feel?" or "What did that Creature seem to be teaching you?"

In every instance, when a person seeking counsel felt safe and like she or he was really being heard, the inner knowing would shine forth. Listening Woman found herself becoming a reflector for those seeking assistance, always recognizing that at some point all of her children needed to be reassured. Some were frightened of the Stillness, others were afraid of the darkness of the Void, still others were scared of what they might hear because they had been denying the truth inside themselves.

Each member of the Human Tribe was an individual who had to follow the path to wholeness that suited him or her, but all of the Human Tribe would have to discover inner hearing before those paths would reach the wholeness they sought. Hearing the voice of the Orenda was the manner in which all humans would eventually realize their potentials. Without that ability to listen to their hearts' desires and inner truths, they were lost. Listening Woman taught them that the first step on every individual path was learning to listen to their bodies and to each other with respect. Later, they were taught the skills of listening to nature; then, how to hear and interpret the unspoken messages of the natural world and the voices of the Ancestors that rode on the winds. Further along the path to wholeness, the Children of Earth learned how to listen to their own spoken words, comparing what they actually said to the truth found in the Orenda's voice. This step was a weeding-out process that struck at the heart of the limitations and illusions found along the Red Road of human life.

As Listening Woman reviewed the skills she had been able to pass along to the Children of earth, the fluttering of her heart caught her attention. She focused on the flutter and found the voice of her Orenda, filled with love. A shudder went through the Clan Mother's body as the voice spoke:

"The Children of Earth will heal their wounds and find the same joy that you have cradled in your heart, self of myself. There is more inner peace available with each passing season because more members of the Human Tribe are discovering the way home. The love is returning. As that flow of life increases, and the Two-leggeds find the Eternal Flame of Love inside of themselves, Hail-oh-way-an, the Language of Love, will return. They will once again be able to hear the pureness of each other's hearts and understand the harmony of Creation that the Great Mystery has given as a legacy of peace. All life forms will live together as one and will support all others without judgment or exception. Listen. Can you hear it?"

As the voice of her Orenda faded, Listening Woman heard the faint murmurs of the breeze, building in pitch, climbing the ridges across Sacred Mountain, encircling the Earth Mother. The voices of the Ancestors rode the Winds of Change, whispering to all who could hear.

"Now is the time of the return of White Buffalo. It is time to set aside your fears and to join us in the quest for wholeness and unity. Children, call to this Grandmother who can teach you the harmony of your heart's inner peace. Listening Woman hears your call and stands ready to show you how to discover the way. Listen for the soft falling footsteps of your Ancestors amid the pounding of White Buffalo's hooves, and know. Know that every night we light the homecoming fires across the great expanse of the Sky Nation. In Tiyoweh we wait. We send you our ancient whispers to mark the Harmony Trail back to your heart's home."

Listening Woman sat in the Stillness and listened. The emerging voices that were calling her name came as no surprise. The time for humans to listen and to reach for spiritual wholeness, discarding separation and limitation, had finally arrived.

STORYTELLER

Tell me a story, sweet Mother,
Of the Ancestors and their days,
Of how they walked with beauty,
Learning the Medicine Ways.

As you relate the stories,
I am allowed to see
The importance of every lesson
And how it applies to me.

Through another's example
I share the laughter and the tears.
Through another's experience
I learn how love can conquer fear.

Together we can journey
Through those other times,
Reclaiming all the wisdom
Of the legacies left behind.

Clan Mother
of the
Sixth Moon Cycle

STORYTELLER is the Clan Mother of the moon cycle that falls in the month of June and is represented by the color red. Storyteller teaches us to have faith, to be humble, and to stay young at heart by keeping our innocence intact. These are some of the Medicines found in the color red. The Sixth Cycle of Truth guarded by this Clan Mother is *speaking the truth*. Storyteller teaches her human children how to speak from their hearts, always saying what they mean, in a truthful, clear, and concise manner. This Clan Mother is the teacher of truth and the pathfinder who shows us the faith we need to find our way through the illusory forests of our own confusions. Storyteller teaches us that speaking the truth is the basis of the Oral Tradition that keeps universal, timeless wisdom alive. The hard-learned lessons that have guided other human beings safely down the Red Road of physical life apply to all humans because they are based on eternal truths.

Storyteller teaches us how to use humor to dispel our fears and how to balance the sacredness with irreverence. When we can laugh at our humanness and our silly attempts to preserve our limitations, we will have conquered

▲▲▲▲▲▲▲▲▲▲▲▲▲▲▲▲▲▲▲▲▲▲▲▲▲▲▲▲▲▲▲▲▲▲▲▲▲▲

the self-created demons that bind us to high drama and our need to create constant upheaval. Through listening to the stories of others and how they handled the lessons presented on their paths, we are able to gain perspective on our own Rites of Passage on Earth.

This Clan Mother is also the holder of Heyokah Medicine, tricking us into growth through laughter. The Heyokah can show us how to achieve the wholeness our Orenda's desire, by going through the back door or contrary side of any lesson. The Spiritual Essence, or the Orenda, sees beyond human tunnel vision and can work with Heyokah Medicine to push us beyond our stubbornness. The Heyokah will clown around, giving us subtle lessons that we can reflect upon or ignore. Storyteller can also weave a story that embodies the characteristics of a person's life lessons without pointing a finger at the individual. The Heyokah personality of Storyteller then tricks the listener into safely seeing his or her situation through the eyes of an observer, instead of having to confront the issue head-on.

Storyteller uses the gifts of wisdom presented by the Ancient Ones, now in spirit, to present the truths that helped those Ancestors. When truth has been used to solve life's problems or challenges, those truths are to be shared with future generations. Storyteller and her moon cycle are connected to the color red because blood is red. The wisdom of all human Ancestors and their lessons are coded in the DNA of the blood. In Traditional Indian Medicine, the blood has always been acknowledged as the river of life that flows through our bodies, allowing us to claim the knowing held by the wise Elders who came before us. Only in modern times have scientists discovered that the DNA carries the genetic imprint, but they have not discovered that the collective mind and spirit of the human race can be accessed through the patterns of DNA in every human cell and in the blood.

Storyteller allows every listener to hear the stories of how others found truth in their lives. Through the words of truth she speaks, this Clan Mother teaches us to know how to speak from our personal truths and from our Sacred Points of View when we are asked for an opinion. When we are *not* asked to make a comment, she teaches us to listen without having to add our unwanted advice. The Guardian of the Medicine Stories reminds us that speaking the truth never hurts another if it is done with love and if we do not include the projections of self-righteousness or the petty judgments we often use to criticize ourselves. Speaking the truth is an art that never includes judging another. Pointing a finger at another always leaves three fingers pointing back at the accuser. This kind of judgment never allows the person who is the target of the criticism to find the truth for himself or herself. Like Storyteller, a person wishing to speak the truth without pointing a finger can share a story of how he or she learned a lesson or passed safely through a crisis. This Teacher of Truth reminds us that people who are passing half-truths, breaking the trust of a confidence, or being rumor factories are doing so because they are wounded. Because of their inability to speak the truth even to themselves, they project the lies and illusions inside their woundedness on to the nearest human reflection or situation they can find.

⩙ ⩙

The Telling of Tales

Storyteller looked into the faces of the children who had gathered around her to listen to the stories she would share with her Tribe's Council of Wee People. The fire was reflected in the expectant faces of the little ones, giving Storyteller an audience of rapt admirers. The love they felt for Storyteller came from the way the Clan Mother treated them with respect. Storyteller had taught the preceding generations of many Clans and Tribes that the children were full-grown spirits in tiny bodies, hence the Council of Children became the Council of Wee People.

The night sky was moonless, bringing thousands of stars into view. This Sleep began the new moon cycle of the Ripening Moon. The Starry Medicine Bowl of the night sky gave everyone a sense that something spectacular was about to happen. The breeze carried the sweet perfume of Mimosa blossoms that dangled from the branches of the Tree People who encircled the Clan Mother's lodge. Lightning Bugs danced in the air around the tall cattails, wild mint, and red clover-lined brook that snaked through the camp. Occasionally Fireflies would flicker and twinkle in the warm summer night.

Storyteller decided that it was a perfect time to share the story of how Firefly got his blinking light. The children who made up the Council of Wee People were entranced by the Clan Mother, the stars, and the dancing Fireflies, trying to decide what was more interesting to their curious minds.

· ·

"*Naweh Skennio*, thank you for being healthy." Storyteller began with the traditional greeting that brought the children's wandering attention back to her. The little ones knew that this greeting was the formal sign that they were to settle down, to be very still, and to listen without interrupting. Storyteller only told short stories to this Council of Wee People because the youngest children, who had passed only three summers, had much shorter attention spans than the older ones who were also a part of the council. When a child passed his or her eleventh summer, the boys moved to the Young Warriors Council and the girls joined the Council of the Butterfly, which prepared them for their budding and blossoming transformation into womanhood.

Storyteller cleared her throat and began her tale. "Many, many long moons ago, the Firefly was known by another name. He was a star and his name was Forgets to Twinkle. This little brother was a part of the Great Star Nation and lived with his Seven Sister Stars, who are still shining brightly there, in the sky." Storyteller pointed to the seven stars inside the constellation of the Great Buffalo, showing the children where to look.

"The Seven Sister Stars held the Seven Sacred Directions of East, South, West, North, Above, Below, and Within, teaching all of us in the Human Tribe to honor the abundance that the Great Buffalo brings to us from every direction. Forgets to Twinkle was always sad because his sisters had the missions of holding the Seven Sacred Directions for the Great Buffalo and he wasn't sure what his mission was. He was so very sad that sometimes he let his light fade away and that is how he earned his name of Forgets to Twinkle.

●●●

"One Sleep, when Grandmother Moon was showing her Full face, Forgets to Twinkle asked her for permission to leave the Sky Nation and go nearer to the Earth Mother to discover more about his purpose in life. Grandmother Moon said that Forgets to Twinkle could go, but that he should be careful not to go too close to the Earth. The Earth Mother's magnetism could hold him and keep him from coming home. Forgets to Twinkle agreed that he would pay attention and only travel where it was safe.

"On the first Sleep, Forgets to Twinkle traveled through the Sky Nation until he was hanging in the clouds above Sacred Mountain. His heart was very happy because he could see all of the Little Sisters and Brothers of the Creature Tribe playing in the moonlight. He shouted down to Brother Coyote and asked if he could join in the play. Coyote was known by all of the other animals as the Trickster, but little Forgets to Twinkle did not know anything about any of the Children of Earth because he had never been anywhere but the Sky Nation. Trickster Coyote shouted back that he would be delighted if his Little Star Brother wanted to play with him, but Coyote thought Forgets to Twinkle was too far away.

"Forgets to Twinkle thought a moment and then decided to come closer, dancing in the sky while Coyote danced with him on the Earth. Coyote started talking to the Little Star Brother very softly, making Forgets to Twinkle come closer to hear what the Trickster was saying. Softer and softer words of friendship brought the Little Star out of the sky until he was floating just over Coyote's head."

Storyteller paused for just a moment, allowing all the children to wonder what would happen next. When she had every wide-eyed face glued to hers, she raised her voice in increments, finally shouting at the scary part, "Then that mean old Trickster grabbed Forgets to Twinkle and gobbled him up!" The children gasped and some squealed, forgetting their manners for a moment.

"Well, I suppose that all of you know how terrified Forgets to Twinkle was when he found himself inside of the Trickster's belly. He was so upset, he forgot to twinkle and did not know how in the world he was going to get out safely.

"Around the same moment that Coyote gobbled up the Little Star Brother, Grandmother Moon looked down and noticed that Forgets to Twinkle was nowhere in sight. She looked and looked but could not see her Little Star Brother anywhere. Because she was concerned, she sent the Stars-with-Tails, who were her scouts, out to look for Little Brother. In those ancient times, the Comet People were messengers who could come and go from the Great Star Nation. These Stars-with-Tails searched high and low for Little Brother without any luck in finding him.

"Inside the Trickster's belly, the Little Star Brother was frightened, but he knew that he had better start remembering all the wisdom his Seven Sisters had taught him or he would never see them again. After a long while, he finally remembered why he was called Forgets to Twinkle. He had always been afraid that his light was not as pretty as his sisters' and so he would only blink a little light here and there. Now that he was trapped inside Coyote's belly, he decided he had better trust his ability to shine brightly. He huffed and puffed and sent all of his light into his little star body, lighting himself and shining as brightly as he could.

"The Trickster suddenly found that the trick was on him when his whole furry body lit up like Grandfather Sun. Coyote ran and ran, trying to hide from the Comet scouts that Grandmother Moon had sent to find Little Brother. The Trickster had seen the Stars-with-Tails circling the prairies, looking for Forgets to Twinkle. Old Coyote had thought he could trick the Star Scouts as easily as he had tricked Little Brother. Now the slippery Trickster was so bright that there was no place he could run to or hide without the Star Scouts finding him. In a panic, the Trickster opened his mouth and spit Little Star Brother out and then ran away.

"The Stars-with-Tails spread the news to the Cloud People, who told the Thunderers, who told the Fire Sticks that the mean old Trickster needed a taste of his own Medicine. The Sky Nation was filled with the Little Star Brother's angry Relations who gathered the storms, filling the Cloud People with Raindrop People and Ice-beings who could wet and punch Coyote with their water and ice bodies. Hinoh, the Thunder Chief, belched his rolling roar, and the Thunderbird flapped his giant wings, bringing such enormous sounds that the Trickster stood quaking in fear.

"Meanwhile, Little Star Brother was trapped in the Earth Mother's magnetism. He could not move from the ground and go home. He was still shining brightly so that his Sky Relations could see where he was, but no one could rescue him because they would be caught in the Planetary Mother's magnetism as well. He called out to the Earth Mother and asked her to release him and waited for her reply.

"The storm was moving across the land, giving the Trickster a chance to run as he finally found his paws and started to dodge the pellets of ice and freezing rain. Lightning bolts crashed around him and one Fire Stick hit him, finally catching his tail on fire. Coyote ran and ran, trying to think how he could trick the Sky Relations and make them leave him alone.

"Little Star Brother finally heard the Earth Mother speak amid the sounds of the Thunderers. Her voice traveled on the raging winds that accompanied the storm his Relations had made. 'Forgets to Twinkle, you are going to have to live with the Children of Earth now. If I release my magnetism, you will be able to go home, but all of my children will fall off the earth and go flying into the sky. You are responsible for forgetting to pay attention to Grandmother Moon's advice and warning. There is no way that I can help you without hurting my other children. You must stay here with us and decide what kind of creature you would like to become.'

"Forgets to Twinkle was sad but he knew that the Earth Mother was right. He had not paid attention and had been tricked into ignoring Grandmother Moon's warning. He wanted to be a part of the Sky Nation and to see the world from above as he had always done when he lived with his Seven Sisters. He knew that he would never again forget to shine his light brightly, because he wanted his Sky Relations to know where he was and that he remembered his family. He decided to tell the Earth Mother that he wanted to be a flying creature who could shine like a star. The Earth Mother agreed and changed him into a flying Creepy-crawler of the Insect Tribe. She put a tiny star in his tail so that he could twinkle at his Sky Relations, reminding all other Little Brothers and Sisters in the Great Star Nation what could happen to them if they did not pay attention to the wisdom of their Elders.

"Even now, if Coyote hears thunder or sees a Firefly, he will run away in fear. The Trickster remembers that the Fire Sticks caught his tail on fire and that he had to jump into a pond to put it out. Some people say that the Fire Sticks and Thunder Beings counted coup on Coyote, bringing victory and honor to Little Star Brother. That is how Forgets to Twinkle earned the name Lightning Bug. His Firefly tail lights up to remind Coyote of the only Relations that ever outtricked the Trickster by catching his tail on fire. When Firefly's tail lights up, we Two-leggeds are reminded to let our Medicine shine and to keep a twinkle in our eyes so the Trickster cannot fool us into following the crooked trail."

All of the children sat with open mouths or wide eyes, gaping at Storyteller, savoring the richness of Little Star Brother's story.

Older sisters and brothers came by to gather the wee ones back to the lodges to make ready for the Sleep Man. They had all heard Storyteller tell the tale of the Sleep Man and knew that after a nightly story, the Sleep Man would come to sprinkle sleep-sand in their eyes. If the children were still awake, the Sleep Man would be angry and their dreams would not be happy dreams. If they were settled for the night, the Sleep Man would bring happy dreams to the little ones. Everybody wanted happy dreams and so the Tribe never had a problem getting the children tucked into warm sleeping robes and off to Dreamland.

Storyteller watched as the Wee Council departed with parents and older siblings. Their tiny voices said, *"Naweh, Aksot, o'gadenetga do,* thank you, Grandmother, I had fun."

The Clan Mother acknowledged the thanks and farewells and prepared to retire to her lodge.

She sent her silent thanks to the Great Mystery for the enrichment that the children brought into her life and the gifts she was able to pass to the little ones, giving them a strong foundation for growth.

She was brought from her thoughts when she heard the howl of Wolf, who always walked beside her in spirit. Her Totem gave her *the ability to create new paths for learning and teaching.* The pack of timber wolves who lived above the river in the hills had been her friends over the many Ripening Moons when her Tribe came to live by the river. Often, she had observed their hunting and their play when she visited the upper meadows. She raised her voice to salute her brothers and sisters, returning their greeting with a howl that matched their own. The Clan Mother's greeting was answered again, signaling that the Sleep Man was beckoning Storyteller to rest and refresh her body so that she could dream the joys to be found in the coming Sun.

Later, when Storyteller was nestled in her sleeping robes, she dreamed of Magpie, who was sometimes called the Little Black Eagle. In her dream, Magpie was riding the back of Buffalo, feasting on the insects that had collected in Buffalo's fur. The black and iridescent midnight blue of Magpie's feathers shone in the sunlight, flashing amid the white touches of feathers gracing her wings and tail. In the dream, Magpie told of her Medicine, which was *the talent of relieving the pain of others.* Little Black Eagle taught Storyteller that discomfort was a warning that showed change in the body. Magpie told Storyteller that some Two-leggeds were not willing to go through any kind of discomfort because they did not understand that chills and fevers were the body's way of shedding limitation. After the Human Tribe understood the lessons of growth found through the challenges of discomfort, Magpie would send her spirit to remove the discomfort and pain. Like her namesake, Eagle, Magpie showed Two-leggeds how to find freedom. Eagle taught the freedom of the Spirit, and Magpie taught how to allow the spirit's understanding and freedom to enter the body.

Storyteller was the listener in her dream, just as the children were her listeners during her waking hours. The Keeper of Humor nearly woke herself when she laughed while listening to Magpie harping about her cousin from the tropical regions of Turtle Island. Magpie described the Winged Cousin as having the biggest beak imaginable and bright-colored feathers. Because the cousin's beak was so big compared to her body, she was known for having her nose in everyone else's business, but in fact she noticed everything that could bring harm. Little Black Eagle called the cousin Toucan and said that this cousin's Medicine was *the warning system of the jungle.* Toucan sometimes visited the dreams of the Human Tribe who lived far, far away in order to make them more observant. When trouble or danger was near, Toucan would fly through the jungle in the tangible world or send her spirit flying through the Dreamtime, calling out a warning to those who needed to heed the danger signal.

Magpie nearly always followed Toucan, flying through dreams, showing human beings how to avoid the painful lessons found by not being aware of the warning signs and dangers along the Red Road of life. Little Black Eagle told the Keeper of the Medicine Stories how her big-beaked cousin's warnings could teach human beings to be aware of situations that could strip them of their physical well-being. Toucan sent a warning in life-threatening situations, reminding unwary daydreamers that paying attention could save them from being physically harmed. Since Toucan lived in a very distant part of Turtle Island, Magpie was introducing the Clan Mother to Toucan's Medicine through the dream, giving Storyteller the knowledge of Toucan's Medicine so that she would have his protection if she ever needed it. Storyteller thanked the Little Black Eagle for the introduction and for the lessons she had discovered in her dream.

When Storyteller awoke, she discovered that Grandfather Sun's light had not yet graced the morning sky and so she lay in silence, reflecting on the Medicine she had received during the night. Story after story filled her head with new ways to share the wisdom that had been presented to her. The Clan Mother felt a sense of newness as she smelled the dew-covered plants on the morning breeze. Storyteller listened to the water song of the river running near her lodge and was content. The Oral Traditions would continue to live, as long as those who spoke their eternal truths passed them from generation to generation, giving the human children of Earth a way to understand their lives. She was happy that she was a part of the oral legacy and that the Creature-teachers were willing to share their Medicine with her so that she could pass that Medicine on through the tales she told.

The Guardian of the Medicine Stories closed her eyes for a moment and saw the spirit of her new friend, Toucan.

Silently, she allowed her thoughts to ask Toucan if the Winged One had sent her spirit for a reason or was just greeting the Clan Mother on this new Sun. Toucan spoke to Storyteller, whispering a message that would always be a part of the Keeper of Humor's memory.

"Mother, I have come to tell you that many changes will befall the Two-leggeds during the passage of worlds. My warning is twofold. If the Children of Earth forget to laugh at themselves, they will perish from the actions they take when seriousness strangles their sense of play and laughter. The Human Tribe needs to be shown how to use humor to diffuse potentially painful or destructive situations. If they forget how to balance the sacredness with the irreverence, the joy of living will be lost.

"The second part of my warning concerns the keeping of Oral Traditions. When a Medicine Story has been passed to many generations and contains truth, those wise ways will support humans in their growth throughout time. To allow those stories to die would be an injustice. The Children of Earth will change and some will lose their connections to the natural world. If only through their dreams, the Medicine Stories will keep them connected to the rest of the Planetary Family. Any person who can speak the truth by telling a tale that will give listeners a way to reflect on their lives without pointing a finger will carry my Medicine of warning. If the warnings allow those listening to come back into balance, unity will be achieved."

Storyteller thanked Toucan for her twofold warning and then showed her feathered friend how well she had heard the message by replying, "So, my big-beaked sky sister, I am to remember that if we do not pay attention to the wisdom found in the telling of tales, we may find ourselves showing our tails to the world!"

Storyteller and the spirit of Toucan laughed and laughed. The sunlight had broken through the predawn grayness. The stern warnings had been taken to heart and understood. The warnings of the hard lessons found in imbalance reflected human pain and sorrow, but laughter had counted coup on the dark clouds that stood as human limitations, seemingly hiding the joys that could be found in being human. Storyteller understood and was willing to face the future with her children, always being mindful that each human being had to find these truths for herself or himself in order to pass through the spirit's evolution. She knew that her stories would be a comfort to the weary on the Sacred Path, and for that reason she would give them away— so that speaking the truth of wisdom and the Sacred Traditions would never die.

LOVES
ALL
THINGS

Mother, show me how to love
Beyond my human fear,
Teach me all the joys of life
Behind the veil of tears.

Let me find the pleasure of
A lover's gentle hands,
Let me know the wisdom of
Respect without demands.

Oh, Keeper of Forgiveness,
Teach me how to see
Beyond the petty judgments,
Supporting human dignity.

I will learn your Medicine
Of Mother, lover, friend,
Teaching others how to love
And broken hearts to mend.

Clan Mother
of the
Seventh Moon Cycle

LOVES ALL THINGS is the Clan Mother of the Seventh
Moon Cycle and the month of July. The color connected
with her Medicine is yellow and her cycle represents *loving
the truth* found in all life forms. She teaches us the wisdom
of compassion and how to be a loving woman and nurturing
mother.

Loves All Things is the Keeper of Sexual Wisdom and
shows us that every action of physical life is as sacred as our
spiritual growth because they are the same. When we be-
have as if all acts are sacred, there is no judgment. This Clan
Mother teaches us to love our bodies and to honor the pleasures of being human. She shows us that breathing, eating,
walking, playing, working, observing a sunrise, making
love, and dancing are all acts of pleasure given by the Earth
Mother to human beings. She asks us to do everything in
life with a happy heart. In her wisdom, Loves All Things
teaches us that we can find the joys of physical life, without
trying to escape our pain through becoming addicted to false
pleasures or compulsive behavior patterns.

Loves All Things is the Guardian of Unconditional Love
and is connected to Grandfather Sun. Like Grandfather's
sunlight, which shines on everything without withholding

▲▲

warmth or life-giving sustenance, this Clan Mother loves all her children equally. Loves All Things uses a form of unconditional love to show us that she does not judge our behaviors. She is willing to love us enough to allow us to go through the hard self-imposed lessons that are the consequences of following the crooked trail. Having to experience the consequences of our unloving actions may not give us pleasure, but remembering and avoiding those pitfalls in the future will always bring us back into balance. This Clan Mother holds the wisdom of allowing and does not smother her children or impose rigid rules. She uses her ability to allow us to go through the hard life lessons on our own but is always waiting to nurture our disappointments and mend our broken hearts.

Loves All Things teaches that every action in life is equal because the reaction is equal to the original deed. If we are good to our bodies, our bodies are healthy and good to us. If we nurture and respect ourselves, we will command that same respect and nurturing from others. If we lie to ourselves, others will lie to us in kind. If we think positive thoughts, good things will happen to support our attitudes. If we apply the love of truth to all things, we find ways to know and love the Self. This Clan Mother instructs us in a way that applies the concept of free will in its purest form. Her foremost understanding is that we will evolve, no matter what happens. Healing and growth may take many cycles of the Medicine Wheel, but she is willing to love us unconditionally through all those Rites of Passage until we love ourselves enough to break the patterns of self-induced slavery.

The freedom found in loving the Self without conditions is the talent that makes Loves All Things the Guardian of Children. She allows children to develop loving self-expression, encouraging them to be their personal best. This Clan Mother uses the child's love of discovering life as the guideline for raising the young. She teaches the child within us to accept love, to give love, to find ways to love the self, and to love the truth above all else.

Loves All Things is the Mother-Nurturer, a sensual lover, the Keeper of All Acts of Pleasure, and the Guardian of Sexual Wisdom. This Clan Mother embodies the attributes of the devoted friend who sees the strength of our personal Medicine, as well as our weaknesses, accepting both sides without judgment. Patiently, she supports us in our growth process by pointing out our talents, urging us to grow. Loves All Things ignores our unwillingness to use the talents we have at hand, because she understands that one day, on our personal healing paths, we will find it in ourselves.

▲▲

The Sacredness of Love

Loves All Things felt a warm shudder move up her body when she relaxed in the light of Grandfather Sun. It felt wonderful to gather that golden warmth into herself and to let her body absorb the goodness of Grandfather Sun's unconditional love. Loves All Things turned the palms of her hands upward to collect the sunbeams as if they were the amber nectar from precious tropical flowers. While the water spirits of the running river sang her a song, she was reminded of the multitude of simple pleasures that could be experienced in a human body. The bubbling rush of water, undulating over the round stones in its path, gurgled a continuous greeting. An occasional spray of tiny water droplets showered her feet with new sensations while she took in every perception her human senses could encompass.

Loves All Things smelled the rich perfume of wet soil at the river's edge mixed with the many fragrances of wild flowers and blooming herbs. The faint scent of wild green onions coming from the shaded woods behind her reminded her of the many savory foods the Earth Mother freely offered. The smell of moist fallen leaves in the undergrowth carried with it the faint odor of blooming berry and grape vines, promising an abundant time of gathering during the ripening moons. She reveled in the perpetual goodness that being human offered.

Loves All Things opened her eyes a crack to gaze at the sunlight and the rainbow prisms it reflected through the lattice created by her eyelashes. The brilliant, effervescent colors danced around her line of vision, giving her yet another pleasure to enjoy. She could see the reflections of colors caught in the moisture of the perspiration on her skin. She noticed that water, like feelings, could reflect any subtle nuance in the changing play of light and shadow. She remembered how she had been amazed by the extensive and varied sensations she had encountered when she first embodied her human, female form. She had been like Hummingbird then, tasting everything that the flowers of human experience offered, flitting from one to another in total delight.

Once she had watched Hummingbird dart and taste all the different nectars he found flowering in a woodland meadow. She decided that the world was to be savored with the same joy. Those early days had taught her the Medicine that Hummingbird offered and that same attitude of love and joy had continued to shape every experience in her Earth Walk. Loves All Things silently sent her thanks to the smallest of all winged creatures, who hummed the song of letting the joys of life chase away negativity and fear. Lost in her feelings, the relaxed Clan Mother barely noticed that she was following the colors of a sunbeam through her eyelashes and into a sparkling set of memories that reminded her of the joys and the trials she had discovered on the Good Red Road.

She remembered how she had been initiated into sexuality, learning the pleasures of coupling, in a field of corn poppies and soft green moss. The day had been a warm one filled with the sounds of her own pounding heart and the calls of thrushes and larks. The birds were circling, then diving into the meadow to feast on wild grass seeds and grains. She was walking next to a man who had touched her heart deeply during the past few moons. Together they had explored the surrounding foothills and had shared many fires. He had protected her, had provided their fires with food to cook, and had shown her the respect due a female. This man knew that every woman was an extension of the Earth Mother and that to harm a woman in any way could bring the consequences of scarcity to all the Children of Earth. The night before, as they sat by a fire, he had spoken to her of the responsibility of pleasuring a woman in a way that would teach and preserve the joys of coupling.

Loves All Things had discovered that being near this man brought many new and curious feelings. Her body would react in the strangest ways if their hands should inadvertently touch or if their eyes should meet. She did not know how to gauge the flood of emotions or the rush of blood that would set her face on fire. She was innocent of the quickening drumbeat of her heart and the warm gush of heat coursing up her thighs. Feathered Dog, the man at her side, was very different from the other men she had encountered. None of them had ever made her feel this way. The attraction she felt for Feathered Dog gave her a sense of longing and excitement, but she did not know how to deal with the flood of emotions that overwhelmed her when she was with him. Some feelings were extremely pleasurable and others bordered on aching pains of longing. She was confused because she did not understand what she was longing for. Sometimes it was difficult to breathe when he placed his arm over her shoulder or smiled when looking deep into her eyes.

The mating dance had lasted three moons, leaving Loves All Things enthralled with the sensuality of touching and feeling nurtured. The pitch of intimacy had grown during that time as she and Feathered Dog had shared their innermost thoughts but not their sleeping robes. Today, in the field of corn poppies that radiated all the salmon-rose colors of a newborn Sun, she would open herself to her man in a new way.

Feathered Dog had earned his name because he carried the Medicine of Feather, symbolizing *a messenger of spirit*, and Dog, who taught *the value of serving humankind with loyalty*. This man embodied the three Medicines needed in any relationship: *respect, trust,* and *intimacy.* Feathered Dog understood the importance of building a strong foundation of mutual respect that then gives birth to trust. He knew that when trust and respect are present in any relationship, intimacy and the sharing of the heart's desires can bloom, rooted in fertile ground. In his wisdom, Feathered Dog had allowed Loves All Things the time she needed to experience building this foundation for their relationship. From this strong and caring base of togetherness, the sexual attraction had naturally evolved.

Loves All Things recalled every gentle caress of that day long ago and relived the beauty and sacredness of that first coupling. She had been given a gift that was the Earth Mother's desire for all her children: discovering the pleasures of human sexuality without guilt, fear, or pain. Over the next few years, Loves All Things and Feathered Dog shared all of the joyous pleasures of life and love in their mated union.

The happy experiences shared with her mate and the birthing of their children had taught Loves All Things the joys of nurturing and being nurtured. Through the sexual Rites of Passage shared with Feathered Dog, she had become the Keeper of Sexual Wisdom. Through mothering their offspring, she had rediscovered the world through the eyes of her children. The wonder of life and the excitement of being alive had allowed her to master the art of being a warm and sensual woman and a nurturing, understanding mother. Her heart filled with overflowing love as she remembered the goodness life had given her through her daughter and three strong sons.

Saying good-bye to Feathered Dog had been difficult when he passed into the Spirit World. She experienced more pain when she buried her children and their children, after watching them all grow old while she still carried a body that did not age. Loves All Things had developed a resentment during those passing winters that brought forth one of her hardest lessons in human life. The Earth Mother had never said that any of the thirteen aspects of herself would find being human an easy task, but Loves All Things had conveniently forgotten the consequences of having a human body that did not die. She resented the fact that she was left to enjoy the pleasures of being human while she buried her loved ones and they went to live in the Other Side Camp of the Spirit World.

The Clan Mother was tested time and again when her resentment would thwart the feelings of joy that she could have experienced had she given the negativity away. She found it hard to love the truth that she was immortal, and harder still to love the life around her while she was grieving the love she had shared in the past. Loves All Things wanted her family back. She wanted to recapture the playful Medicine of her daughter, Little Otter, to fill those lonely times when the shadow of resentment darkened her path. The Earth Mother spoke to Loves All Things, reminding her of the Medicine carried by Otter, her daughter's namesake. The Clan Mother was not ready to reclaim the balanced Woman's Medicine of *being an adult who was young at heart, playing or working with the same inno-cence and delight.* She could not see the value of reclaiming the balance needed in her life by accepting what had passed and, like a child, deciding to live the happiness of the present. Loves All Things was focused on all the love she felt she had lost, forgetting to notice the gifts of renewal and abundance she was being offered through the Earth Mother's wisdom.

Loves All Things found herself judging all acts of life as never being enough to fill the growing hole in her heart. She insisted on living in the past and forgot the joy she had once found in being alive. She marched for many Suns and Sleeps to visit the sea, where she intended to share her salty tears of regret and remorse with the ocean. Once she arrived at the home of endless water, she tossed herself into the brine wanting to die, forgetting that this, too, was impossible. As her body sank beneath the frothy waves, she was stung by Eel, making her humiliation complete. Dragging herself to the sandy dunes, she screamed in pain and started to accuse herself of all of the victimlike tendencies she had gathered during her shadowy passage into sorrow.

Loves All Things began blaming herself for never growing old; she blamed her family for being human; she blamed the Earth Mother for giving her the experiences of pleasure and now this intolerable pain. She ranted and raved, sending her disgust and revulsion to the Four Winds as she cried out in her anger. The growing red welt on her leg where Eel had stung her reflected the rage she was feeling toward herself and toward the world. She was furious that such love and such pleasure had carried any consequences. Loves All

Things had intended to live life seeking nothing but ultimate happiness. There was not supposed to be another, upsetting side to human experience. Life with pain was not fair. She was helplessly unable to stop the sorrowful existence she abhorred, even by trying to take her own life.

Lost in her own misery, Loves All Things noticed nothing around her until a gale brought crashing waves and the sound of the Thunderbird's wings slammed her back into the moment. Hinoh, the Thunder Chief, had sent the Thunderbird with his clapping rolls of thunder to teach Loves All Things how her own feelings had affected the balance in nature. She heard the voice of Hinoh, as he bellowed into her ears.

"Daughter, you have created these icy winds because your heart has grown cold. You have forsaken your name and brought your own wrath to bear on the other Children of Earth who depended on you for love and nurturing. In your anger, you have created a storm that will send many to their deaths, and yet you have learned nothing of the scarcity you bring when you refuse to love. You, too, must weather the storm that you have brought forth and you must see for yourself the kind of pain you have created inside your body and how that pain can harm the natural world."

As soon as Hinoh's voice faded, Loves All Things was struck by a crashing wave of water that dragged her body into the raging sea. Down she went, being tumbled and rolled by the onslaught of pummeling waves. Spinning amid the currents, being tossed to and fro, she slipped into the darkness of her own unconsciousness and self-pity. The last thing she remembered was that something was very, very wrong.

The burning sensation in her leg and the unpleasant smell of rotting flesh brought Loves All Things to her senses. She struggled to get her stomach under control but wretched anyway. Salt water poured from her mouth as she felt her insides knot and release, time and again. When she could finally prop herself up on a nearby boulder, she was amazed by the wreckage around her. The beach was covered with the bodies of all sorts of creatures who had died in the storm. Silent tears etched their way down her cheeks as Love All Things took in the horror of her own creation. The wreckage in front of her was wrought by her compulsive self-pity. She had come to a place within herself where she hated who and what she was.

After Feathered Dog had died, she had fed her self-pity by taking lovers whom she did not love. She had used them for the pleasure they could give her. She had broken some hearts along the way and had fallen into projecting her own pain onto others by denying how her actions were literally destroying all of the lessons of respect, trust, and intimacy that had been her mate's Medicine. Now she had come to this piteous ebb: the beach filled with broken bodies, littering the sands around her.

As she touched the angry welt on her leg, Eel's voice filtered through the lapping waves, reaching her waterlogged senses.

"Loves All Things, listen to me, hear me with your heart. I am the *conductor of love,* this is my Medicine. The electric bolts of my sting were not meant to harm you. The shock was necessary to show you that sometimes through pain, love can be reclaimed. If you will accept my Medicine, I may be able to help you."

"Why would anyone want to help me, Eel? I have nearly destroyed myself and all of those whom I pledged to love before I came to walk the Earth."

Eel replied: "I have not forgotten the true meaning of love, Mother. It knows no boundaries, finds no faults, and waits not on time to make it right. The fire of Grandfather Sun mixes with the water of the Earth Mother inside of me. I choose to be the conductor of the unconditional love of both. Can't you accept their love and mine?"

Loves All Things sobbed as she nodded, feeling like she was being given the opportunity to come home to who she really was. The Clan Mother fully realized that she had punished herself and everyone around her while she walked with the shadow. More than anything, she now wanted to reclaim the love, releasing the darkness of blame and fear. Eel felt the change in the Clan Mother's heart and continued to speak.

"Loves All Things, to reclaim the abundance you once had in your life, you must cross a bridge that you create between the shadow side of your nature and your loving heart. The bridge may appear to you like a rainbow because it reflects all of the beautiful colors found in life. The bridge is made of forgiveness and spans the abyss of human fear, bitterness, hatred, and jealousy. Those hurtful emotions are adopted when the heart is broken, in order to mask the pain. You must cross that bridge willingly. To make that journey, you must drop all negative judgments and/or blame you have about yourself and/or any other person, place, event, location, or idea that you have ever experienced."

Loves All Things' mind was suddenly flooded with the memories of blame, shame, regret, wrongdoing, and senseless pain she had caused herself and others. Forgiving all those things would be an unbelievably challenging task, but she realized that she must start somewhere to reclaim the love that had once been her guiding light. She spent many Suns and Sleeps walking by the seaside, washing away the shadowy side of her nature. She felt every emotion, without letting herself be drawn into them again. Slowly, she observed a change in her sense of well-being and practiced finding something she could love about herself and the world around her. She whispered words of thanksgiving every time she encountered a new breakthrough, destroying the chains of heartbreak that had bound her to a lifeless existence. The aliveness began returning, as she fortified each forward step in her healing process by thanking the Great Mystery for the gift of life.

Her changed attitude toward the world around her brought back the vibrancy of the colors in nature that had come to seem so lackluster. When she swam beneath the waves, the coral reefs were treasure troves of creatures who sought her company, reflecting the rainbow colors of the bridge that forgiving had created in her life. As she reached out to life once again, the eight arms of Octopus taught her that she was enveloped with love, in all directions, as long as she desired it. The purple ink that Octopus sprayed into the water to protect himself from preying marauders showed Loves All Things that the color purple, representing gratitude and healing, was also her protection against the shadow's destructive nature. As long as she returned thanks for every healing step she took, the healing would continue.

Every so often, a gray day would bring foggy memories of the past into Loves All Things' experience. At first, she resisted the thoughts that brought up the fear of her shadow side, but unlike her past solution, which was denying the existence of her troubled mind, she confronted the memories by finding ways she could have solved those past situations. Her newly developed skill of being grateful for every lesson in life kept her from returning to the reckless behavior that had once forced her to use pleasure as an escape, numbing everything into oblivion. Loves All Things was learning to be accountable for her actions, realizing that every time she fed the positive side of a challenge by looking for ways to express her natural ability to love all experiences equally, she could easily find needed solutions. She noticed that the opposite, negative reaction would also make her accountable by throwing her into old feelings of unworthiness that made her want to run and hide from life.

Soon the day came when Loves All Things was confident that she was ready to walk among her fellow human beings without reflecting her past upon them. She started out on her trek, moving through foothills and valleys, traversing forests, and crossing streams. In the dawn light, on the sixth Sun of her journey, she woke to the sounds of thirsty Deer taking a drink. Loves All Things intently watched Deer as she nudged her fawn toward the embankment of moss growing close to the brook. Loves All Things fought back the tears welling in her eyes as memories of Little Otter, her daughter, surfaced in her mind. Her little girl had first learned to walk on moss-covered knolls near a brook very similar to the one in the clearing. Deer felt the Clan Mother's anguish and turned, speaking to Loves All Things.

"You are the Mother of All Acts of Pleasure, Loves All Things, and yet you have forgotten to be gentle with yourself. You would be kind and caring to me and my fawn, but you are merciless toward yourself. We creatures have heard of your torment and of your healing and we have rejoiced in your progress. I was sent to cross your path, reminding you of the *tender and sensitive gentleness* of my Medicine, not so that you will apply that comforting calmness to others but so you will stop being so hard on yourself. In all ways but one, you are human. The fact that you will not experience the aging and death of your body does not mean that you have to push yourself beyond the capacities of other humans. Sweet Mother, there is no fault in being human. Your feelings will always be a part of you, they will never vanish, but it is not wrong to touch them from time to time with gentleness. You have crossed the bridge of forgiveness and now you must rediscover the way to be gentle with yourself. Finding the balance between strength and gentleness is a delicate matter. You may call on my Medicine anytime you need me."

With those words, Deer and Fawn were gone. The forest enveloped them, leaving Loves All Things to her thoughts. The words spoken by Deer had bolstered the Clan Mother's resolve to find the tenderness with herself that she needed in order to carry on. In gentleness, Loves All Things sent her words of thanksgiving to all of her creature children and to the Great Mystery. Then she washed in the stream, ate some berries, and looked toward the pathway, starting her trek once again.

Two moons later, she reached an encampment of Two-leggeds who were busy demonstrating all of the hurtful actions that humans could inflict on one another. She realized that her time with them would test everything she had learned. This lesson in life would provide Loves All Things with the opportunity to walk through the final Rite of Passage of *loving the truth* in all things. As the Keeper of Forgiveness, she would be called upon to show these members of the Earth Tribe how to heal their hearts. The challenge of completing the task that had been placed in her path brought up fleeting thoughts of wanting to run from her mission, but instead she gave thanks for this opportunity for growth.

Every time a member of this band of humans tried to pass rumors to the Clan Mother about someone else, she countered with a comment about the positive nature or traits of the person being talked about. When someone was feeling dejected, she was the first to show gentleness and loving encouragement. When a man was on the rampage, spitting anger at those nearest to him, she chased the clouds away by teaching how all anger is really directed at the self. Forgiving the self for being human or for depending on another to do the things one should have taken care of on his or her own usually dissolved the anger instantly. Winters passed, and new generations of this Tribe were born, learning the gifts of forgiveness, gentleness, and love that Loves All Things freely offered.

Loves All Things traveled to different Clans and Tribes, sharing the experiences of her Earth Walk and the wisdom she had gathered through her healing process. She taught young women to respect their bodies and to nurture their children. She shared the lessons of sacred sexuality (respect, trust, and intimacy) with the young men, who would then use their understanding of sexual wisdom and relationships to form lasting bonds with their mates. The Mother-Nurturer taught the children how to enjoy the pleasures of being human by loving the coldness on their feet when standing in a mountain stream or by savoring the steaming aroma of a hot stew as much as its delicious flavors. The senses were to be honored and respected, because those skills of perception gave humankind the pleasures of life.

Through example, Loves All Things showed her human children that every act of physical life was sacred. When it was approached in a loving and meaningful way, nothing having to do with sexuality was judged as dirty or wrong by the Keeper of Sexual Wisdom. The Mother of All Acts of Pleasure taught that the functions of the human body were honored natural processes that kept the body healthy and full of life. She showed the young adults the way male bodies gave from the genitals and received through the heart and how the female body received through the genitals and gave from the heart. When a female and a male stood face to face, this process of giving and receiving created a circle between the two. If one or the other was cold, unfeeling, or afraid, the circle was not allowed to complete itself. When this type of disconnection occurred, it was time to find out which of the three points of respect, trust, and intimacy had been lost.

For the circle of sexual sharing between male and female to be restored, both partners had to be willing to open themselves to giving and receiving. This sacred bond could only be achieved if mutual respect, trust, and intimacy formed the foundation that supported their love. Loves All Things taught her children that coupling was a physical form of communication between humans that represented the male and female sides of each individual. If the individual was unhappy with himself or herself, that feeling was then used to fracture the person's internal sense of wholeness, forming a barrier to the sharing that could be experienced with another. Through loving the self and through forgiveness, healing the heart's hurts could take place. When one was able to forgive the self, it was much easier to forgive others for insensitive words or unconscious actions.

Loves All Things reviewed her own path of joy, pain, self-destruction, and ultimately, forgiveness and healing, every time she watched another human being go through similar lessons. Each time she saw herself in another, the reassuring pleasure of being able to direct her energy in a positive fashion came forth. She had become a healed healer through facing her shadow with love. When she had learned to love the truth found in every lesson in life, she had learned to love the part of herself that had driven her nearly to destruction. She could own her name now because she did *love all things*. She had put aside the shadow's need to be critical of the self and others and had donned the ability to love the truth in every person on every spoke of the Wheel of Life. She had gained the compassion of a once-tormented woman who had loved and lost, nearly losing herself in the process. She had walked in the moccasins of every brokenhearted Two-legged who had been hardened by pain, and through experience she had learned to reclaim the precious gift of love.

Loves All Things had learned that salty tears were the beginnings of transformation and that through these droplets of anguish, the waters of forgiveness began to flow. The Clan Mother of the Seventh Moon Cycle had come to understand that healing begins with forgiving the self for the could-have-beens and should-have-beens found on the Good Red Road. Compassion was born from the hurts of the Clan Mother's life, and in gently finding compassion for herself, her healing was accomplished. The road back from her pain and into the light of love had been a long one, but the restored pleasure she found in life was worth the effort. The sounds of the river at her side brought her from her memories and helped her focus on the pleasurable warmth moving up her arms from her open hands.

The rainbow colors of Grandfather Sun filtering through her eyelashes displayed curious images of human forms dancing. Loves All Things felt a tug on her heart as she recognized Feathered Dog, Little Otter, and her three strong sons, dancing in the rainbow lights. In her vision, the Earth Mother called to Loves All Things, letting her know that her Earth Walk was complete.

A deafening hum filled her ears and she was floating over the river. When the Clan Mother looked down again, she caught her own reflection in the glassy waters of a still pond. She had become Hummingbird and was flying on the streaming light of a sunbeam. Upward she traveled, traversing the deep cornflower blue of space, until she passed through a flaming wall of fire, being propelled into the body of Grandfather Sun. The fire had burned away her Hummingbird body and once again she transformed into her female human form and found herself in the arms of Feathered Dog.

As the circle of their love was made complete through the reunion of their hearts, the two lovers became one dazzling star. The burning star flew from Grandfather Sun and took its place in the Sky Nation. For six moons, the star of love lights the twilight sky and is called the Evening Star; then for the following six moons, the star of love appears at dawn and is called the Morning Star.

Through the story of Loves All Things and Feathered Dog, we are enabled to see both sides of our natures. That wholeness is reflected in the bird of love and joy who knows that there is no separation in the human spirit, except the illusions we impose upon ourselves. Hummingbird hums now and flies in circles because he knows the lovers' secret— to love all things is to love every reflection of *who* and *what* you are.

SHE WHO HEALS

Mother, sing me a song
That will ease my pain,
Mend broken bones,
Bring wholeness again.

Catch my babies
When they are born,
Sing my death song,
Teach me how to mourn.

Show me the Medicine
Of the healing herbs,
The value of spirit,
The way I can serve.

Mother, heal my heart
So that I can see
The gifts of yours
That can live through me.

Clan Mother
of the
Eighth Moon Cycle

SHE WHO HEALS is the Clan Mother of the Eighth Moon Cycle in August and is the Guardian of *serving the truth*. She Who Heals serves the Children of Earth by being the Keeper of the Healing Arts, Mother of All Rites of Passage, Guardian of the mysteries of Life and Death, and Singer of the Death Song. She is a midwife, herbalist, Medicine Woman, spirit healer, and teacher of the cycles of the Earth Walk. Her color is blue, representing intuition, truth, water, and feelings.

As Guardian of the Healing Plants and Roots, she is closely connected to all of the Plant Spirits who comprise the Tribe of all things green and growing. This Tribe is sometimes called the Earth Blanket Tribe because together the Plant and Tree People form the covering that protects the Earth Mother's soil from erosion and keeps the cycles of regeneration in balance. She Who Heals is the Keeper of all the healing uses of every plant in the Earth Blanket Tribe. She knows which parts of each plant to use in her healing remedies as well as how and when they are to be gathered.

As Keeper of the Life and Death Mysteries, she welcomes new spirits into the world when they take their

▲▲

human bodies. When an individual Earth Walk is complete, she sings the beings who are Dropping Their Robes, or dying, into the Spirit World. She also serves the Children of Earth by sewing their cuts, setting their bones, birthing their babies, and doctoring their bodies and spirits during their Earth Walks.

She Who Heals is also the Keeper of the growing cycles of the Medicine Wheel and all Rites of Passage. She teaches us the steps of gestation, birth, growth, death, and rebirth. She shows us how the Great Medicine Wheel of Life turns; when to fight for life, when to let go, when to allow our spirits to make the choice, and how to accept death as another step that leads to rebirth. She Who Heals invests every human being she teaches with the ability to drop fear of death and accept the change as a new adventure in living. Whether the death is the end of a relationship, the end of a job, or the end of physical life, she shows us how to see beyond the illusion of finality and to celebrate each turn in the road as another step that leads to wholeness.

This Eighth Clan Mother is the embodiment of the feminine principle that serves the Children of Earth in truth by assisting them through the healing process of being human. She sees their Orendas or Spiritual Essences come inside their bodies at birth. She sees the illnesses created when they lose connection to their Spiritual Essence during their lives. She helps them reconnect to the Eternal Flame of Love when they decide to heal their physical forms and continue walking the Earth. She shows them how to know when their missions on the Earth are complete and when they are ready to move on by becoming one with the Orenda and preparing for rebirth in the Spirit World. Her Medicine Story is one way we can understand the vastness of the wisdom she freely gives us all.

⚠ ⚠
The Turning of
the Medicine Wheel

Beads of sweat trickled down her face as She Who Heals kneaded the knotted muscles in the calves of the woman in labor stretched before her. The birthing cave was echoing with the keening cries and mourning trills that floated in from the mass of women gathered outside, burying their dead. It was the time of the Starving Moon, the last moon cycle before the Earth Mother shook off her blanket of snow and ice and welcomed the new shoots of green growth.

If it had been any other time, the frail Sister in front of her would have had the strength to go through this exhausting labor. As it was, her Clan had not had fresh meat in many Suns and the pregnant women and their unborn babies had suffered along with the others. She Who Heals wished that the mourners would move a little farther away from the birthing cave, because their voices were implying to her laboring charge that there was no reason to bring new life into the world of hunger that surrounded them. The last of the food store of tubers, grains, and berries had been used four Sleeps ago along with one stringy squirrel who was too weak to avoid the hunters.

The children and the Elders had been the first ones to die during the last of this moon's cycle. She Who Heals had fulfilled her duties during that time when none of her healing herbs could prevent starvation and none of her talents could give them the strength to fight for life. She had learned the lessons of serving others in many ways since she had taken a human body. Still, she grieved when one of her children lost the will to live.

Distractedly she added a handful of twigs to the fire at her side and gave thanks for that small handful of warmth that had been gathered far from the birthing cave, at such a great expense, by those who traveled with empty bellies. The hollow eyes of Squash Moon, the laboring mother, implored her for some comfort and reassurance. She responded by gently wiping Squash Moon's brow and giving her an encouraging smile. She could not give any more herbs to ease the labor because Squash Moon's belly was empty and the remedy could send her into eternal sleep. She Who Heals needed Squash Moon to help with the labor by fighting for the life of her unborn baby, but the Medicine Woman realized that this was one of the times that the choice of life and death was in the hands of Swennio, the Great Mystery, and in Squash Moon's will to live.

She Who Heals smiled at Squash Moon and gently took the laboring Mother's hand, feeding her strength as another onslaught of contractions began to wrack the young woman's body. She Who Heals realized that Squash Moon's connection to her own Orenda was the only hope for mother and child. If Squash Moon could connect to her Spiritual Essence, the Great Mystery could feed her the strength she needed. Without that precious connection, her starved body would succumb and her spirit's connection would have to be made when Squash Moon reached the Other Side Camp in the Spirit World. She Who Heals put on her stoic mask of support, never letting Squash Moon see the painful concern and helplessness she felt.

The burial of the family members who had starved must have been completed because the mourning trills had mercifully stopped. During the Starving Moon, the bodies were deeply buried in snow, preventing them from becoming food for wandering carnivores. Until the ground was thawed enough for the Planetary Mother to finally receive the dead into her earthen breast, the ice mounds in back of the lodges served as temporary burial cairns. It was difficult to use the last reserves of life force to bury the dead, but this band of the Human Tribe was willing to endure the hardship for their loved ones. The silence was a signal to She Who Heals that two women would soon be returning to the birthing cave to assist her with the tasks at hand. The labor had already been a long one, but the Keeper of the Medicine Roots had insisted that the other two women go and say good-bye to their relations who had Dropped Their Robes.

Between labor pains, She Who Heals began to think of how many generations she had brought into the world and how many she had sung over into the Spirit World. In the beginning, it had been necessary to teach these human children the purpose of mourning. She remembered how the mourning wails and trills had relieved those grieving family members in the early winters of her Earth Walk. It was easy to recall the way in which the songs of mourning had removed the burden baskets of grief from the shoulders of the families of the dead. She had watched the letting go that occurred when the mourners were allowed to express their sorrow and she had observed the spirits of their loved ones, who used those wails of grieving like bowstrings to direct the arrows of their spirit forms onto the Blue Road. It seemed like long ago, but allowing the truth of the pain in their hearts to be expressed had served her children well.

She Who Heals traveled farther into her memories while her body, with its confident and caring mask in place, instinctively attended to Squash Moon's needs. Her abilities as a midwife were impeccable, derived as they were from hundreds of births, patience, compassion, and her talent for taking charge and never showing panic no matter how desperate the situation. If her total attention was needed, the voice of her Orenda would bring her from her memories into instant readiness.

Pictures of long-ago moons flashed across her mind, bringing memories of Harvest Feasts, weddings, births, deaths, Council Fires, Rites of Passage celebrations, and nights spent around the lodge fires when stories were told. The faces of all the Two-legged human Tribes and Clans she had known and the special times they had shared whirled before her while the flickering of her twig fire reminded her that she must add another handful of fuel, lest it grow cold.

Among the harvest basket of memories, one picture began to emerge, taking She Who Heals into another time. She had spent many passing cycles of snows and ripenings learning the healing missions of each root, leaf, and flower of the Plant Tribe. Although she had come to walk the earth in an adult body that did not age like the other Two-leggeds, she had felt younger then, due to her lack of experience. Every lesson taught to her by the Green and Growing Tribe was a tribute to Plant Nation's desire to assist their Human Relations in surviving.

She recalled Badger's lessons on using the Medicine Roots and the assistance given when She Who Heals encountered her first human with a broken bone. The Clan Mother smiled inwardly when she remembered how Badger had shared her Medicine of *taking charge and aggressively showing competence* in difficult situations. Badger never once showed aggression toward another, except when she was protecting the weak or injured from some outside hostile force. Mother Badger had shown She Who Heals how to use the ability of taking charge to get any task done with drive and vigor. Badger taught She Who Heals how to competently complete anything with efficiency, never wasting time or energy.

Badger had introduced many other Creature-beings to She Who Heals in those early days. Through Aardvark's Medicine of *prolonging life,* She Who Heals had learned the secrets of longevity. When she met Stork, she was shown the Medicine of *easing labor and giving birth.* Stork showed her how to position a woman's body so that the laboring mother would not fight the rhythms of pain but could put aside her fears and then allow the flows of her contractions to bring her child forth.

Memory after memory came forward as reminders of the passage of She Who Heals into knowing how to serve her children. The Medicine Woman felt the deep gratitude her heart held and sent that thanks to each of her teachers as her memories brought them forth one by one. She silently thanked Osprey, who by breaking the bones of his prey had shown her his Medicine of *breaking and setting bones*. She sent her heart's gratitude to Beetle, who had shown her the process of healing and rebirth through his Medicine of *regeneration*. Beetle had shown her how all things are regenerated into other forms and that nothing in the universe is ever lost. New plants grow from the soil fertilized by decayed fallen leaves, new suns are born from the dust of exploded stars, new cells are grown to mend wounds of the flesh, and the Orenda is eternal, taking many physical forms throughout time. These lessons were the foundation that gave She Who Heals her inner strength, and she was honored to be able to share those skills to serve her children.

Snake had taught her how to transmute poisons, negativity, and limiting ideas to shed the skin of the old. Snake had also taught her the art of using tiny amounts of poisonous plants to render a person or animal immobile while she set a bone or sewed an open gash. Her patient's body would then transmute the poison and be stronger because of it. Snake had shown her the wonders of life force and its flows in the body. Together they had explored the spirit's ability to heal and the mind's ability to thwart or compel the healing process. Snake's Medicine of *transmutation* was another gift to be grateful for, because it had served her well over the years.

She Who Heals stirred from her thoughts and brought her attention back to the birthing cave. Squash Moon was weaker than before; when the contractions came, a groan would barely escape the laboring mother's lips. She Who

Heals knew that something had to be done or the labor would soon come to a halt, leaving mother and child helplessly stranded in the Void or slipping into the Eternal Land.

She Who Heals began to vigorously massage Squash Moon's body as she silently sent her plea for the lives of her charges to the Earth Mother and Swennio, the Great Mystery. As she turned her eyes upward, the midwife noticed her own Totem hanging from the top of the birthing cave. The upside-down face of Bat changed as he slowly opened his eyes and gazed into the face of She Who Heals. Without stopping her hands from caressing Squash Moon's arms and legs, She Who Heals listened for Bat's voice as it spoke to her heart.

"Mother, we are not alone in this cave," Bat said. "Look at the far corner and see who is watching your efforts."

Near the top of the cave, She Who Heals spied a pale blue light. She recognized a spirit form like the ones she had seen during every birth. The Medicine Woman was relieved and extremely happy. The Orenda of the child waiting to be born was in the birthing cave. This was the sign that She Who Heals had been waiting for. The child's Orenda was ready to enter the soft spot of its new body the moment the baby's head crowned the birth canal. The Keeper of the Healing Arts had seen the miracle of spirit taking form a thousand times or more and was always filled to exaltation when she experienced it again.

She Who Heals glanced back to Squash Moon and saw that the massage was helping the mother-to-be maintain some small connection to her body, but she was wavering in and out of consciousness and needed to be more aware of what was occurring. The midwife moved into a position where she could support Squash Moon's shoulders, raising her head and cradling the half-conscious girl in her arms. She Who Heals began to hum a sweet tune that comforted Squash Moon. Intermittently, the midwife squeezed the hands, then the arms of her charge to urge the life force to flow into them. After a moment or two, Squash Moon opened her eyes and whispered, "Am I dead?"

She Who Heals replied, "No, little mother, you are not dead. Someone is here to see you and so you must pay close attention."

The labor pains had stopped and it was imperative that Squash Moon be revived enough for her body to continue the birthing process. She Who Heals began to speak to Squash Moon in a stronger voice that commanded the girl's attention. "You see, little mother, the spirit of your unborn baby is here in the cave and you must open your heart to hear it."

A flicker of fiery recognition briefly flashed across Squash Moon's face as she summoned as much life force as she could before whispering, "Please help me, show me how to see my child's spirit, Mother."

She Who Heals felt a wave of relief flow through her limbs as she directed Squash Moon's eyes to the far corner of the birthing cave's ceiling. She Who Heals began to believe that maybe there was some hidden resource still buried deep inside the mother-to-be that would bring them all through this precarious moment of life and death.

The Medicine Woman began describing what she saw and how the pale blue spirit form moved until Squash Moon could see it as well. Then She Who Heals talked Squash Moon into the silence where she could actually hear the voice of her unborn child. She Who Heals was able to hear the voice of the child's Orenda as clearly as Squash Moon did when the voice spoke to its mother's heart.

"You are to be my mother, Squash Moon, but I will be your teacher as well. We must begin our journey together in this moment before my birth. You have forgotten how to connect to your Orenda and how to pull the strength you need from the Great Mystery. I have come to remind you of the time before your own birth when you knew that connection well. If you whisper your own name and picture what that name means, you will rediscover your personal Medicine. That set of gifts is held in trust inside your Orenda, awaiting your discovery."

"Squash Moon, Squash Moon, Squash Moon," the young mother whispered to herself.

Pictures of the yellow-orange squash blossom floated through the mother-to-be's mind, transforming itself into a harvest moon brimming with golden light. The scene changed and the harvest moon took on the qualities of a lovely woman bathed in the light of flowing melon- and salmon-colored rays. Upon the head of the dream woman was a wreath of autumn leaves and ripened wheat, woven with yellow buffalo grasses and wild green mustang grapes. Purple berries and wild pink primroses spilled from the wreath, interwoven with clusters of orange berries gathered from the mountain ash tree. In the woman's arms, she held a basket woven of river reeds and pine needles. Coming from the basket was another light whose pale blue rays danced across the face of the smiling woman of the moon. Once again the vision transformed itself as the woman then reached inside the basket and cupped the blue ball of light and brought it to her heart. Lightning bolts came from the ball of energy and connected the Earth Mother and Sky Father, below and above the dream woman. Radiant beams of light of all colors encircled the vision and Squash Moon could feel the Great Mystery's love reaching for her from the dream.

At that exact moment, Squash Moon felt a burst of life explode inside her own heart. She inhaled with a gasp, as rivers of bubbling energy shot through her tired limbs. She could feel pulsating waves of warmth bring her nearly lifeless body back from the brink of the Eternal Land. Her amazed eyes looked from the face of She Who Heals to the Orenda of her unborn child. Tears of joy spilled from her eyes onto her cheeks and her face began to show some color. She Who Heals smiled and gently rocked Squash Moon in her arms, allowing the rhythm to encourage the girl's body to bring the contractions back into play so the baby could be born.

As if on cue, the two women who had mourned their dead parted the hides hanging at the cave's entrance and entered. They had washed the soot of mourning from their faces and smudged their bodies with cedar smoke as She Who Heals had instructed, leaving their thoughts of death outside the birthing cave. Clear Lake and Has Courage took their places beside She Who Heals as the Medicine Woman gently stroked Squash Moon's distended belly with circular motions, moving in the direction of the sun's path across the sky. She Who Heals then motioned for Clear Lake to support Squash Moon's shoulders while the midwife moved in front of the mother-to-be to stroke her belly from the front.

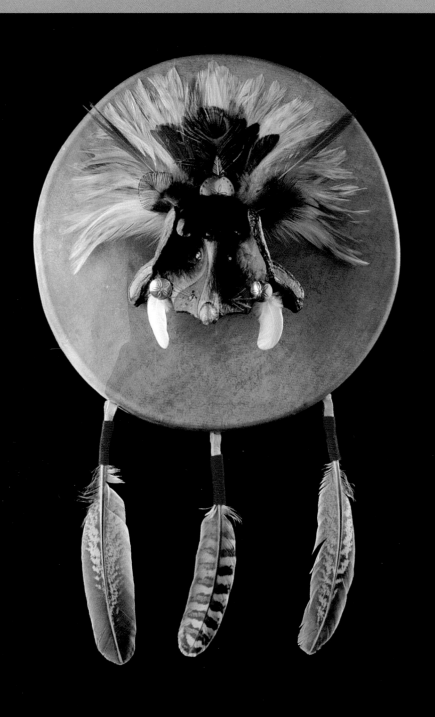

FEBRUARY
SECOND MOON CYCLE
WISDOM KEEPER

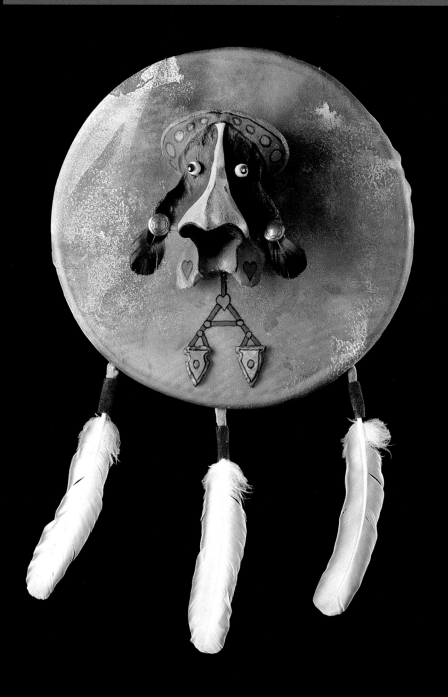

MARCH
THIRD MOON CYCLE
WEIGHS THE TRUTH

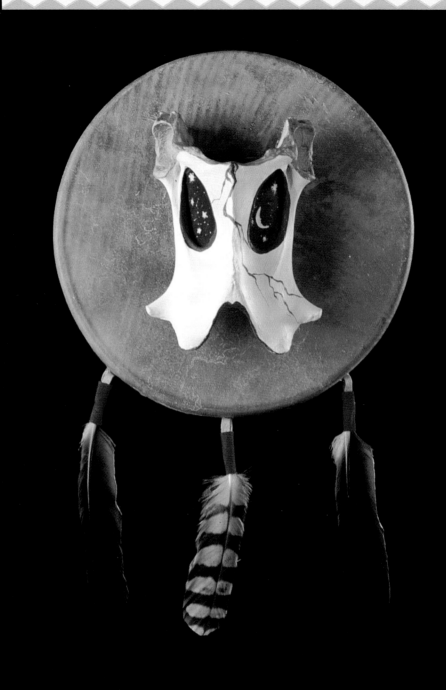

MAY
FIFTH MOON CYCLE
LISTENING WOMAN

JUNE
SIXTH MOON CYCLE
STORYTELLER

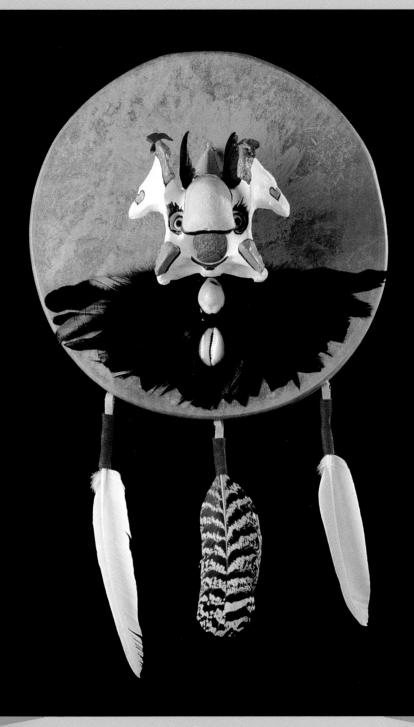

JULY
SEVENTH MOON CYCLE
LOVES ALL THINGS

AUGUST
EIGHTH MOON CYCLE
SHE WHO HEALS

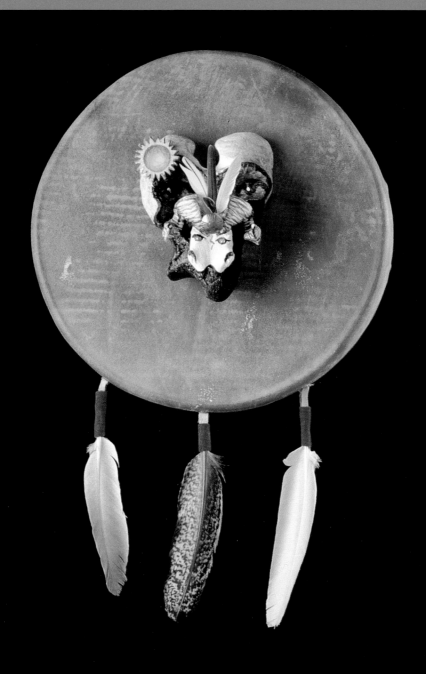

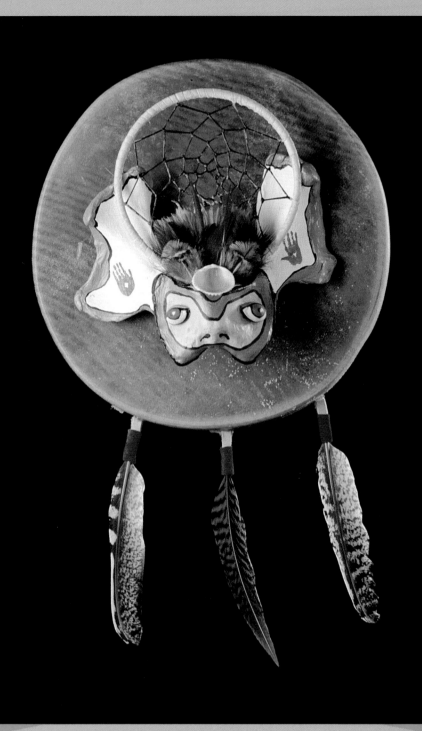

OCTOBER
TENTH MOON CYCLE
WEAVES THE WEB

NOVEMBER
ELEVENTH MOON CYCLE
WALKS TALL WOMAN

DECEMBER
TWELFTH MOON CYCLE
GIVES PRAISE

BLUE MOON OF TRANSFORMATION
THIRTEENTH MOON CYCLE
BECOMES HER VISION

Gives Praise

Wisdom Keeper

Setting Sun Woman

Loves All Things

She Who Heals

Jamie Sams

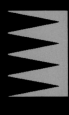

Becomes Her Vision was taken aback by the beast appearing
before her eyes. A giant Rainbow Lizard with eyes of flame
and the wings of Condor came crashing through the
Great Smoking Mirror, shattering the surface
as if it had been made of solidified smoke. In the
eyes of flame, the good and evil of the world parted,
and all illusions were shattered, revealing
the purity of the Eternal Flame of Love.

The descendant of giant Rainbow Lizard still
walks our Earth to remind us how to
shatter the illusions, and receive
the Eternal Flame of Love.

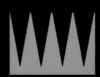

After a few moments of massaging Squash Moon's belly, She Who Heals grabbed her rattle and shook it over the belly in the same sun's path circles. The Medicine Woman began to sing the song of the Bat to restart the contractions.

> Bat Mother hear me as I sing
> In the cave of this one's womb,
> Out of the darkness you must fly
> To bring this child forth soon.
> River of life, waters come forth,
> Ease the way for this babe.
> Bat Mother, symbol of rebirth,
> Release what has been stayed.

Over and over she sang the chant while she kept looking to the top of the birthing cave. At the end of the seventh refrain, Bat, who had been watching the scene below while hanging upside down like the child in Squash Moon's womb, took flight and dodged through the hides at the cave's entrance. She Who Heals placed her hand over Squash Moon's navel and felt the beginning rumble of a contraction that brought with it the breaking waters, flowing from the mother-to-be's womb. The Medicine Woman smiled because Bat had given her a sign that her song had reached the Seven Sacred Directions. When Bat flew, She Who Heals knew that the baby would be born.

This was the beginning of the hardest part of labor and She Who Heals was grateful that the near-starvation had not caused Squash Moon to lose her child through a dry birth. The waters of life had broken much later than usual, but under these circumstances, later had been a blessing. If the waters had broken earlier, the Sun and Sleep and second Sun of Squash Moon's intermittent labor could have killed both mother and child.

Grandfather Sun would be rising again soon, bringing the grueling labor to a joyous close. Clear Lake and Has Courage were working as diligently as She Who Heals when the baby's head came into sight. Squash Moon was being held in a squatting position, allowing the Earth Mother's magnetism to draw the child to its Earth Walk. Squash Moon cried out in wonder rather than pain when she saw the Orenda of her child enter the soft spot in its skull. With the next push, the baby's body turned and the shoulders were released. The hips gently followed without effort. She Who Heals caught the child and whispered, "We have a girl, Squash Moon."

The young mother was relieved and happy when the baby girl sounded an echo through the birthing cave, letting the world know that she had arrived with a fine voice. She Who Heals cut the cord, washed the child in the water made from melted snow that Clear Lake had prepared by the twig fire, and then wrapped the baby in soft furs, placing her next to Squash Moon. Has Courage began kneading Squash Moon's belly to release the afterbirth, while Clear Lake took the birthing robes out to be buried in the snow.

She Who Heals began to think about Squash Moon's mate, Grey Stag, who had been killed by a stampeding Musk Ox four moons before her time to give birth. Squash Moon had been taken into her sister's lodge, but now that sister and all her family were dead from starvation. The Medicine Woman made a decision. Squash Moon would come to live at her fire. She was always given plenty of meat by the hunters in exchange for her services and so there was no reason not to enlarge her family circle with the young mother and newborn girl-child.

She Who Heals was about to tell Squash Moon of her decision when Has Courage passed by, handing the washed umbilical cord to the Medicine Woman before she walked out into the snow to bury the afterbirth at the foot of Grandmother Mountain. She Who Heals took a minute to tightly wrap the umbilical cord into a circle, then hung it on the deer antler perched near the fire to dry it out. Later, the fully dried cord would be placed in a pouch made of hide and then would be sewn tightly inside the tiny Medicine Bundle for good. The Umbilical Medicine Pouch would belong to the newborn child and would be a constant reminder of her physical connection to the Earth Mother and her spiritual connection to the Sky Father. None of the Children of Earth feared being alone or orphaned when they carried their umbilical cord over their hearts, because they understood that the physical cord was replaced with a spiritual umbilical cord that kept them connected to their true Father and Mother as long as they walked the Earth.

Squash Moon called the name of She Who Heals and the midwife moved to her side. "Healing Mother, I am going to name my little girl Earth Blanket because her Orenda showed me her Medicine as she was born. It is her wish that you become her teacher as she grows tall. Earth Blanket has reminded me that the cycles and seasons always change and that from the snows of the Starving Moon, the green blanket of the Earth Mother is born. This child is the promise of spring who has taught me faith. She told me that faith is the

Robin who sings of flowers while the Earth is still blanketed in snow. Earth Blanket explained to me that her birth, which is her first Rite of Passage, has been a Rite of Passage for me too because I reconnected to my Orenda and to the Great Mystery. I thank you for bringing us both through the birthing process, Healing Mother."

She Who Heals was touched by Squash Moon's words and shared her decision to bring them both to live at her fire. The Medicine Woman had known about the lessons that Earth Blanket had taught her mother, but hearing them expressed, as they were experienced and understood, gave the Guardian of the Healing Arts further joy.

She Who Heals, Squash Moon, and her newborn were surrounded with delicious aromas of sizzling meat as Has Courage entered the cave. An Elk had fallen from the cliff of Grandmother Mountain to the base, where he was discovered by Has Courage when she went to bury the placenta. Has Courage cooked many strips of meat and carried them to the birthing cave so the women could fill their bellies.

The women knew that it was very important to eat small amounts and to chew well, lest the dinner be rejected by their stomachs. After the meal, it was Earth Blanket who wanted to be fed, sending a warning cry that she would not be forgotten. She Who Heals smiled as Earth Blanket suckled at her mother's breast. The Clan Mother returned to her thoughts as she imagined how life would be for little Earth Blanket. Like the Green and Growing Tribe, this child would learn the cycles of life, death, and regeneration by becoming a sister to the Plant and Tree People. She would learn the healing uses of all parts of every plant. She Who

Heals would teach Earth Blanket the way to birth babies, mend bones, sew cuts, and heal wounded spirits.

Earth Blanket would have to be taught the ways of the spirit even though her Orenda knew them before she was born. Forgetting was almost always a part of the human life process, but reclaiming the Remembering was one of the most important Rites of Passage during any human's Earth Walk. It would be a joy to experience Earth Blanket's passage into womanhood and her tapping of the memories that would bring her Orenda fully into her body.

The Eternal Flame of Love was the guiding light of every life form's Orenda. When and how each Two-legged rediscovered her or his connection to the Creative Source was up to the individual. Birth always brought growth, change, death, and rebirth as the Great Medicine Wheel turned. Every cycle and spoke on the wheel brought the lessons that allowed all of the Human Tribe to find meaning in their lives. The will to continue and to learn more was fueled by the Orenda and the spirit's connection to the Great Mystery.

Through the Medicine experienced this day, Squash Moon and Earth Blanket had reclaimed their connections to the life force found in their Spiritual Essences. Because of those connections, Bat had flown from the birthing cave and had called to Elk to sacrifice his body in order that the *stamina and persistence* of his Medicine could be shared with this band of human beings. The relationships between the caring members of the Planetary Family were strong again. From near-starvation and death, this Clan of Two-leggeds had been reborn, because one among them had fed her faith with the Eternal Flame of Love found in her Orenda.

She Who Heals sang a song of thanksgiving for the miracles of this day and for the miracles that awaited them all on the Good Red Road of life. She was reminded again of the seasons and reasons that brought opportunities for growth and change. Through every turn of the Medicine Wheel, change was always present. The eternal, undaunted human spirit would forever sing the song of life, growth, death, and rebirth inside the bodies of those Two-leggeds who chose to change or heal. She Who Heals saw a bright future for the Human Tribe just beyond the horizon, in her mind. The Clan Mother of the Healing Arts gave thanks for the time she was given to know and understand these Children of Earth. She found joy in knowing that after her Earth Walk, her spirit would always be available for those who had the courage to reach out to her, healing their broken bodies, minds, or spirits. The Medicine Wheel would turn, life would continue to grow and change, death would bring rebirth, and she would assist that healing process until the end of time.

SETTING SUN WOMAN

Keeper of tomorrow's dreams,
Mother of the star-filled night,
Show me how to live my truth
And bring my dreams to light.

Teach me how to use my will,
Living the truth I find within,
Discovering all the parts of me
Where light and shadow blend.

Let me sing the song of future
With concern for what will be,
Upholding all of nature's laws
For creatures, stones, and trees.

Mother, I see you in the sunset
And I hear you in the rain.
You teach me inner knowing
Through your heart's sweet refrain.

Clan Mother of the Ninth Moon Cycle

SETTING SUN WOMAN is the Keeper of Tomorrow's Goals and Dreams. She is the Clan Mother of the Ninth Moon Cycle, which falls in September and is connected to the color green. Green is the color of will; Setting Sun Woman shows us how to properly use our wills to insure the abundance of the future. She teaches us that the will to live, the will to survive, the will to be impeccable in preserving the Earth Mother's resources are paramount parts of our Earth Walk.

This Clan Mother teaches us how to *live the truth* and sits in the West of the Medicine Wheel. The West direction is the home of the feminine principle, the Earth Mother, the setting sun and night sky. The abilities we gain from learning the lessons of the West are concern, dependability, nurturing, inner knowing, achievements, and goals. The West is sometimes called the Looking-within Place because the feminine principle is naturally intuitive and is willing to be receptive.

As the Guardian of Unborn Generations, Setting Sun Woman gives us many lessons on how to use only what we need. She teaches us the sacredness of using every part of anything we harvest; never wasting anything usable. This Ninth Clan Mother shows us how we can depend upon the Mother Earth to provide for our needs if we are also dependable children who honor and give thanks for that abundance. She shows us how to provide for the next Seven Generations by saving seeds for next year's planting. She is the Keeper of Preservation and the Guardian of all species of seeds, plants, creatures, and stones. She guards against the extinction of any part of our Planetary Family by allowing those species that would naturally transmute to evolve into the forms that are more adapted to the world's conditions.

Setting Sun Woman teaches us how to go within and find our personal truths. This Clan Mother shows us how to meet the future without fear because we have taken steps daily to ensure a bright tomorrow. The darkness of the night sky is the Starry Medicine Bowl or womb of the feminine principle that holds all of the potential of our future. The stars are points of light that represent the Sacred Fire of our dreams. When we find our personal truths in the darkness inside ourselves, we determine which visions we will bring to Earth in manifested form. Setting Sun Woman walks with us across the Milky Way, which is comprised of the campfires of the Ancestors. When we travel with her, we rediscover the ancient truths of preservation and inner knowing that guided those who walked the Red Road before us. Through Setting Sun Woman, we rediscover the universe as it lives inside our Spiritual Essences. This discovery of worlds within worlds teaches us that we are not our bodies, but that we are vast beings and that our bodies exist inside of the limitless space of our Orendas.

⋀ ⋀
Evening Star, Promise of Tomorrow

Setting Sun Woman sat on a cliff overlooking the ocean, peering at the tide pools below. The tide pools nestled in the jagged rocks housed hundreds of life forms that sent reflections of bright colors up through the water when touched by the sun. Grandfather Sun's light was strong because he had nearly reached the zenith of his path across the Sky Nation. The smell of salty brine and washed-up ocean plants permeated Setting Sun Woman's senses and she took a deep breath to fill her lungs with salty air. The rhythms of the tides soothed her senses, with an occasional crashing wave bringing her thoughts home to her heart.

The path down the cliff to the water's edge was one she had traveled many times, but in her present reflective mood she preferred the expansive view from high above the sea. She had passed many winters in her Earth Walk and had learned much about having a human body. Still, she was fascinated by the feelings she could touch inside herself when she sought the ocean's shore. The waves, moving to the sand and running back to the sea in an endless rhythm, were like gentle fingers caressing her spirit, filling her with a sense of well-being.

A vulture circled the cliff to her right, giving her a memory of how he had come to find his mission on the Earth. Although he was not very pleasing to those who feared death, he carried important Medicine in the Clan Mother's understanding. Vulture was a good teacher for the Children of Earth because he wasted nothing. He picked the bones of those who had Dropped Their Robes or died, leaving no part to rot. Vulture was happy with his Medicine, which taught the Children of Earth the idea of *waste not, want not.* Setting Sun Woman followed her memory to another time, recalling one of her greatest lessons, which had changed the course of her Sacred Path. She reflected on that other time as her thoughts drifted like the tides into that memory.

The dense forest gave way to a rolling set of hills that were covered in wild flowers of every color, proudly showing their little faces above the deep emerald blanket of clover that covered the Earth Mother's sensuous form. Setting Sun Woman was standing on the crest of a hill, looking to the West, waiting for Grandfather Sun's light to fade as the Pipe was passed to the evening sky and Grandmother Moon. It was a time of stillness when the little flowers began to nod, some closing their petals, making ready for rest. The brilliant colors of sunset were fading to pastels, giving the hills far off, near the southern horizon, robes of deep purple to cover them while they slept.

In the distance, Setting Sun Woman could hear Frog singing his Medicine Song, signaling to all listening that it was time to *cleanse* the activities of this Sun in order to *refresh and replenish* themselves during the coming Sleep. The Clan Mother could smell the marshy vapors of the pond down in the meadow as the cooling soil wafted the

Earth Mother's perfume her way. Frog was not singing his rain song and the Cloud People had traveled to other camps in their Sky Nation home. The sky would be clear during this Sleep, and the Earth would be alive with all her Children who sought the darkness to hunt or prowl.

Wata-jis, the Evening Star, would soon poke her head through the purple sage blossom blanket of the night sky. Setting Sun Woman always relished the moment when her sister Wata-jis appeared, signaling the emergence of the Starry Medicine Bowl in all of its glory. When the Star Nation came awake after sleeping during the brightness of Grandfather Sun's journey across the sky, Setting Sun Woman could see the forms of some of her Totems outlined in the Sacred Fire of the stars. Bear lumbered across the Sky Nation while the world slept, teaching everyone his Medicine. In the darkness, he reminded the Children of Earth to go within, *reflecting and introspecting.* His raw strength and huge form spoke of the benefits of retreat and hibernation. The Mountain Ram also traveled the heavens, traversing the peaks and valleys of purple space. This big-horned sheep was the keeper of *tenacity and the willingness to meet challenges head-on.* The Medicines of these two Creature-teachers had served Setting Sun Woman well during her Earth Walk and she anxiously sought the star forms of these Totems, returning her thanks to them every time the inky darkness covered the sky.

Setting Sun Woman came from her thoughts, peering at the place in the sky where Wata-jis would appear. She raised her voice in song, sending her heartfelt welcome to the star she called sister.

Hi-nay, hi-nay, Wata-jis,
Hi-nay, hi-nay, Wata-jis,
Ya-ta-hey, Ya-ta-hey.
Dey-whey-no-de, no-way,
Dey-whey-no-de, no-way,
Wata-jis, Wata-jis.

Greetings, Greetings, Evening Star,
Greetings, Greetings, Evening Star,
I greet the fire spirit in you.
We are sisters, you and I,
We are sisters, you and I,
Evening Star, Evening Star.

As Setting Sun Woman finished her song, Wata-jis's fiery face poked through the night sky's robe, twinkling with fiery light. The Clan Mother was always in awe of the Evening Star's sparkling form, but on this night, Setting Sun Woman saw a spirit canoe moving on a river of fog, coming toward the Earth. The blue streak of light from Wata-jis lit the crests of the fog-river's waves, rocking the canoe until it slid to the Earth at Setting Sun Woman's feet.

The luminous form of the canoe was made of milky moonlight and opalescent star fire. Setting Sun Woman saw that no one was paddling the spirit canoe and wondered if she should get inside. She peered over the canoe's edge, looking into the bottom, and discovered a child laced inside a cradleboard, nestled in white fur robes, peering back at her. The baby smiled and looked directly into the Clan Mother's eyes. Setting Sun Woman realized that this was no ordinary child and finally found her voice. "Thank you for being," she said, formally greeting the child in the cradle-board.

The child replied by smiling and then spoke, "I am the child of tomorrow, Setting Sun Woman. I have come in this spirit canoe, sent by the Evening Star. I have traveled on the trail of campfires lit by the Ancestors that some Children of Earth will one day call the Milky Way. I have come to show you the hidden feelings of future that you hold in your heart."

Setting Sun Woman was standing in the stillness, notic-ing that the sounds of the night creatures had ceased. She took a breath and then asked, "What shall I call you?"

"I am Wata-jis, the Evening Star, your sister."

Setting Sun Woman saw the twinkle in the girl-child's ebony eyes and was filled with an inner knowing that re-laxed her. She could see that this child was a gift from the Starry Medicine Bowl and that there was only loving intent in the child's eyes.

The child began speaking again as the Clan Mother lis-tened. "I am wrapped in the Cradleboard of Creation, Mother. If you are willing to carry me on your back, you will begin to understand the many purposes of your Earth Walk. I am the promise of all the tomorrows that will ever be. All dreams of wholeness and harmony are embodied in me. I represent every spirit that will travel from the breath of the Great Mystery to the Womb of Creation called the Starry Medicine Bowl and then to Earth to be born as human Two-leggeds."

Setting Sun Woman reached into the spirit canoe and lifted the Cradleboard of Creation with care. Gently she pulled the harness across her shoulders and settled the child securely on her back before she spoke. "Wata-jis, I thank you for coming to be my teacher. What do you want me to do now?"

A giggle escaped the tiny girl's lips and then she replied, "We are going to play a kind of game, Mother. Do you notice that you cannot see me but that my weight is like a reminder, always present but not seen?"

"Why, yes, it does seem that way. I can already see that the children of the future are like that. I cannot see them because they have not been born, but I always consider their needs. They will need food, shelter, fire, water, air, fertile soil, and the companionship of All Their Relations."

Wata-jis continued, pleased with the Clan Mother's quick reasoning. "Mother, what senses must you use when you cannot see me?"

"I must hear your voice, feel your weight, smell the fragrance of your sweet hair, and allow my body to align with your rhythms, anticipating your movements so that we can walk in balance as I carry your cradleboard."

Wata-jis smiled. "Those are the same abilities that human Children of Earth must develop in order to prepare for the future, Mother. They must sense the weight of future generations' needs in order to find harmony and balance now. If they waste the precious resources of the Earth Mother, there will not be an abundant future for the generations yet unborn. As the Human Tribe learns to carry the Cradleboard of Creation as an unseen part of themselves, there will be no separation between the present and the future. All that is needed for survival on the Good Red Road will naturally be there, because everyone alive today will take responsibility for the needs of the next Seven Generations."

Setting Sun Woman asked, "Evening Star, what if some members of the Human Tribe forget these Teachings?"

"Unfortunately, that time will come, Mother. The Medicine of Elk will give the *persistence and stamina* needed for the Faithful to continue guarding the needs of future generations. We may also call upon the Medicine of Opossum to assist the Faithful in *planning and strategy.* Two-leggeds must be flexible and willing to grow and change for the future. The needs of some will be confused with the desires of others to own material possessions. Some will adopt greed and wish to control the masses. Every human being will have the opportunity to meet those challenges by rediscovering inner knowing. The solution will fall into your hands. You are the Clan Mother of the West who can assist the meek and faithful Children of Earth by showing them how to go within."

Setting Sun Woman agreed with Wata-jis and added her own thoughts. "I noticed that you were nestled in the snowy fur robes of the Great White Bear. Those robes are very sacred to me. The Bear has taught me how to enter the cave inside myself and to find my own truths. Through those lessons I am able to live my truth every Sun and Sleep. If every Child of Earth could find that same inner knowing, we would assure the future generations of a legacy of harmony and life abundant."

"That's right, Mother, we could also teach them the lessons of the humpbacked traveler of the deserts. Camel shares his Medicine of *conservation and proper use of resources* even in situations of scarcity. One of the gifts of inner knowing is knowing how and when to use available resources. The Bear lives on stored fat when she hibernates, the Camel lives on stored water when he travels the deserts, and the Human Tribe lives abundantly when they gather and eat just what they need."

Setting Sun Woman understood the lessons of preparing for tomorrow. The resources of the Earth Mother would abundantly serve the Children of Earth if they learned to conserve them.

"Mother, you know that I am the Evening Star, but did you know that I am the Promise of Tomorrow because I am also the Morning Star during six moon cycles?"

Setting Sun Woman was startled by Wata-jis's revelation. "Why no, I did not know that," she replied.

"I become the Morning Star and ride the currents of the sunlit morning sky. For eight days during the thirteen moon cycles, I am not seen in morning or evening. It is during that time that I go into the void of the Great Medicine Bowl of the night sky to be reborn. I travel the Sacred Spiral of the Eight Powers, visiting the East, Southeast, South, Southwest, West, Northwest, North, and Northeast. I live for one Sun and Sleep in each of those directions, learning the steps of transformation that will teach me how to change my path and focus.

"The Sacred Spiral leads from one Medicine Wheel of experience to the other. If we were to look at a wheel lying on the ground and another one a few feet directly above it in the same position, we would see two different circles of experience. The void in between the two is made of thin air, but there is an imaginary spiral of steps formed by each direction's lessons. All life forms walk those spiral stairs when they are ready to evolve into their next set of life's experiences."

Setting Sun Woman thought a moment and then said, "Are you saying that each flower that buds and blooms and then sheds its petals would, at the end of its cycle, then go through eight Suns and Sleeps of lessons before moving to its next experience?"

"Yes. The Spiritual Essence of every living thing moves through that Sacred Spiral for eight Suns and Sleeps before beginning the next life cycle. It can be a time of reviewing the past, counting the lessons learned and the victories achieved. It can be a time of preparation and planning as well as a time of saying good-bye to the past and greeting the future. Many of the Human Tribe forget this period of completion, reaching their next set of life's experiences either unprepared or out of balance. They encounter many difficulties when they do not honor the Void and the Sacred Spiral."

"Wata-jis, when you go through the Sacred Spiral, what happens to you?"

"I reconnect to my Orenda and let go of the past by being grateful for all that I have learned. I see the spiral around me because I am in the center of my Sacred Space, but I also see the steps formed by each direction of the spiral inside of myself. In the night sky, as the Evening Star, I am living the feminine side of my nature. In the void of the spiral, I am all and nothing—pure spirit. After eight days, as the Morning Star, I live the masculine, demonstrative side of my nature. The Directions of the Eight Powers inside the spiral teach me that I am both feminine and masculine. When I ride the night sky, I go within and seek the truth of my free will and my will to show my gifts to the world. As the Morning Star, I bring all those personal truths to light, sharing what I am with all those who seek the breaking dawn."

Setting Sun Woman understood. "Both sides of our natures are present in your journey. The West direction is the feminine and the East is the masculine. In the Absence of the eight Suns and Sleeps when you are not seen in the Sky Nation, you show humankind the way to connect to the Orenda. Your lesson to humankind is how to balance the female, male, and divine energy of the Great Mystery that lives in all things, is it not?"

"Yes. I also show the infinite possibilities found in the number 8. When humankind develops the understanding of how the Spirit World and the tangible world form two Medicine Wheels, they will find that the two are really one infinite set of lessons."

Setting Sun Woman saw the goodness the Great Mystery had placed in every part of Creation and was thankful that her role in the expansive plan had brought Wata-jis into her path. The Cradleboard of Creation not only held the potential of the unborn children of all tomorrows but also had given every child the ability to express a female and a male side no matter what gender the child's body was. All of her human children would be able to express their personal wills, because all Children of Earth carried the potential to be guided by their Orendas. Like Wata-jis, the Evening Star, the promise of tomorrow lived inside of every human being. The Earth Tribe could be assured of a bright future by balancing both sides of their natures with the Spiritual Essence

that connected them to their infinite capacity to create tomorrow by living in harmony today.

Setting Sun Woman felt Wata-jis shift her weight in the
cradleboard and release a little sigh. The Clan Mother gently removed the cradleboard and rocked Wata-jis in her arms
for a moment. The child's eyes were fluttering and growing
heavy. Setting Sun Woman smiled, noting that even a child
woven of starlight needed sleep. She kissed the child's
cheek and silently promised to keep the lessons she had
learned close to her heart. The Sleep Man had sprinkled
sand over the baby's eyes, sending her into the realms of
happy dreams. Setting Sun Woman tucked the cradleboard
into the robes of the Great White Bear, nestled in the bottom of the spirit canoe. Before stepping back, the Clan
Mother slipped a sleeping wild flower into the baby's lacing,
trusting that the fragrance would fill the child's dreams and
senses with memories of their time together.

Slowly the spirit canoe was lifted by moonlit hands
formed of the starshine coming from the Evening Star. The
spirit canoe entered the river of light and vanished into the
night sky, leaving Setting Sun Woman feeling wistful. She
perceived the sounds of her night traveling creatures as they
started to prowl again. The occasional hoots and howls of
her nocturnal children comforted her and gave her a sense
of company. As the Clan Mother turned to walk toward the
lodge she had built on the edge of the forest, she saw a white
reflection out of the corner of her eye. She turned and faced
the direction of the light. There was the robe of the Great
White Bear resting on the clover and wild flowers—a gift
from Wata-jis.

Setting Sun Woman lifted the robe and placed it across her shoulders, shedding tears of joy and gratitude. She looked to the place in the sky where Wata-jis had been before. The fiery light of the Evening Star sparkled in recognition and then disappeared and reappeared as if reminding the Clan Mother of both sides of its nature. Receiving and giving were both sacred ways of finding balance. Meeting the future needs of the next Seven Generations depended on the ability to go within and walk in balance every living moment. The robe of the Great White Bear of the West represented the spirit of all species of bears on the planet. Setting Sun Woman would always remember the lessons found in Bear's cave and would nestle in the white fur robe every time she retreated into herself.

That special memory had carried Setting Sun Woman through many troubling seasons as the Children of Earth had weathered the greed in some human hearts. She felt the ocean breeze on her bare arms and thought of how the bright-colored Finned Ones, swimming in the tide pools below, were the colors of the Whirling Rainbow of Peace. The common goal of the Earth Tribe was to reclaim the legacy of harmony and peace that the Great Mystery placed inside all life forms. Inner peace is found inside the Self. Setting Sun Woman gazed at the horizon where the ocean met the sky and gave thanks for the human children who had rediscovered the Looking-within Place.

The Keeper of Tomorrow's Dreams was drawn from her thoughts as Walrus waddled onto the beach below and croaked a greeting. Setting Sun Woman laughed because she had just been sternly reminded not to allow negativity to slip into her thoughts regarding the future. Walrus is the Creature-teacher who reminds humans of the cycles and changes in life. This big-tusked creature of the ocean's edge carries the Medicine of *altering actions and feelings in order to interact with the changes life offers.* Setting Sun Woman understood: it was time to keep her eyes on the goal, not on the waywardness of the Human Tribe. Their growth is by trial and error. Sooner or later, all human Two-leggeds will seek to understand their feelings and find the Cave of Bear.

The sea's tides change with the passage of Suns and Sleeps, the seasons, Grandmother Moon's cycles, and weather. The Clan Mother saw how the waters of the Earth Mother reflect the human journey as well. When the Human Tribe allows the flow of life to set the rhythm, like the tides, instead of fighting each new wave of experience, harmony is found through subtle adjustments. The pounding waves of stormy seas that wreck the shoreline reflect the imbalance found in human stubbornness and rigidity. Setting Sun Woman understood that the natural examples of worlds within worlds are endless reflections of how to live in harmony. She looked forward to the day when this same inner knowing would be claimed by all her human children.

Grandfather Sun was putting the light to rest, painting the sky with the colors of harvest leaves. Setting Sun Woman watched until the flaming mass of his pumpkinlike body touched the horizon, sinking into the sea. She was feeling the stillness of eventide when she heard the Wind Chief hiss as if the fire of Grandfather Sun's body had melded with the waters of the Earth Mother, signaling with invisible smoke that the Sacred Pipe had been passed from day to night. The sunbeams that had carried the human words of thanksgiving to the Great Mystery during the day were now giving that sacred duty over to the beams of light coming from the Starry Medicine Bowl of the night sky.

Setting Sun Woman stood and raised her arms to the Sky Nation and returned thanks for all that she had experienced during that Sun. She greeted the falling robe of the night sky and imagined the Cradleboard of Creation resting in her hands, being offered to the heavens. Wata-jis appeared, as if to receive the cradleboard from Setting Sun Woman's outstretched arms. The Clan Mother felt the bond of Sisterhood between herself and the Evening Star. That bond was forever strong, because it was woven with love and made of the fibers of tomorrow's promises.

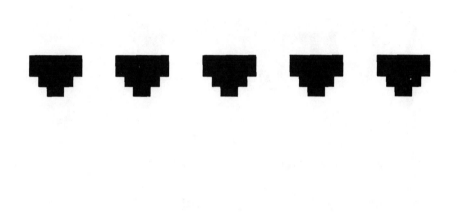

WEAVES THE WEB

Gossamer threads of life hold me,
Perched between Earth and Sky,
Weaving the web, dreaming the dream,
Through the two worlds I will fly.
With you as my muse, Mother,
I create the substance of dreams,
Allowing the artist within me
To fashion my life with esteem.
I mold the clay of experiences
Into a sacred Medicine Bowl,
Capturing the essence of living
As it sings deep in my soul.
Your secrets of creation, Mother,
Have taught me when to destroy
The chains that have bound me,
Limiting the expression of my joy.
You have taught me how to labor,
Giving birth to the visions within,
Setting them free like silver arrows,
Kindling the fire of Creation again.

Clan Mother
of the
Tenth Moon Cycle

WEAVES THE WEB represents the creative principle within all things. Her moon cycle falls in the month of October and is connected to the color pink. *Working with the truth* is her Cycle of Truth. She teaches us how to use our hands to create beauty and truth in tangible forms. Pink is the color of creativity. Weaves the Web shows us how to use crafts and art to create our ideas and dreams in the physical world. Through using our hands, we show our willingness to be of service to All Our Relations.

Weaves the Web is the Guardian of the Creative Force in all things. She helps us express our creativity in a positive manner and use the energy available to us. This Clan Mother is also the Keeper of Life Force and instructs us to create health, to manifest our dreams, to develop and use our talents, and to access our spiritual potentials.

The Clan Mother of the Tenth Moon Cycle is the Mother of the Creative and Destructive principles; she shows us when to destroy limitations and create anew. She also teaches us when to nurture our creations, because she is the Keeper of Survival Instinct. When our physical, emotional, mental, or spiritual survival is at risk, Weaves the Web shows us how to tap into the life force to grow beyond

▲▲

this stagnation. She is an artist, a creatress, and the muse who beckons and inspires us to create the beauty found in our heart's desire. Through making something tangible and filling that creation with beauty, we are shown that the stuff of dreams can be expressed, giving form to our visions. She is the Clan Mother we turn to when we are afraid of failure or lack self-expression.

When we follow the steps necessary to bring our dreams to life, Weaves the Web shows us how to use the life force found in the four elements of air, earth, water, and fire. We learn how to mix these elements with the creative essence that is our gift from the Great Mystery. This creative spark is called the Eternal Flame of Love and lives inside our Spiritual Essences. When the desire to create is in place, we are then able to make the decision TO BE. We then give form to our Spiritual Essences or Orendas through self-expression.

Weaves the Web, like Grandmother Spider who wove the web of the universe, teaches us how to weave the web of our experiences. She shows us how every circle we create grows to touch the circles created by all other life forms. The webs we create can trap us, if we do not create them in truth. We are asked by this Clan Mother to work with and for the truth in order to manifest a world dream that all living things can share. A web that is created in greed will eventually trap and devour the one who wove it because it was woven too tightly to allow giving, receiving, and sharing. A web woven too loosely, without care, lacks the craftsmanship that is necessary to make it strong and durable. A web woven from fear will attract the lessons needed to overcome that fear. A web woven from the love of creating and the desire to share the abundance caught in the web's silvery fibers is a web that will endure until the dream is fulfilled.

Weaves the Web is the Clan Mother we turn to when we need the skills to make our dreams real. She shows us how to take the actions necessary to tap our creativity and go with the flow. Giving birth to our dreams is always accomplished by having the *desire* to create, *deciding* to create, and *taking the actions* necessary by using the flow of life force to give birth to the dream in the tangible world.

▲▲

Grandmother Spider
Came Down

Weaves the Web scooped the rich white clay from the river's embankment below the chalky bluffs and placed the lumps of alabaster earth into her river reed basket. The leaves of the scrub oak had turned bright red in contrast to the yellow pollen that clung to the deep forest green of the surrounding cedars. The leaves of these Standing People would bring forth many colors when added to her oven to fire the bowl she would create from the clay. She would climb the limestone cliffs to gather the flat-leafed cedar and red-orange oak leaves, but she was happy to do it.

Weaves the Web found such a joy in making objects of beauty and experimenting with new designs that she often lost herself in the creative process. Sometimes when she was out walking on the land, she would find herself deep in the tall forests covered with vines and chirping birds and would have no idea where her wanderings had taken her. Weaves the Web had a natural ability to retrace her trek by looking into her basket and working with the gathered objects that she had placed in a specific order. She could begin with the last object she had gathered and walk back to the area where she found it; then one by one, the locations of her collected bounty would take her back to familiar surroundings. From those often-traveled locations the Clan Mother could easily find her way home.

Weaves the Web used the bark, berries, tubers, leaves, and mosses she gathered in the same way Grandmother Spider used the silvery threads of her web. It made no difference if the Mother of Creativity traveled in a circle or in a straight line, she could always find her way back to her camp. Each location where Weaves the Web gathered something from the land contained a spot where she had connected her creative threads of self-expression with the living plants, earth, or stones of sunlit forest. The Clan Mother always left a gift for the spirits of the forest when she took something for her own use. The loving exchange, showing gratitude, left a trail through the lush growth that formed a homecoming trail back to her camp, nestled in the limestone outcroppings that towered over the river's bend.

As Weaves the Web dug more clay from the embankment, using a sharp piece of stone as a hand tool, she saw in her mind's eye the Medicine Bowl she would fashion from the clay. The enjoyment she felt when she used her hands to make pots coursed through her arms, bringing her a sense of satisfaction that made the hard work of digging the clay seem easy. The hole carved by spring runoff that gaped like an open mouth in the slanting ridge reminded Weaves the Web that the Earth Mother would need to be fed after sharing the cloud-colored clay with her Two-legged daughter. Weaves the Web had carried several large stones down the bluff to place inside the orifice where she had dug her clay.

Squirrel scampered down the trunk of a pecan tree on the other side of the river, exposing his nut-laden cheeks to Weaves the Web. He tried valiantly to give the Clan Mother a smile without spitting out the pecans. Weaves the Web giggled at Squirrel's predicament, thinking of the lessons he had taught her through his natural Medicine of *gathering energy and saving a little extra for lean times.* In the early seasons of her Earth Walk, the Clan Mother had learned to pack dried fruits, tubers, and meat in underground storage holes, saving the food for use in the winter. Squirrel was once again preparing for the coming snows.

Weaves the Web noticed that Mother Beaver and her clan had made ready for the coming White Moons because they were busy stopping the river's flow, adding saplings to the dam they had built across the inlet, just downstream from where she was digging clay. The changing temperatures were a sign to the Clan Mother that it was time to gather all the materials she would need to keep busy during the winter when her activities were limited by the biting White Winds of the north. She had filled her food stores, gathered herbs for cooking and medicinal purposes, and tanned the green pelts needed for a new parka, and now she was collecting the supplies she would need to make usable implements for her life in camp.

She silently thanked Mother Beaver for showing her how to use her time to build or make things during periods of long inactivity. Beaver was the keeper of Builder Medicine, who showed humankind *how to keep busy by being productive,* bringing their visions and dreams of a better life into reality. The Tribe that walked through the Clan Mother's forest in summer following the trail to their Ripening Moons Gathering was always happy to trade with the artist because her creations were so unusual. Weaves the Web always had a storehouse of handmade toys, baskets, clothing, clay pots, and cooking utensils finished by the time the snows had been replaced with clear green shoots of new undergrowth. By the Moon of Ripening Berries, the Clan Mother had bartered for the items that would fill her own needs, assuring her that she could meet the challenges of living alone during the falling snows.

Every Moon of Falling Leaves, Weaves the Web would see which raw materials were available and would plan all of the things she could make during the time her Creature friends would be hibernating. The clay she was now digging would be a part of her cache of art supplies, as would the leaves she intended to gather later before Grandfather Sun went down. For the next two moons, the Clan Mother would complete her gathering and store all her needed supplies in the cavern she called home. The blowholes in her cavern created by the Earth Mother's metamorphic growth and cooling cycle in ages past had provided the Clan Mother of Creativity a few excellent places to keep her things. She could even fire her pots in a blowhole that had a natural chimney through the limestone roof, high above the cave's entrance.

Winter came with all its blustery glory. The northern winds exhaled the snows in swirling patterns, covering everything with glistening Ice-beings and downy snowflake blankets. Inside the cavern, Weaves the Web was happy and warm. Each new Sun brought new ideas and the continued joy of whittling, making pots, fashioning dolls from old bones, basket weaving, or sewing hides into clothing. Weaves the Web put her love and expertise into each item she made and in so doing, gave each creation the gift of life and purpose, similar to the way the Great Mystery gave life and purpose to all of Creation. She looked forward to the coming days of trading during the Ripening Moons that would bring her a way to share her artistic endeavors with other Twoleggeds. Just imagining the expressions of joy that would light up their faces after the trade was completed warmed her heart even now in the deep cold of winter. The ones she traded with would never show how much they liked something before a trade was complete, fearing the barterer would ask too high a price, but afterward the gleam in their eyes was a welcome reward for the Mother of Creativity.

One Sun, after the first few snows had blanketed the Earth Mother in her white robes, Weaves the Web awoke to find the most exquisite spider's web she had ever seen, covering the opening of a blowhole. In the center of the web was a most unusual spider, completely white except for one red spot on the upper portion of her body. Weaves the Web marveled at the unusual appearance of her eight-legged friend. Spiders did not usually appear during the cold of winter. Perhaps the warmth of the cavern had brought her visit, but it was doubtful. Weaves the Web thought it was a sign from Grandmother Spider, who wove the web of the universe. Grandmother Spider was the special creature that the Great Mystery had chosen to weave the original webs of the tangible world, making a skeleton of concentric circles that would hold the flesh and realities of all life forms in Creation.

Weaves the Web asked Spider if she had a special message. She was startled by the Creepy-crawler's answer echoing as a voice inside her human thoughts.

"I have been sent from Grandmother Spider to tell you that you have created many things of beauty and have woven a new web of experience because your heart has expressed the desire to share that creativity with others. Use your new Medicine Bowl and seek the visions that will reflect the desires hidden within your heart. Seek answers to what is coming into the web you have woven out of your hidden desires. Trust that you have chosen well and that your dreams will be fulfilled."

Weaves the Web went to the far corner of her cave where she kept her Medicine objects to retrieve her latest creation. The bowl was hard-fired and blackened with smoke from the leaves she had gathered. Here and there were flecks of color from trace minerals in the clay. She retraced her steps across the cave, lit a fire, and filled the bowl with melted snow. It was not long before her efforts brought the vision of three Two-leggeds stumbling through the snow at the edge of a forest. One larger and two smaller forms struggled against the pounding winds of a storm. The vision changed and Weaves the Web saw the smiling faces of two children—then nothing.

That night Weaves the Web dreamed she was seining for food in the sea and as she looked down into her woven net, she spied a starfish. It was an unusual starfish, colored a brilliant purple-red. Starfish spoke to her and told her that its body represented the creative life force that Two-leggeds could use when they tapped into the Clan Chiefs of Air, Earth, Water, and Fire and then mixed those elements with the Creative Force of the Great Mystery. Starfish showed Weaves the Web how the Clan Mother had employed that same use of energy in making her crafts and in the ingenuity she had used in fashioning the cavern into a warm home.

Starfish whispered to the Clan Mother's heart, "Weaves the Web, you have used your creativity to fill your life with beauty, but you have become lonely. The hidden desire in your heart is weaving a dream that can change that aloneness, if you pay attention. The abundance of creative talent that you possess can be shared with others if you give birth to your dream of having a family."

The Clan Mother was startled by Starfish's revelation, but she could not pull her senses away from the dream. She tried to wake up, struggling with her desire to remember, but as the dreamscape changed, she went even deeper into the pictures being presented. The Keeper of Survival Instinct knew on some level of consciousness that she needed to surrender and follow the dream vision in order to understand why she had not allowed the feelings of being alone to surface. She sighed in her sleep and then plunged into the watery world around her. Fathoms of ocean traveled past as she slipped beneath the waves, discovering that she could breathe under the dream water. When she reached the ocean floor, Starfish, riding on her shoulder, whispered to her again.

"Weaves the Web, you are immersed in the watery womb of the Earth Mother. Here you can give birth to your dreams and allow yourself to be reborn in the process. You never allowed the aloneness to surface because you were busy giving life to your other creations."

The Clan Mother focused her attention on her womb and saw all the pent-up feelings she had hidden from herself with her desire to create. She wanted children. She wanted to share the toys she had made and to teach the young to use their imaginations, allowing them to create to their hearts' content. She wanted to share the wisdom she carried regarding every human's ability to create as much as her or his imagination would allow. Children knew how to make that kind of magic and so did Weaves the Web. A deep cry rose in her throat as she screamed her loneliness into the water. Suddenly, the Clan Mother felt a movement in her belly. She had the urge to spread her legs and push hard. She allowed her body to do the work, and a big iridescent bubble came from her womb into the water and rose to the surface. She caught a brief glimpse of bright eyes and two smiles looking back at her. Her body jerked involuntarily and she woke up.

It was an unusually chilly predawn and so she decided she would make a big fire to warm her shivering body. There was no use in trying to go back to sleep. She looked at the blowhole where Spider had been and was astonished to discover the figures of three Two-leggeds woven into the outer edge of the web. Spider was gone. The fire was having trouble getting started because a draft was coming into the cavern from around the hides that covered the entrance. The Clan Mother threw a heavy robe around her shoulders and stumbled to the doorway.

When Weaves the Web tried to cover the cave's entrance with the hides, pulling the rocks over the bottom of the skins to anchor them, she saw, not far from the trail that led to her home, a large mound covered in snow that was not usually there. Thinking that some lost creature had broken its leg and could provide her with fresh meat, she grabbed her flint knife and braved the foggy grayness of predawn. Upon reaching the mound, she placed her fur-wrapped foot on the side and gently nudged it to see if the animal was still alive. After a second, firmer nudge, the Guardian of Creativity heard a human groan. The next few moments were spent in a furious endeavor to dig the body out of the snow.

Upon reaching a nearly frozen Buffalo Robe, Weaves the Web cast it aside and found the blue body of a woman sheltering two children. The Clan Mother bent close and listened, realizing the woman was no longer alive but was now walking in the Spirit World. She tried to reach beneath the frozen mother to see if the children were still breathing. She wrestled with the frozen arms of the woman's body and pulled a boy of four summers into her arms and then his older sister. She placed both children on her robe and covered them with two smaller robes that had been beneath them, keeping their bodies from lying directly on the frozen snow.

She fought and tugged, dragging her load up the trail to the cave. The bodies of the children were ice cold, but they were breathing. She returned her thanks to the North Wind for not bringing more snow and for the lives of her two charges. She had covered the woman's body, but she would have to return later to bury the body deeper to keep it from being food for wandering carnivores. Finally she reached the hides at the cave's entrance. The fire blazed brightly, giving all three people the warmth they desperately needed.

Amid whimpers and moans, Weaves the Web worked diligently to rub the life back into the children's half-frozen limbs. The Clan Mother was reassured that the children would recover by the smiling faces she had seen in her two visions, but she hurriedly continued to administer her healing salves, stopping only once to hang a pot of stew over the fire.

After the children had been rubbed, fed, and then tucked in extra heavy sleeping robes, the Clan Mother rested. Tiny sighs and moans came from the Buffalo Robes nestled near the fire. Assured that the children were asleep the Keeper of Survival Instinct donned her fur parka and went to bury the children's mother in the fading light. Later, bone-weary, after stoking the fire for the night, she collapsed into a dreamless sleep, but had some part of herself still listening to make sure the children were all right.

Sound of Rain was a young girl of eleven summers who found comfort in being with Weaves the Web. From the first instant that the girl resigned herself to the fact her mother was in the Spirit World, she began calling the Clan Mother "aunt." This term of endearment was the way tribal children showed respect for their Elders, acknowledging extended family as well as blood kin. Sun Behind the Clouds, her little brother, had only passed four summers but was precocious, bold, and interested in everything he came into contact with. The little warrior was fascinated with the things his new aunt could do and the way she included him in all the activities of life inside the cavern.

Weaves the Web was overjoyed with the company of her new niece and nephew. The children were always looking for ways they could assist in the daily routine. Sound of Rain was very creative and willing to talk about the ideas that poured from her imagination when she was learning how to make things. Sun Behind the Clouds was a quick learner and was the quieter of the two, hiding his bright smile behind an unusually thoughtful manner. Together the three would spend hours making new and wonderful toys, clay pots, and paintings, as well as participating in stories and games. Weaves the Web felt that she had been given a gift that made her life complete. The children had replaced their sense of loss with a magical world that filled every passing Sun with new games, fun, and a sense of family, living with an aunt who cared for them very deeply. The storms of winter howled and groaned outside the cavern, but inside the fire was warm, the food was plentiful, and the loving new experiences seemingly inexhaustible to the two little ones.

Weaves the Web assisted Sun Behind the Clouds in making a child-sized shield out of rawhide and a tiny set of arrows to go with a little bow. The young warrior would spend hours at the back of the cavern, shooting the giant Four-leggeds that the Clan Mother had painted on the walls of the cave. Sun Behind the Clouds would silently stalk his prey, hiding behind the boulders scattered here and there along the limestone floor; then he would pretend he was a fully grown hunter who was capable of downing the Buffalo or Elk with one arrow. Often he would mimic hauling the meat home to his aunt and sister. Weaves the Web always thanked Sun Behind the Clouds for his prowess and for the imaginary meat he brought to their fire. In a very serious manner, she would ask the little warrior what great Four-legged he had downed that day and he would name the creature. The aunt would then teach the boy how to apologize to the beast, giving thanks to the creature's spirit for the food provided, and then she would show the boy how to release the animal's spirit. Every time Sun Behind the Clouds brought fresh invisible meat home, Weaves the Web would cook some dried meat from her stores for the evening meal.

Sound of Rain was impressed with her aunt's ability to support both children's vivid imaginations. The Clan Mother encouraged any kind of creativity that either child cared to employ when playing, making things, or helping with chores. If the children could find an easier or more self-expressive way of doing something, Weaves the Web was happy to go along. The Clan Mother showed both her charges how to work with their hands and how they could create a beautiful life in the same manner they created crafts of beauty. She showed them how to take care of materials, how to be proud of their handiwork, and how to put love into everything they created. She reminded both children of how the Great Mystery had put love into every life form and how they, as Two-leggeds, were asked to continue that legacy of loving creativity.

Weaves the Web taught the children that every painted symbol had meaning to an artist and that every color had a significance when an artist created an object of beauty. The Medicine Story behind each pot or toy gave those items a mission or something to teach a Two-legged who looked upon those creations. The self-expression of the artists who created the items always reflected how those craftspeople felt about themselves, how well they had developed their skills, and how they saw the world around them. Weaves the Web became a muse for the two children, always urging them to use their imaginations and reasoning powers by putting their creativity into workable methods that would allow the pictures in their minds to match the crafts or playthings they made.

Sound of Rain was a striking example of how quickly a child could learn to become as skilled as an adult. The girl's keen ability of observation and repetition astounded Weaves the Web. The young girl's imagination and sense of self shined through every new endeavor she undertook and then accomplished. Weaves the Web could clearly see from the way Sound of Rain used her materials and took painstaking efforts to make and paint pots that the girl would become a masterful artist and craftsperson. Symbols were delicately and precisely painted by Sound of Rain's unswerving hands, guided by the girl's natural sense of proportion and composition.

Weaves the Web realized that her heart's hidden desire had brought the dream of having loving, artistic children into her life. As the Warming Moons approached, the Clan Mother found herself weaving future dreams that included her niece and nephew, sharing the magic of creating a life full of rich potential. Daily, Weaves the Web returned thanks for the fullness she felt in being privileged to observe the children's growth and joyful self-expression. She forgot what it had been like to pass winters alone and in silence, with only her pots, crafts, and toys for company.

One Sleep during the Warming Moons, the voice of the Earth Mother permeated Weaves the Web's dreams. "Daughter of my spirit, hear my voice. The gift you have given yourself in the form of these two children is a gift of the Dreamweaver, Grandmother Spider. You will nurture these children into adulthood. You will share their exuberance and their tears. You will find yourself reflected in them, as you observe them passing through the cycles of growth and change. These memories are the living treasures that every mother carries inside her heart. While they grow, the children will also use their creativity to test your authority, to test your wisdom, and to test your resolve. Know that they need a firm hand, as well as a loving aunt who teaches them how to destroy limitation through using their self-expression and creativity."

The Clan Mother thought of all the times she had shown the youngsters how to make something new from a pot or a toy that did not turn out as it should. Creation and destruction could always be re-invented if one used imagination. Weaves the Web took the Earth Mother's words of wisdom to heart, making note in the dream to remember all she heard and perceived. Then the Earth Mother continued.

"You have birthed your heart's hidden desire through weaving your dreams with the invisible webs of the Creative Force, daughter. You have created a loving family circle that will touch the circles of every other life form when life's experiences are shared. When your hoops of creation come together with the circles of life's experiences created by others, new ideas and creativity are available to everyone who is willing to share. Sun Behind the Clouds is a living extension of the male side of your nature and Sound of Rain is a reflection of the female part of yourself. As you love them into adulthood, you will be creating the patterns of self-expression and webs of creativity that will serve them throughout their Earth Walks. Through their experiences you will be able to see how your own creativity can meld with theirs to manifest the dreams you have shared in common. Teach your children well, Weaves the Web, and you will show others how the spirit of the artist living inside every human can fashion a world that respects the creativity that the Great Mystery placed inside all living things."

As the Earth Mother's voice faded, Weaves the Web found herself riding through her dream on the back of Cheetah. Cheetah's Medicine of *accomplishing tasks with speed and agility* brought the Clan Mother visions that seemed to fly through her mind's eye as if in fast motion. Images of showing the children how to accomplish new tasks, avoiding the laziness and procrastination that comes from lack of inspiration, flashed through the Clan Mother's mind. The future would be good, the horizon was bright with possibilities, and Weaves the Web had found an unlimited source of inspiration, seeing the world through the eyes of Sound of Rain and Sun Behind the Clouds.

Weaves the Web silently thanked the Great Mystery for allowing her to express the beauty found in being a Mother of the Creative Force. Her path would grow and change, along with the lives of her children. Every object she had ever created was an extension of her love and self-expression, each having a purpose and a mission of serving. Her children would find their own purposes and missions through their individual forms of self-expression. As the Keeper of Survival Instinct, the Clan Mother realized that she had created a way for the wisdom and love she carried in her Orenda to be passed on, surviving the tests of time, because she had woven a web of creation that allowed her to give life, longevity, and permanence to her manifested dreams.

WALKS
TALL
WOMAN

You walk in beauty, Mother,
Allowing all to see
The glory of Great Mystery
That sets your spirit free.

Guided by the bliss inside you,
Walking it through your deeds,
Never needing another's approval,
Your heart's truth takes the lead.

With focus and directness
You teach me how to walk,
Balancing thought and action
Instead of misusing talk.

I stand straight in your presence,
I hold my head up high,
With my feet rooted in Mother Earth,
My arms embracing Father Sky.

Clan Mother
of the
Eleventh Moon Cycle

WALKS TALL WOMAN is the Clan Mother of November's moon cycle, who teaches us how to Walk Our Talk. Her Cycle of Truth is *walking the truth* and is connected to the color white. Through the color white, we learn magnetism and how to use authority and will properly. Walks Tall Woman shows the Children of Earth how to lead through example instead of insisting that others follow the leader. This Clan Mother teaches us how to change life's situations through taking action ourselves, not depending on others to do it for us.

Walks Tall Woman teaches us how to be proud of our accomplishments through self-esteem, not self-importance. She shows us that the more we refine our skills, the happier we are with ourselves. Walks Tall Woman understands that actions always speak louder than words and that when we are living examples of our philosophies, we are walking our personal truths. When we walk with truth, there is no need to fear what others think of us. Reputation is based upon integrity and inner knowing, not on the opinions of others, who may be jealous or insecure about themselves. Walks Tall Woman teaches us that it is through our relationship to

▲▲▲▲▲▲▲▲▲▲▲▲▲▲▲▲▲▲▲▲▲▲▲▲▲▲▲▲▲▲▲▲▲▲▲▲▲

the Great Mystery and to life that we know and honor our selves and our spirits.

This Eleventh Clan Mother is the Guardian of Leadership and the Keeper of New Pathways. She shows us the value of leading through example, being our personal best, and exploring all our options, and the importance of innovation. If there is a more appropriate or more efficient way to do something, Walks Tall Woman will apply those new ideas to her Earth Walk, to see if the new way will assist her in Walking Her Truth. Through this Medicine, she has earned the right to be the Mother of Innovation. This type of innovation does not destroy the Traditions of the past but rather adds new truths to those Traditions, giving the ancient ways of the Ancestors new growth potential.

The Eleventh Clan Mother is also the Mother of Perseverance and Stamina, who teaches us the value of health. The needs of our physical bodies and the use of exercise to make them strong are part of her teaching. Walking tall and in truth is exemplified by our ability to be graceful and to find the point of gravity in the human form. To do this we must use the natural flexibility of the human body. Walks Tall Woman shows us that we must be flexible enough to allow others to follow their paths. A healthy mind will support the body's health. A mind riddled with half-truths and negativity can thwart the body to the point where disease is created. Walks Tall Woman shows us how to honor the body's needs by balancing physical activity, proper attitudes, good eating and sleeping habits, and hygiene.

Walks Tall Woman also teaches us that we can persevere, meeting our goals when the body is healthy. Stamina comes from treating the body with care. To use persistence in a proper way, we are taught how to be tenacious, using all our gifts of health, attitude, self-reflection, and spirit to meet challenges head-on. Walks Tall shows us how to keep our eyes on the goal, our feet on the path, and the truth in our hearts, never waiting for another to do it for us. Leading through example by being personally responsible in thought, action, and deed is the way we find the Medicine of Walking Our Talk. Our challenges are to be willing to drop our fears of taking action and to balance our work activities with rest, relaxation, and retreat.

▲ ▲

Scouting the Trail of Truth

Walks Tall Woman could hear the sound of wind rushing past her ears and the thundering of her heart, filling her whole body. She saw the passing blur of green as she ran across the meadow to the forest's edge. Entering the forest, she slowed her pace a bit, lithely dodging the brambles without breaking a twig or disturbing the undergrowth. Swiftly and silently she traversed the deep woodlands, pushing toward her goal.

The chirping of the Winged Ones suddenly stopped and Walks Tall came to a soundless but abrupt halt. When her heart slowed its drum-shattering rhythm, she could hear the faint, stealthful sounds of a large Creature-being coming from somewhere near her. Cautiously she turned, raising her head to look into the treetops. Her gaze was met by piercing golden eyes. The great cat was perched, poised, and ready to jump from the stout limb of Sycamore. Walks Tall Woman mustered the courage she needed to gaze back into those unwavering eyes, showing her natural boldness, even when she was confronted with Mountain Lion's prowess. For reasons unknown to Walks Tall, Puma simply sat on the branch and showed no further interest in the woman below. The Mountain Lion began licking her paws and preening.

Walks Tall was not going to wait to see what would happen next. She bolted through the glen and continued her journey with great haste. Soon she had once again hit her stride, allowing her body to find its natural balance and center of gravity. Never once did she stumble or displace a twig as her feet seemingly flew across the floor of the primeval forest. She cut through the outlying scrub and made her way to a path strewn with wild violets and strawberries that ran along the edge of the woods by a shallow river. Walks Tall Woman took the river in three leaps, sending sprays of water flying in every direction as she lithely bounded up the opposite shore covered with goldenrod and red clover.

The Clan Mother knew that she was hitting the homestretch and poured all her strength into her powerful legs. She ran and ran, crossing the corner of a prairie filled with wild golden grains, bounding up the last hill. The incline was difficult to traverse but the Mother of Perseverance met the challenge by changing her strides, breathing more deeply despite the ache in her chest, pushing her body to adjust to the new rhythms she had created on the homestretch.

When Walks Tall Woman reached the summit she was greeted by the astonished faces of the people of the Water Clan that she had wintered with. Grandfather Sun then passed a quarter of his journey across the Sky Nation before another runner appeared. This was a summer game of constructive competition and comradeship, and the Clan Mother had used the race to teach the Water Clan many other lessons about stamina and perseverance.

That night around the communal fire, with stars twinkling and bellies full from feasting, Walks Tall Woman took the opportunity to speak. Because she was known as a woman of few words, the members of the Water Clan listened intensely to her. Walks Tall Woman told them about the value of finding alternate paths through the forest, new ways of approaching their daily tasks, and how she was able to win the race because she had scouted the trail, making a new, shorter route to use during the footrace. Now that the Warming and Planting Moons had passed, she offered to teach the humans of the Water Clan how she could move through any terrain without disturbing as much as a leaf.

The hunters and trackers had been unsure of letting a woman teach them the skills they were usually taught by other males, but the Clan Mother had won the footrace, and therefore had won the bet that she could beat all the men who entered the contest. The amazed men began to look at Walks Tall Woman in a new way. Some were even happy that she could teach them new skills that would surely stand them in good stead at the Harvest Festival when all the Clans of their Tribe gathered to return thanks for the abundant harvest.

Walks Tall Woman worked with the men of the Water Clan all through the summer moons. They spent time watching her each day, learning new skills as she showed them how to make the most of the actions they set in motion. The Clan Mother showed the men how Antelope when hunted on the plains used grace and balance to bound through tall grasses. Her students practiced on the balls of their feet to create a spring in their steps and change their running gaits. Together, using Antelope's Medicine of *grace, readiness, and taking action,* they practiced walking the length of fallen logs that would roll, making the students adjust their balance every few feet. The Water Clan men found the body's center of gravity in their hips and learned to use their inner vision to make their bodies lighter by seeing themselves as Antelope, who could spring forward, seemingly fly through the air, and land lightly without a sound.

Walks Tall Woman continued the training, teaching the arts of changing stride, using the intent to propel the body, understanding the body's rhythms in motion, and scouting. Never once did the Clan Mother try to show that she was superior to the men. She was always encouraging and supportive in her teaching role, insuring that other men did not belittle the ones who were bold enough to try a new skill for the first time.

Walks Tall Woman taught the whole Clan how action counts double when one is honing new skills. Even the smallest children were imitating their Elders by finding new ways to assist in the chores that were necessary to keep camp life moving smoothly. The Mother of Innovation was pleased that the youngsters had scouted new ways to be productive, as well as finding new games that included all of the children. The women were elated that their men came back to the lodges each sunset smiling and feeling self-assured about the accomplishments made during each Sun. With every member of the Clan making ready for the gathering and the competitions, only Walks Tall Woman noticed that the usual gossip and petty arguments had stopped. When everyone was productive, they were happy and did not have the desire or the time to waste on idle chatter.

Walks Tall Woman had worked hard preparing the Water Clan for the games to be held at the Tribe's gathering. The Mother of Perseverance's talents paid off when the Water Clan took the lead, counting coup on the other astonished Clans of their Nation. For her efforts, the men of the Water Clan presented the Clan Mother with a horse. Walks Tall was deeply touched by the gesture because horses were rare in those times. Most Clans and Tribes had a dozen or so horses for more than a hundred human beings, with most possessions and packs being carried by their faithful dogs.

The Clan Mother decided to accept the gift by speaking a few words about the Medicine of Horse. She explained to the Water Clan that the power of Horse's Medicine was in *the proper use of gifts, talents, and abilities.* Horse taught Two-leggeds to balance the gifts of the tangible and intangible worlds. Like Horse, Two-leggeds were being taught to be of the Earth and to be at one with the wind. When the two worlds came together, balance was attained, allowing humans to see the beauty of spirit living and working through their physical forms. In that balance, physical and spiritual power could be used. Horse taught how to use *will, endurance, authority, and talents in a proper manner without abuse or misuse.* Walks Tall Woman thanked the men of the Clan for their gift and returned thanks to the Great Mystery for their combined successes and all of the new skills they had attained. She was particularly grateful for the letting go of the fear of taking action and learning new skills that could have robbed them of their victories at the games.

The Moon of Red Leaves followed, bringing many new lessons to the Water Clan. After the harvest and gathering of wild foods from the forest, the Clan prepared for the coming winter. The spirit of victory was still keeping the Clan productive, with the reminders of those innovative ways of accomplishing tasks still fresh in their minds, but Walks Tall Woman sensed an unsettling change. The subtle shift was not apparent to the members of her Clan, but the Guardian of Leadership was very aware that something was amiss. The situation needed to become clearer before the proper solution could be applied, so Walks Tall Woman watched and waited, continuing her own activities but not speaking until the time was appropriate.

The brilliant colors of sunset were painted on the leaves by Mother Nature, carrying with them the first frosts that signaled the approach of winter. Walks Tall Woman walked to the forest to be alone and to ponder the ways she could help the Children of Earth through the changes that could rob them of having the right attitudes toward life. The bickering had begun again among the women, and the men were disgruntled. Spats had replaced the former comradeship of the Yellow Moons of summer between the children. Walks Tall Woman lay her body down on a bed of bright fallen leaves and allowed Grandfather Sun's light to warm her skin. This rare time of inactivity and reflection took her into a state of heightened awareness where she was riding Horse through a Dreamtime landscape on the open plains.

Faster and faster they galloped as her body became a living extension of her steed. Walks Tall Woman's head was bent forward, her hair mingling with the mane of her Four-legged companion, named Runs with the Winds. Together they rode through the steppes of golden, windswept grasses as she urged the stallion forward with a slight pressure from her knees. The forests of the foothills drew closer as she melded her spirit with the stallion's powerful rhythms and strides. Her perceptions changed and she saw through Runs with the Winds' eyes. The shape shifting was complete as Walks Tall Woman melded with her galloping companion, feeling the power of four legs thundering across the distance, closing in on the foothills. A surge of energy flowed through her body as together they approached the wooded hills.

Runs with the Winds came to a halt among the trees of the forest and the magical spell was broken as Walks Tall Woman's perceptions returned to her human form. The exuberance and overwhelming feeling of intense power still coursed through her veins as she dismounted. When she tethered the stallion to graze, she felt as if she were being watched. Walks Tall Woman followed her feelings and gazed up into the branches of a sturdy oak just in time to see Mountain Lion pounce, coming to rest gracefully at her feet. Quickly, she looked toward her stallion, finding him uninterested in the great cat. She was startled by the horse's

behavior, but in the Dreamtime there was no threat between creatures, so she relaxed.

Mountain Lion spoke and caught her by surprise.
"Mother, you have walked with me since the beginning of
your physical life, but it is only now that you have slowed
down enough for me to be able to speak to you. Have you
forgotten my Medicine of *leading through example?*"

Walks Tall Woman was stunned and speechless for a
moment. "What do you mean, Puma? I walk in balance and
always allow my actions to speak for my intentions. Have I
forgotten to perform some duty or to take some action that
would show others the integrity of my walk?"

"No, Mother, you have been a fine example to your
children. You have taken the actions needed. You have always been compassionate, caring, and forthright. You have
showed your children new paths and innovative ways of
correcting wrong attitudes and how to follow their heart's
desires; but you have not balanced action with the strength
of inaction. You have been so busy doing, you have forgotten to take the time you need to reflect and regroup your
thoughts, dreams, and energy. This is the first time during
your Earth Walk that you have rested and released enough
of your need to be a perfect example, to let down the barri-
ers that keep you from being human."

Walks Tall Woman sat on the ground in stunned silence, realizing that Mountain Lion was right. The tears she
had been holding for all the winters of her human life began
to flow and sobs racked her body until she could utter no
sound, trying to get her breath. The multitude of sorrows
she had felt when she was frustrated or hurt by the actions

of others had been buried in the snows of her frozen heart. Walks Tall Woman was ready to release the illusion that she needed to be superhuman. In her efforts to be an impeccable example, she had masked her human needs with action. The drive and ambition to be her personal best had led her down a lonely trail that insisted she never show her feelings. She had placed all of her spiritual experience outside of herself, never allowing time-out for the lessons to be felt and integrated as a part of her humanness. When she finally caught her breath and the tears had been exhausted, Mountain Lion continued.

"Leading through example is a Beauty Trail, Mother. If you are being an example to other human beings, it is necessary to show them that being human is not to be judged as having weaknesses. Allowing the tears to flow is the first step in transformation. Making mistakes is the way that skills are honed to precision. You have mastered perseverance, you have mastered innovation, you have mastered taking action; now it is time you make the commitment to allow yourself to become a female, feeling, human being. That vulnerability is a strength, not a weakness. Buried deep inside of you is the truth you have feared. You felt that if you slowed down and took a retreat when you needed it, the truth would be able to catch up with you. That truth is that you are human."

Puma waited a moment for her words to reach the Clan Mother's heart before she continued. "You have developed your stamina, your excellence, your ability to comfort others, but you are frightened to death of being comforted yourself. When you can allow yourself to show vulnerability by trusting another, you will have finally learned to trust your-self. When you push yourself beyond your endurance, run-ning from the truth of your humanness, the signal you send to the world is not the one you think you are sending. You tell others that you are untouchable when you keep moving from early morning to late at night. You fear Tiyoweh, the Stillness, because you are afraid to confront the fears and criticism of your Shadow. That Shadow-self would love to tell you that you are not worthy of rest, pleasure, or a life that includes true friends who respect your humanness and a supportive mate who will love you for who you are, not the deeds you accomplish."

Walks Tall Woman felt the tears of transformation run like slow-moving, lazy rivers down her cheeks. The truth had taken root in her heart and the impregnated seed of change had been planted in her womb. It would gestate until it was time in the future for the Clan Mother to give birth to her new, more vulnerable self. She quietly sat and reflected on the words Mountain Lion had spoken before she asked a question. "How can I be an example to other women, Mountain Lion, when I have to learn these lessons for myself?"

"You are the Mother of Innovation, Walks Tall Woman. In the present world of time, woman has come to take the role of nurturing others. A balance must be found. The Earth Mother is ready and willing to nurture her daughters but her daughters must insist on taking the time they need to receive that nurturance themselves.

"You have taught your human children that the place of gravity in the human form is in the pelvis. For men, that space is where their testicles were housed before puberty.

For females, that space is the womb. As Mothers of the Creative Force, women must understand their role of nurturing the seeds of all of tomorrow's dreams for the Planetary Family as well as birthing new generations of children. To accomplish this task, every woman must commit to herself to take the time she needs to retreat during her menstrual flow, when her womb is open to the light.

"This special Moontime is when the Earth Mother feeds all women if they are willing to spend three Suns and Sleeps during their flows in total silence, becoming the receptive vessels of love created by the Great Mystery. During the other days of their flows, they can be with their sisters, sharing experiences, handcrafts, and inner thoughts. During their Moontimes, women have the power to claim any available energy in their midst because their wombs are open to receive. This is one new Tradition that you can start for the Human Tribe that will also serve you in discovering your own humanness."

Walks Tall Woman saw the possibilities of creating a new Woman's Tradition that would allow all women to find balance. She understood that some of the bickering was probably caused from exhaustion, and that because women did not take the time to be refueled with the Earth Mother's loving energy, they were often bound by old, cranky, and petty habits that took root in the moments when they were overtired. A broad vista of opportunity spread before the Clan Mother in her dream. The Dreamtime always seemed to provide parallel ways to change old and limiting habits, and Walks Tall Woman was now still enough to access those opportunities. As the Mother of Persistence returned from her realizations, Mountain Lion spoke to her again.

"There has never been a time when you showed mercy toward yourself, Walks Tall Woman. You have enjoyed being active and have masked your Shadow well. The Shadow has shown you no mercy by driving you beyond all that is humanly possible. You have made promises that have actually forced you into the Shadow's keeping. You have not abused your leadership ability by hurting others, but you have abused the trust other women placed in you as a role model. You have set an example that would break the back of any beast of burden. Donkey carries his Medicine of *shouldering his load of responsibility*, but he also knows how to refuse and become stubborn when the burden is too much. There is great inner strength to be found in showing mercy to yourself and in allowing yourself to be an example to other women by showing them that all humans are worthy of rest and pleasure. The example you set through making time for your needs will liberate you and every other woman who looks to you for guidance. The excuse that you do not have the time or the space to be nurtured will harm more people than yourself, giving the Shadow the upper hand."

Mountain Lion waited for Walks Tall Woman to take in her words before she continued. "Do you remember the day you passed me in the forest, running like a prairie grass fire?" The Clan Mother nodded in affirmation and Mountain Lion spoke again.

"I was standing on a branch, watching you as you cut through the bracken and undergrowth. I was not surprised because I had seen you scouting that trail earlier. I wondered if you would run from the Totem who protected you, and sure enough, you did. The other runners would be a long time in catching up with you, but still you had to run on, making sure that you would outshine all others in an embarrassing, overachieving manner. You showed no mercy toward yourself or toward the dignity of your male counterparts. I licked my paws and showed you that you could slow down, but you were single-minded and my example was lost on you.

"Skunk could teach you a lesson, Walks Tall Woman, if you would take the time to listen. Skunk's Medicine has to do with *reputation and the ability to attract or to repel what you need in your life.* You have been so worried about your reputation of taking action that you have attracted the unmerciful Shadow-self and have repelled the inner voice that cries out for you to take the rest you need. Like Skunk, the whole situation stinks, Mother."

Walks Tall Woman broke her seriousness and laughed at Mountain Lion's description of the smelly set of circumstances. The tension was relieved and the Clan Mother forgot to berate herself for a moment and to blame herself for her overachieving drive. Walks Tall Woman tried to shake off her shame as she made the firm decision to be merciful toward herself and thus give her sisters permission to be kind to themselves, through her example. She asked Mountain Lion a final question she trusted would expel the heaviness in her chest that had caused her to breathe shallowly for many moons.

"I am tired of being my only support system and being afraid to trust and be vulnerable. Mountain Lion, when I find the merciful part of myself and take my retreats and times of silence, will you be my companion and Ally?"

Mountain Lion stretched and yawned, then replied, "I have always walked with you, Mother. You were just too busy to notice. You were afraid to be still and alone with yourself, so you could not hear my voice. Nothing will change in my devotion to you and to your spiritual growth. We are Sisters and are bound together by the bonds that make all females kin. Grandmother Moon shows her full face to illuminate our hidden fears as well as our strengths. In the Moontime cycle, we find our balance, confront our Shadow-selves, share our joys and sorrows, and then face the world as Sisters of the heart."

Walks Tall Woman was deeply touched and tears began to flow again, as she was drawn from her Dreamtime vision back to the tangible world by someone licking the real tears from her face. She opened her eyes and saw the physical embodiment of Mountain Lion, licking her cheeks and reassuring her that the vision had been real. The Guardian of Leadership placed her hand gently on Mountain Lion's neck and caressed her Sister's soft fur. Mountain Lion's green-gold eyes pierced Walks Tall Woman's heart and the final barrier came crashing down when the Clan Mother saw the softness and vulnerability of her own face mirrored in Mountain Lion's eyes. There was the face of the merciful self, being comforted by a Creature-teacher of the wild.

Mountain Lion placed a paw on Walks Tall Woman's chest, forcing the breath the Clan Mother had been holding in apprehension out of her lungs. Mountain Lion did not let up until Walks Tall Woman gasped; then the giant cat moved to lie at the Clan Mother's side. Walks Tall Woman took the deepest breath she remembered taking in many winters and felt the life force explode inside her, bringing a new sense of relaxed comfort to her weary, emotionally spent body.

• •

They lay side by side until the full face of Grandmother Moon rose high in the purple blanket of the Sky Nation. In the magnificent light of the full moon, a cloud changed form to show Walks Tall Woman the seeds of transformation that her tears had planted in the tangible world. She had returned from the Dreamtime to begin a new Tradition for women that would serve all of her Sisters until the end of time. The Cloud Person shape-shifted into the form of a quetzal, reminding the Mother of Innovation that Quetzal carries the Medicine of *the totally free, uninhibited spirit who is willing to express all aspects of the Self.* If caught and caged, Quetzal dies.

Walks Tall Woman thought of the cage she had created for herself and how the Shadow-self had placed a stranglehold on her freedom to express her needs and to trust that others would understand her humanness. The cloud form of Quetzal also reminded her that it was time to lead other women through Quetzal's example. In Walking Her Talk, the Clan Mother would never again impose her own limitations or impossible expectations on another human being. The uninhibited freedom found in accepting her humanness without judgment would light Walks Tall Woman's path. She had discovered the strength found in retreat and the wisdom of letting go.

Mountain Lion stayed with her through the night and allowed the warmth and comfort of a true Ally to be understood. When Grandfather Sun rose to shine his light on all of his children, Walks Tall Woman went back to camp. She was greeted by all of the members of the Water Clan as if she had never been absent. They had not been concerned because she had only projected the invincible side of herself in their presence. The lesson stung but forced the Clan Mother to realize how many ways she had sabotaged herself. She had been too independent and aloof.

During the next few Suns, Walks Tall Woman called a Council of Women and was vulnerable enough to tell her story and let go of the former untouchable self. She was surprised by her Sister's tears of joy and relief, and their hugs of thanks shocked her into further realizations. Many were grateful for the new example she was setting. Others took her aside and gave her gifts they had made to celebrate her Rite of Passage. Some Sisters were eager to share their fears that they could never live up to her former example, while others spoke of the resentment they had carried when the Clan Mother had been used by complaining husbands as an example to chastise them. Those days were very healing to all of the women of the Water Clan, creating new bonds of Sisterhood that would continue.

The Council of Women came together as one, as equals, in a circle, each having a single vote. Through unity, they decided how to run their Moon Lodges, assuring every woman of having her time for retreat. Each woman would cover the responsibilities of a friend while the other was on her moon. Grandmothers committed to watching the young, while aunts and sisters volunteered to cook and see to the fires. The Sisterhood of the Moon Lodge was formed during that long-ago season of changing leaves, leaving a legacy to all women that would form bonds of undying trust throughout the coming worlds.

Walks Tall Woman marveled at the changes in herself and the strength she found in the Medicine of her Sisters. In discovering herself, she had unwittingly gained a large family and support system. The Mother of Innovation understood that some new ways of living could create Traditions that would serve all of humankind. She sang her song of gratitude to the Earth Mother and to Grandmother Moon, understanding for perhaps the first time what it was like to be a strong leader *and* a vulnerable woman.

Now, Walks Tall Woman listens for the voices of her Sisters who are learning the lessons of Walking Their Talk. With compassion, she waits for some to slow down and for others to let go of their fears and take the actions needed to take charge of their lives. Her heart remains open and her spirit is now filled with the tender mercy she learned and earned through the painful lessons of her own passage. Through example, the only conquest she teaches is the conquest of the Shadow-self. Like Quetzal, she beckons her Sisters to express the freedom of who they are and to follow their hearts' desires, discovering those heart dreams through the strength they find in retreat. Walks Tall Woman whispers to women everywhere that the nurturance and support of the Sisterhood and the Earth Mother are available to any woman who is willing to honor her right to be by making the commitment to herself.

GIVES PRAISE

Thank you, Mother, for teaching me
To lift my heart in praise
Filling my spirit with gladness
For the blessings of the Beauty Way.

You have taught me how to sing,
How to rejoice, dance, and drum,
And how to show my gratitude
For the abundance that will come.

You have shown me the magic of
A change in the mind and heart,
An attitude made of the wisdom
That celebration of life imparts.

I sing the truth of thankfulness
When I greet Grandfather Sun,
Then send my love to Mother Earth
For the life force that makes us one.

Clan Mother
of the
Twelfth Moon Cycle

GIVES PRAISE is the Clan Mother of the Twelfth Moon Cycle, who teaches us how to be grateful for everything we experience in life. In returning thanks, we are shown how to make space in our lives for future abundance. Gives Praise teaches us to see how we are healing through every lesson we encounter on the Good Red Road. This Clan Mother reminds us to be grateful for the challenges we are given, no matter how difficult, since they show us how to develop our inner strength.

The Twelfth Cycle of Truth is *giving thanks for the truth*. The moon cycle of this Clan Mother falls in December. The Medicines of Gives Praise and of the color purple are healing and gratitude. Through this Guardian of Ritual and Ceremony we rediscover the importance of setting aside time for celebrating the gifts in our lives. When we show the Great Mystery that we are thankful for all that life gives, we are completing the circle of blessings we have received. Gives Praise reminds us that habitual ritual performed by rote and without a happy heart does not show gratitude and cannot bring healing into our lives. For instance, saying grace over a meal in the same manner each time, does not express true gratitude and can become meaningless.

▲▲

Gives Praise teaches us that sharing our abundance is another way that we can keep our lives flourishing. As the Mother of Abundance, Gives Praise instructs us in the value of giving as well as receiving. She reminds us that we are to be grateful for what we are able to give away as well as being thankful for the gifts of life we receive. In this manner, the circle of giving and receiving is created, allowing us to share. The simple joys of the Earth Walk are gifts we often take for granted. The warmth of Grandfather Sun, the ability to breathe, our health, free will, clean water, food, shelter, and the love of friends and family are blessings. If a few of these basic privileges were taken away, human beings would quickly understand their importance. Gives Praise points out the crooked trail followed by those who have forgotten these blessings and who only want to fill their emptiness with material objects or pretended wisdom that will never make them happy or whole.

The Twelfth Clan Mother shows humankind that magic is no more than a change in consciousness. Right attitude and a change of heart have created more miracles in people's lives than all the sorcery ever performed throughout time. When Gives Praise was learning the lessons of being human, she discovered that celebrating life and being grateful for everything one encountered created a completion. Then the Wheel of Life could turn again, creating new abundance, new experiences, and further joy. Tangible results always follow thoughts. Negative thoughts and fears will magnetize difficult life lessons. Discovering the truth that negativity robs us of our joy and learning how to change those patterns can shift the experience. This Clan Mother teaches us that being grateful for the truth found in our lives gives us the right attitudes and produces miraculous healing and new paths to follow. Because of her discovery, Gives Praise earned the right to become the Keeper of Magic, showing us how a change in perception, attitude, or consciousness can create magic and miracles.

Gives Praise encourages all Children of Earth through praising what is best in their natures. She shows us that when we celebrate who we are and give thanks for the lives we are leading, we then open our hearts to continue the healing process of being human. The truth we find in every experience of our spiritual evolution marks a forward step on our individual Pathway of Peace. Giving thanks for every victory we achieve and encouraging others by praising and being grateful for their victories ensures the continued movement of humankind toward unity.

▲▲

Dancing the Dance of Celebration

Gives Praise stood outside the Turtle Council House, waiting for the family who was coming for a Naming Ceremony. The Clan Mother had rejoiced when one of the members of her Tribe had delivered twins during the two moons past. The tiny boy and girl were given names by the mother in the first moments after birth, but the inner names or spiritual names were to be given by a wisewoman. The feasting that would follow the Naming Ceremony was open to all Tribe Members but the ceremony itself would only be attended by the Clan Mother, the twins, and their natural mother.

Spiritual or inner names were never spoken out loud and only the mother of the child was allowed to hear the name the Clan Mother or Wisewoman bestowed, in order to protect the child's vulnerable Sacred Space from harmful trickster spirits. The inner name was the way that a human being would be recognized in the Spirit World. Any spirit who called a Two-legged by a name other than the secret spiritual name was not to be trusted. The Ancestors' spirits and the spirits of the Totems, who were allied to humankind by offering assistance, always used the person's secret name to make contact.

This Sun of celebrations would begin the twins' connections to the Spirit World. Gives Praise had spent much time in Tiyoweh, the Stillness, looking at the Orenda of each child. Each one of the twins had a different set of talents and abilities, as well as unique and individual Spiritual Essences. The boy child was guarded by the spirit of Jaguar, whose Medicine was *secular and spiritual leadership potential.* The little boy had the potential to become a great Chief and the added ability to carry the talents of a Medicine Man. The girl child was guarded by Raven, *the Keeper of Magic, who sought the Void of the Unknown to effect change.* Together, these special twins could accomplish great things for the Tribe, who celebrated their arrival with open arms and best intentions.

Gives Praise turned, surveying the surrounding area, admiring all of the lush green grasses and wild flowers that covered the land around the Turtle Council House. Gives

Praise could see the rolling hills on the other side of the high meadow, the tall standing pines, and the sloping meadowlands that led down to the high mountain lake. The Council House looked like a giant turtle walking in deep grass, coming down the hills toward the water. The domed roof was made of sod and covered with large flat stones, giving the appearance of the turtle's shell. The turtle's head was made of an enormous stone that had been carved to accent the eyes, but the natural shape was exactly like the head of the sea tortoise. Gives Praise took in all the beauty around her and returned thanks for the glorious vistas of the Mother Planet.

The twins would have a wonderful time as they tested, tasted, touched, and smelled the natural world around them. Gives Praise could imagine what it would be like to be born into such a world, blessed and cursed with such a tiny helpless human body. She often thought of how she had come to walk the Earth in her already adult body that would stay forever young. *"It must be difficult to experience growing up in a human form,"* she mused, *"and yet, it could be a wonderful time of discovery and loving experience given the right environment."* She decided to follow the twins' growth and to put herself in their places in order to capture the lessons of a childhood she had never experienced.

When Twilight Moon came walking up the path from the lake, bringing her twins bundled on the front of her chest in fur-lined hides, Gives Praise observed the young mother's light step and bright countenance. Twilight Moon had a good sense of balance and the extra weight of the babies seemed to bolster her rather than weigh her down. The long strides the young woman made along the path to the Council House were a sure sign that she was healthy and vital, letting any observer see that the birth of twins had been taken in stride. Twilight Moon's radiant smile flashed across the closing distance between the young mother and Gives Praise. The Clan Mother could sense the pride and joy Twilight Moon felt as she continued the journey to the Council House to properly start the twins on the path of spiritual wholeness. The Naming Ceremony would assure that her little boy and girl would find protection on their spiritual journeys while their physical growth was monitored by two loving parents and a family full of doting relatives.

The two women gingerly embraced, making sure not to crush the twins, and Gives Praise assisted Twilight Moon in untying the halters that held the babies against the young mother's chest. As Gives Praise looked into the eyes of the tiny infant boy, she was pleased to find an open-eyed, level stare gazing back at her. The child was already living up to his Jaguar Medicine. Gives Praise smiled and nodded, then reached for the girl child. The ebony eyes of the little girl sparkled in the early morning light, mirroring a hidden magic that did not waver in the sunlight. Gives Praise laughed when the infant girl half closed one eyelid in an involuntary wink.

A descending path had been cut in the meadow to allow access to the interior of the Turtle Lodge. The shell roof was above the earth but the oval-shaped council room was below. Inside two fires, one at either end, gave off a welcoming warmth. Gives Praise had Twilight Moon sit facing her on the fur robes that had been placed in the center of the lodge. The light from Grandfather Sun filtered through three smoke holes, one above each fire and the third one of-fering light in the area where the women sat with the babies. Gives Praise lit a braid of Sweetgrass and smoked all four of them to bring in the spirits of childlike sweetness be-fore she spoke.

"On this Sun, we come before the light of Grandfather Sun's love as it enters the body of the Earth Mother, lighting our ways. This Guardian of Ceremony gives thanks for the health and life of Twilight Moon, who will nurture these two littles ones during their Earth Walks. These women thank Swennio, the Great Mystery, for the gift of life and breath and for all the goodness that can be found on the Good Red Road. These mothers here thank Yeodaze, the Earth Mother, for the abundance she freely gives to support our human ways. We return thanks to the Creature-teachers who guard the spirits of these twins and have offered to be Totems for the babies. This one, who seeks answers, humbly asks that the Ancestor Spirits guide her in finding the inner names of these two little ones so that they may be recognized in the Spirit World."

Silence fell in the lodge and Grandfather Sun's light briefly flashed as if a cloud had rolled away, bringing an il-luminating beam of light into the circle created by the two women and the twins. Gives Praise smiled and then closed her eyes as if she was looking into her own heart, being en-lightened by the flash of love that Grandfather Sun had sent through the opening in the roof. Gives Praise laid the girl child in a hollowed-out log filled with soft rabbit pelts and continued.

"This Wisewoman asks that the spirit of this baby girl be recognized by the Ancestors and that the Ancient Ones bless her with a name that will carry and uplift her spirit at all times during her Earth Walk. This Clan Mother asks that the Spirits of Nature who will be the child's devoted teachers come into this lodge so that they will know her inner name and honor it for all the Suns and Sleeps of her human life, bringing comfort and courage until it is time to Drop Her Robe and return to the Other Side Camp of the Spirit World. For these requests, this woman gives thanks and praises the Beauty Way, followed by all the spirits called into this Sacred Lodge."

The girl child gurgled and cooed as if she understood and then began looking at something invisible hovering above her. Gives Praise felt and saw the spirits who came to honor the life of this child, circling the four gathered. The Guardian of Ceremony and Ritual was pleased to see that Twilight Moon had sensed the change as the spirits entered the lodge and was trying to cover her nervousness by patting the little boy she held to her shoulder. Gives Praise assured the young mother that all was as it should be and that the spirits who had gathered were benevolent and kind.

The Clan Mother watched as every spirit gathered, filed past the tiny girl, and blessed the child's spirit by touching her Orenda or Spiritual Essence. Then, Gives Praise felt the baby's spiritual name form inside the inner knowing of her heart, and like a bubble, the name rose from her heart to her lips, spilling into the lodge like the sound of clear water.

"Twilight Moon, the Ancient Ones have blessed your daughter with a name that she will be known by in the Spirit World. She shall be called Pipe Song and the Raven is her protector. Pipe Song is the song that flows through the smoke of All Our Relations, bringing oneness with all things. This oneness, found through the song of the Pipe, is the magic that allows Two-leggeds to change and open themselves to the miracles of human life that come from right attitude. This girl child will be an example for those around her. Through her ability to live her life, like the song of oneness that comes from the Pipe, others will observe ways that they can touch the magic of life that comes when humility and thankfulness are present."

After returning thanks for the blessings given to Pipe Song by the Ancient Ones and thanking the Spirits of Nature for coming to be a part of Pipe Song's ceremony, the Clan Mother gave all the spirits who had gathered permission to go on their ways. When the Turtle Lodge was cleared, the Wisewoman handed Pipe Song to her mother and took the boy child into her arms. As she met his bold stare, Gives Praise was struck by the knowing gaze of the infant. It was as if he could see through her body and into the vastness of her Orenda. This child was not afraid of anything and would make a fine leader and Medicine Man for his Tribe. Like his sister, this little brother was one of the Ancestors who had returned to continue the next turn of the Medicine Wheel by walking in human form once again.

As the Wisewoman placed the tiny boy in the log cradle, his little hand reached for the Clan Mother's finger, making a fist, holding it as if he intended to keep the Mother of Abundance's attention. The Wisewoman reached out with her mind and tried to connect to the intent sent her way by this Ancestor in a tiny body. As their minds met in the melding of their Sacred Spaces, she heard his thoughts.

"Grandmother, I have come to teach my people the importance of balancing their spiritual paths with the roles they choose to walk in life. I intend to be a living example of a man who has balanced his reasoning powers and good judgment with the spiritual receptivity of the feminine principle. Will you assist me in this journey and be my teacher?"

Gives Praise answered the Ancient One in the baby body with a nod, allowing the warmth in her heart to course through her hand and into the tiny fist that held her finger. Then she began the same ceremonial thanksgivings used with his sister's naming, inviting all of the boy's Spirit Allies to come into the lodge. When all were gathered, the Wisewoman began her requests to the Great Mystery.

"Swennio, Great and Eternal Mystery, this woman here asks that you bless the path of this Ancient One who has returned. This Wisewoman requests that my influence in this child's life be helpful, caring, and nurturing, supporting his intent in this Earth Walk. This Clan Mother thanks the Earth Mother for the gift of his body, which will carry this child's spirit through the many summers of his life. This humble servant asks that her heart be blessed by the Ancestors, who have chosen the spiritual name of the boy. May those Ancestors find this woman's heart pure and send that name for her heart to understand and for her lips to speak."

A gust of wind flew down the smoke holes over the two fires at the ends of the lodge and created a burst of flame that startled Twilight Moon. Gives Praise reached over and patted the young mother's hand to reassure her that all was well, then briefly closed her eyes to look into her own heart. The emergence of a fiery ball in the center of the Clan Mother's heart quickened her pulse and caused her to take a deep breath. The smell of wood smoke wafted through the lodge, the reflections of light from the smoke holes danced, and the walls of the lodge, made of the Earth Mother's body, gave off a rich perfume. The smell of moist soil mingled with the straw and leaves that were compressed into each mud brick surrounded the infants, signaling the love being sent as a blessing from the Planetary Mother.

Gives Praise opened her eyes and said, "Twilight Moon, the Earth Mother and the Ancestors have blessed your boy with a spiritual name. His path will reflect the Medicine he carries and he will be recognized in the Spirit World by the name of Talking Arrow. The arrow is the symbol of the path of truth, perfectly balanced for flight, directed toward a goal. This boy will grow tall and will speak with truth on his tongue. Talking Arrow will lead the people through example, as he uses his Medicine to heal and his wisdom to show others how to give thanks for the truth in their lives. Together, your children will have many opportunities to show our Tribe how to follow the Beauty Way."

Twilight Moon sat in the stillness of the moment, taking in all that the Clan Mother had said. Her babies would need to be nurtured and loved in a way that would support the development of their abilities. The young mother's mind was filled with memories of her own childhood and how she had passed through the uncertainty of growing up. She remembered all the discomforts of those adolescent years and how she felt so out of place among the other young women of the Tribe. Then, she had believed that she would never find a mate or have children. Now, she had become the mate of a strong, brave, and gentle man who loved her deeply, and she was proudly sitting in the Turtle Council House at the Naming Ceremony of her two beautiful children. She felt that the abundance in her life was due to the guidance and loving encouragement of the Clan Mother who sat in front of her, sharing one of the most precious moments in the young mother's life.

Gives Praise was having the same thoughts as she remembered how the path of life had changed for Twilight Moon. As a young girl, Twilight Moon had been all elbows and eyes. No matter how hard the girl had tried to be graceful, she had fallen over her own feet, knocking over everything in her path. She was made fun of unmercifully by the other girls her age who had dubbed Twilight Moon, "Stumbling Crane." It was true that the girl had looked like a crane with long skinny legs and full lips that always seemed to be pursed in a pout that held back a flood of lonely tears. The only person who ever saw those tears was Gives Praise.

In the fourteenth summer of Twilight Moon's life, she had run to the forest after one particularly cruel name-calling session when she was not included in other girls' games. Gives Praise had found the girl sobbing uncontrollably with her arms wrapped around a giant cottonwood. The Clan Mother's heart had gone out to the child, knowing that she had no relations who would comfort her. Twilight Moon's mother had Dropped Her Robe, leaving her earthly form to walk in the Spirit World, in the third summer of the girl's life. The child's father had married a widowed woman with three daughters who were the beauties of the Tribe, leaving the rearing of his own daughter to his new wife. Twilight Moon's new mother was not a mean woman but was prideful and constantly boasting about the talents of her three eligible daughters, never giving a word of encouragement to her lonely stepdaughter.

Growing up in a lodge full of seemingly perfect stepsisters had taken its toll on Twilight Moon's self-esteem, particularly when tribal Law dictated that adolescent girls were not supposed to worry their fathers with anything. Women were responsible for the traditional training of the females in the Tribe. Being ignored or occasionally spoken to as an afterthought, coupled with the degrading remarks passed by three stepsisters when adults were not present, had created an empty and nearly unbearable life for Twilight Moon.

The Giver of Encouragement found the situation to be a challenge. Gives Praise took Twilight Moon into her heart that day in the forest and spent many passing seasons nurturing the girl's broken heart, showing her how to regain the magic of life. In the beginning, the Clan Mother held and rocked the girl, letting her know that someone loved her and that there was a safe place to come to let her tears flow. The Keeper of Magic showed Twilight Moon how to count every blessing and how to be grateful for every lesson of life. Sometimes Gives Praise cringed when she heard the blessings Twilight Moon gave thanks for. Hearing her thanking Swennio, the Great Mystery, for the passing of a Sun when nobody purposely tripped her or stripped Twilight Moon of her sense of self with cruel remarks, caused the Clan Mother to feel the hurt still deep inside the child. The Clan Mother continued to give Twilight Moon loving encouragement and praise for every accomplishment the girl mastered.

Finally, in the sixteenth summer of her life, Twilight Moon began to blossom. The gracefulness that had evaded her during her younger years suddenly bloomed, giving the young woman the reward of learning to believe in the magic of life. All of Gives Praise's lessons of returning thanks in order to make space for the abundance found in the Beauty Way had come to fruition. In learning to give thanks, Twilight Moon had also learned to make space for and to receive the blessings sent her way. The magic of becoming a self-assured young woman was brought to fullness through the compassionate and caring guidance of Gives Praise. The nights of silently crying herself to sleep were a thing of the past. Twilight Moon had become a young woman full of willowy grace, exhibiting a strength within herself, her connection to her Orenda and the Great Mystery. Out of her former pain, the girl had developed a sensitivity for the feelings of others that gave her a gentleness that attracted every young warrior in the Tribe.

It was no great surprise to Gives Praise when the Chief's son, Dancing Fire, brought seven horses and ten buffalo robes to Twilight Moon's father and asked for her hand. There was something very special about the young woman that now caused others to turn and look in admiration when she passed. The imprint of old pain was transformed into much more than her physical beauty. True to her name, an inner light shone from Twilight Moon's eyes. Grandfather Sun's peach-colored rays at sunset and the silver light of the rising form of Grandmother Moon blended inside the young woman's Orenda.

When the twins were born, Twilight Moon saw her children as the manifestation of the blessings that she had been grateful for, nurtured inside her body like seeds of the future during the years it had taken her to heal the hurts of growing up. The birth names she had chosen for the twins reflected aspects of herself and her mate, Dancing Fire. She named her son Sun on Fire and her daughter Rising Melon Moon. These were the names that would be used by the Tribe, identifying the twins on their Earth Walks.

The memories of the journey that had led to this Naming Ceremony in the Turtle Council House were noted and honored by both women. Twilight Moon's story represented the potential of the human spirit. Those Two-leggeds who knew how to have faith and be grateful for every blessing and lesson of life created the space to receive the Great Mystery's abundance. The gradual shift in Twilight Moon's attitude during her years of emotional pain gave birth to a dream of fulfillment that would bring continued happiness throughout her Earth Walk.

Gives Praise spoke, bringing both women from their memories and into the special feeling of the moment. "These women give thanks to All Our Relations for the gifts of abundant life brought by the Great Mystery. These women, as Mothers of the Creative Force, humbly ask for the continued blessings of life and breath so that our love may be felt in the lives of these twins. This Clan Mother gives thanks for the opportunity to share this rare moment and for the blessings bestowed by all the spirits who will guide the ways of these children. This Wisewoman gives thanks for the Good Medicine that the Creator placed inside the hearts of these family members and for the way those gifts of love will touch everyone around them for the length of their Earth Walks. *Da nahoe,* it is said."

The two women finished the Ceremony by sitting in Tiyoweh, the Stillness, saying their personal words of thanksgiving in silence. Then each woman carried a twin and walked clockwise around the Turtle Lodge, stopping at each Clan Mother's Shield. The twins were ritually introduced to the gifts that each Clan Mother carried and were blessed by the presence of each Clan Mother's Crystal Skull, which held the spiritual lessons and wisdom that each of the Thirteen Clan Mothers could impart.

When Twilight Moon and Gives Praise emerged from the Turtle Council House with the twins, Dancing Fire was waiting. The beaming father took his daughter from Gives Praise and walked with his family and the Wisewoman down the path to the lake. The ceremonial grounds had been prepared and all members of the Tribe had worn their best ceremonial buckskins for the occasion. Elk, deer, and buffalo meat roasted over open fires and the sweet smells of pumpkin and berry soup wafted through the air. Roasted corn and wild tubers were being served by the women into long, hollowed-out log bowls along with steamed squash and wild greens. The dance grounds were cleared and the Powwow drums lined the circle, awaiting the eager Tribe Members who would express their joy for the family through dancing.

After a full Sun of feasting, the last rays of Grandfather Sun touched the western horizon of the Sky Nation, bringing all of the glorious colors of twilight. In the eastern sky, Grandmother Moon had already risen to face Grandfather Sun. Like two dancers offering to share hearts and hands, the sun and moon blessed the occasion with the same heavenly display they had shown the Human Tribe on the evening that Twilight Moon was born. Gives Praise was not the only one to notice the significance of the portents found in the Great Star Nation. Dancing Fire's father, the Chief named Bear Shield, silently watched the celestial grandparents of the Human Tribe as they shared the dance of their combined lights.

Bear Shield spoke these words, announcing to his Tribe the prelude to the dancing: "We have gathered here to celebrate the births and beginnings of the spiritual lives of my grandchildren. As with every new addition to our Tribe, we thank the Great Mystery for the newborn generations that represent the continuation of life. We trust that their lives will bless and enrich all circles of life maintained by All Our Relations. We return thanks for the celebration of being living, breathing human beings who have been given all we will ever need through the abundance of our Earth Mother. Our grandparents, Grandfather Sun and Grandmother Moon, have blessed this occasion by showing us their faces, dancing together in the evening sky. The twins will grow like these sky dancers, bringing Good Medicine to our Tribe in different but equally beautiful ways. As we dance and celebrate this new beginning, let us be reminded of the precious gift of life and how our celebration shows the Earth Mother and Sky Father our gratitude. Da Nahoe."

Cries of happy celebration and the rhythm of the Tom-toms began calling the dancers to the dance. The men entered the circle first as the protectors of the women, children, and elders. As always, the men scouted ahead to secure a safe trail for the others to follow. Then the women came forward, some with cradleboards on their backs, allowing their infants to feel the rhythm of Earth Mother's heartbeat through the beat of the drums. The children followed, and the Elders took their places of honor around the circle, representing the years of wisdom that held the Tribal Circle together in unity, as one large, extended family.

Gives Praise stood next to Bear Shield, admiring the dancers and the way each one expressed his or her gratitude through steps or dips. Deep into the night, the fires lit the happy faces of the dancers. It seemed as if the whole world were sharing the gladness of this night of happy hearts. The Clan Mother, who was the Guardian of Ceremony and Ritual, looked at her tribal children and saw the goodness in each and every one. She silently returned thanks for the blessing that the Great Mystery had placed in her keeping. The Wisewoman held the knowledge that every Ceremony and Ritual was cause for celebration and that every celebration was a way to give gratitude back to the Maker of All Things. When her human children opened their hearts to return thanks, they also opened their hearts to receive and claim the joys of the Good Red Road.

Twilight Moon touched the Medicine pouch around her neck, which was made of moose hide and turkey feathers. The young mother was remembering how she had reclaimed her true self through understanding Moose's Medicine of *self-esteem* and later through Turkey's Medicine of how to *release and give away* her pain. Twilight Moon's faithful gratitude had brought to her the life she had always dreamed of, finding a loving mate who honored who she was. Having seen the sky dance of Grandfather Sun and Grandmother Moon, Gives Praise was assured that the two strong children being honored with this celebration would bless the Tribe by continuing the legacy of love and mutual respect begun by their parents.

••

The Clan Mother looked to the Great Star Nation and saw a Cloud Person drifting close to the light of Grandmother Moon. As Gives Praise noticed that no other clouds graced the Sky Nation, the lone cloud changed into the form of the Clan Mother's Totem, Buffalo. The billowy, white cloud Buffalo walked in front of the full face of Grandmother Moon, touching Gives Praise in a profound way. The White Buffalo signaled to the Clan Mother that her gifts to Twilight Moon of encouragement, nurturing praise, and love had created the fertile, magical ground for the seeds of a lonely little girl's dreams to be brought to harvest. Tears of gratitude spilled from the Wisewoman's eyes, allowing the Clan Mother to receive the thanks being sent to her from the Great Mystery. The Great White Buffalo of abundance was showing her that throughout time, her loving gifts could restore the lost magic to the lives of those human beings who were willing to show gratitude for the unseen miracles of life yet to come.

BECOMES HER VISION

The waking dream comes to life
And lives her vision through me.
Emerging from the chrysalis,
She sets her healed heart free.

Mother of the seeds of change,
Who nurtures them as they grow,
You planted a dream in my heart
To illuminate all that I know.

You taught me how to give away
My fear of becoming the dream,
Showing me how to walk my truth,
Reclaiming self-love and esteem.

As I become all that I am,
Then together we shall fly,
The spirit of transformation
Reflected in Condor's eye.

Clan Mother
of the
Thirteenth Moon Cycle

BECOMES HER VISION is the Guardian of All Cycles of Transformation and is the Clan Mother of the Thirteenth Moon Cycle. She is the Emerging Spirit Keeper who teaches the Children of Earth how to bring their Spiritual Essences or Orendas into their physical forms in order to become the living vessels of love that the Great Mystery intended. Through becoming their personal visions and using their talents for the whole, the members of the Human Tribe can then claim the Fifth World of Peace and Illumination as their own.

Becomes Her Vision is the Mother of Change, who teaches us how to go through every lesson and cycle of transformation in order to spiritually evolve. She shows us the importance of staying on our chosen paths and not being drawn into the limiting illusions that could destroy our personal visions. This process of change transforms the human body, heart, mind, and spirit from a finite sense of Self into an infinite, universal, creative extension of the Great Mystery's love. When this transforming change occurs, human beings can fully understand the Orenda, finding that our Spiritual Essences are vast and are an extension of the Great Mystery. Inside the Orenda is a body, heart, mind, and spirit

▲▲

that comprises a whole human. Until all of the parts come into balance, owning the vastness of the total, there is not a full understanding of how the Great Mystery's Eternal Flame of Love lives inside of every human's potential.

Becomes Her Vision teaches us that we are all and nothingness and that all worlds exist inside us as well as outside us. This Clan Mother tells us that every time we transform, becoming our visions, we are then shown a new vision and a more expansive point of view. The spiral of the evolving spirit continues to take us from one level of understanding to the next Medicine Wheel of experience and is eternal. For this reason, Becomes Her Vision is also the Guardian of Personal Myth. The history of each spirit comprises a personal legend that marks the Rites of Passage into wholeness. Every decision we make and every goal we choose is how we determine the content of our personal myths. Since every spirit's path is a Sacred Path made up of that spirit's desire to BE, we see the uniqueness of every individual represented in her or his personal myth. Every living thing has a place in Creation and because all are given free will, the unified whole is made up of the combined personal paths of all living things. Becomes Her Vision keeps a record of every choice made by each life form in Creation, noting how those choices alter and/or assist each individual's path to wholeness.

Becomes Her Vision teaches the Human Tribe that the ultimate transforming vision is the decision to simply BE. During our spiritual evolution we tend to place labels on who or what we want to become. We usually discover that we do not need labels; we can become our visions by being who and what we are at any given moment. The decision to be all things and nothing takes away the labels that limit our sense of wholeness. All of Creation lives inside and outside of every human being. Becomes Her Vision shows us that we are all extensions of the Great Mystery's dream, as well as tangible, living examples of the visions that we have created to express the Self.

Becomes Her Vision reminds all of her human children that the dreams they hold for themselves grow and change with every decision made and every lesson learned. The evolving dream is constantly present in our lives. We are who and what we are being at any given moment in time. As we make the choices that alter the course of how we manifest our dreams, we express our individualities. This uniqueness is a part of the Great Mystery's plan for wholeness. When every individual walks the Earth as a realized dream of his or her spiritual and human potential, the Whirling Rainbow Dream of world peace and spiritual illumination will be complete. Becomes Her Vision is the Guardian of the Prophesy of Wholeness, who assists humankind in manifesting that Whirling Rainbow Dream.

▲▲

The Dream Comes
to Walk the Earth

Becomes Her Vision sat in the foggy realms of the Dreamtime, waiting for her Twelve Sisters to complete the first lessons of their Earth Walks. From time to time she was presented with a vision of the lessons each had learned so that she could share in their feelings and their experiences. As each lesson was completed in the tangible world, Becomes Her Vision took the essence of each of her Sister's gathered lessons of wisdom deep into her heart. She savored each feeling and experience, making note of the precious and rare opportunities that she was being given to learn all of the lessons that her Sisters had completed during their first Rites of Passage, understanding their humanness through their Earth Walks.

As the stings and disappointments of their human sorrows penetrated her senses, Becomes Her Vision was forced to look at her own fears about taking a human body. She had briefly come into a human form when all of the Thirteen had dreamed together, finding their roles and creating their bond of Life, Unity, and Equality for Eternity, but she had returned to the Dreamtime alone. The Earth Mother had explained to Becomes Her Vision that the combined gifts, talents, and abilities of all of her Sisters would need to be understood and completed before she could come to walk the Earth as Womankind's realized dream.

During the time she was to spend alone in the formless and timeless spaces of the Thought World, Spirit World, and Dreamtime, she would have to integrate every feeling, idea, and experience that every one of the other Twelve Clan Mothers had completed as if it had been her own. The only thing that kept Becomes Her Vision from giving into her fears was the knowing that if her Sisters had empowered themselves and had conquered the lessons of being human, so could she. The massive store of information and feelings that was presented to Becomes Her Vision had been filtered through her memories of the sensations of having had a physical form for one brief moment in time. It was easy for her to remember the exaltation of the Whirling Rainbow Dream or the bond of Sisterhood created by the Thirteen Sisters, but it was very difficult to feel the pain and sorrow, even when it was mixed with her Sisters' later successes.

Becomes Her Vision understood that the bitter had to be taken with the sweet when she was chosen as one of the thirteen aspects that would represent the Earth Mother's unconditional love for humanity. All of the Thirteen Clan Mothers were given the particulars of what it meant to be human before they took human bodies. They all chose to make their Earth Walks with their eyes wide open. The Earth Mother had not spared her daughters any of the details of human life. The Earth Mother had been very careful to instruct her thirteen aspects in the arts of changing their perspectives in order to restore beauty to any difficult situation. Becomes Her Vision could see how easy it was to get caught up in the storm of human emotions and drama by observing the difficult lessons her Sisters had walked through.

Now that all of the lessons of her Twelve Sisters' first Rites of Passage were completed, Becomes Her Vision was to weave a cocoon for herself in order to take all that had been experienced into her total being as a Knowing System. Inside the chrysalis, the visions of the passages of the others would be fully experienced by the Thirteenth Clan Mother.

Becomes Her Vision was the catalyst that would transform all of the poisons of pain and sorrow into new understandings, translating all beliefs and illusions into a healing Knowing System. From her human body, which would be formed inside the cocoon, Thirteen Crystal Skulls would be born. The Orendas of all twelve other Clan Mothers would merge into her own, combining the Thirteen Spiritual Essences into wholeness. The Thirteen Crystal Skulls would then be fashioned to hold the Knowing Systems of the Earth Mother and the Female Principle for humankind until the end of time.

Becomes Her Vision wrapped herself in the gossamer threads of Grandmother Moon's light, allowing Grand-mother Spider to weave them into the webs of a cocoon when the spirit chrysalis was brought from the Dreamtime into the tangible world. When the cocoon was made physi-cal, Hinoh, the Thunder Chief, carried the precious bundle in his arms across the Sky Nation, protecting the daughter of the Earth Mother from harm. As a Warrior Chief of the Sky Nation and Brother of the mighty Thunderbird, his honored role of protector was seen by hundreds of human beings. To the Two-leggeds watching the sky, it seemed as if an enormous cloud formation had embodied a giant warrior who carried a cradleboard in his arms as he glided across the broad expanse of periwinkle space without another cloud in sight. The Cloud-warrior's form was illuminated by the bright golden rays of Grandfather Sun's light, creating a vi-sion that signaled a momentous event to those humans who could read the omens in the sky.

Inside the cocoon, Becomes Her Vision was sleeping, nestled in a cradleboard made of downy clouds. The inner journey had begun for the Thirteenth Clan Mother as soon as the chrysalis had come into the magnetism of the Earth Mother's force field, drawing the Mother of Personal Myth closer and closer to her Earth Mother's heart. Hinoh could feel the serenity of his sleeping charge through the fine woven webs of her cocoon and was very careful not to disturb her inner calm as he laid her to rest on the back of Condor, the largest Winged One in the natural world.

Condor was equally careful as he spread his mighty wings for flight, carrying Becomes Her Vision around the girth of the Planetary Mother and finally into the giant cavern that led to the Inner Earth. Condor took his role as the Creature-guardian of the Whirling Rainbow Dream. His Medicine of *life, unity, and equality for eternity* shone forth as he delivered the cocoon that held the promise of that future world of peace into the cavernous heart-space of the Earth Mother.

Moons passed while Becomes Her Vision dreamed of Moth, hovering close to the Eternal Flame of Love. Using Moth's Medicine of *bringing the intangible of spirit into the tangible world,* she fed the light of spirit into the forming human body that she had nestled in her chrysalis. Flamingo came into her dreams, bringing its Medicine of *opening the human heart,* allowing the Clan Mother to accept the Eternal Flame into her being, developing the talents of compassion and unconditional love. The clucking of Hen sang her further into his core, teaching her to *tend the unhatched eggs of her own Medicine* while she nested inside the cocoon. Gazelle came to teach her *surefootedness,* allowing her to vanquish the last remnants of her uncertainty and fear. Leopard bounded through her chrysalis visions, showing her the Medicine of *understanding the patterns that lead to self-mastery* that would allow her to learn from and to master all the wisdom that her fellow Clan Mothers had made available. Each one of the Creatures that would become her Totems when she walked the Earth generously shared their Medicines with Becomes Her Vision while she grew into the awakened dream.

Some time around the eleventh moon of her passage, Becomes Her Vision was visited by Butterfly, who signaled the final stages of the Clan Mother's Rite of Passage. Becomes Her Vision realized that the time for emergence from her cocoon was nearly at hand. Butterfly spoke to the Mother of Transformation, teaching her all of the secrets of the process of transformation that would enable the Clan Mother to teach others the art of transforming and changing their lives.

Together, Becomes Her Vision and Butterfly saw the mask that the Clan Mother would one day wear when she sat in Council with the other Twelve Clan Mothers. The central part of the mask was in the form of a butterfly whose antennae were made of feathers. Sprouting from beneath the four fragile wings of Butterfly were Condor's mighty wings, giving support for his little insect Sister's delicate form as she rode on his shoulders. On each side of Butterfly's body, where it rested on the broad back of Condor's wings, were two large, fiery eyes, emerging from the feathers.

Becomes Her Vision and Butterfly had never seen eyes like those red orbs. They both thought it curious that they had dreamed the same thing, and yet, neither could place those unfamiliar eyes that pierced the darkness with an all-knowing directness, set aflame. The two friends decided that it was time to allow the understanding of that part of their dream to emerge in the Clan Mother's inner knowing during the final stages of development, before Becomes Her Vision emerged.

The Mother of Change was aware of the components that made up every particle of Creation, and so she called out to the Clan Chiefs of Air, Earth, Water, and Fire to assist her on the journey that she would undertake. The Clan Chiefs told Becomes Her Vision that this journey would not be outside of herself and into the Dreamtime; this journey would take her into the very core of her own being. They explained that the Four Elements would be melded according to her thoughts and that their direction would come from her ability to focus on the vision that would transform her into the truth. With fuller understanding, Becomes Her Vision realized that she was to use her own Medicine to create the emerging vision of her true Self and that the Great Mystery had given her the free will that she needed to accomplish that task. She was the Creatress of the truth she would become, and that truth lived inside of her Orenda.

Becomes Her Vision had lost track of anything so unimportant as time, and so she traveled into the vastness of her Orenda for an everlasting moment that could actually have been in between the in-breath and the out-breath of her own body's respiration. Once inside her own imagination, she saw herself on an open plain covered with low-hanging fog. She stood inside a circle of Sacred Stones that comprised a giant Medicine Wheel. She faced the first moon cycle position of the Wheel and saw her Sister, Talks with Relations, smiling back into her eyes. Talks with Relations walked forward through the fog and came to embrace Becomes Her Vision in the center of the Medicine Wheel. In silence,

Talks with Relations presented her Sister with a gift and then returned to her place on the outer edge of the Medicine Wheel.

Becomes Her Vision looked into her hands and saw that she had received a beautiful orange, fan-shaped, flat shell, suspended from a leather thong. As she placed the necklace around her neck, the voice of Talks with Relations echoed in Becomes Her Vision's heart.

"This shell is a symbol that teaches us to listen to the voices of all that we have made kin. Through them, we will always find the wisdom of the natural world. Through hearing their rhythms and the rhythms of our own feelings, we come to *learn the truth* about ourselves and All Our Relations in the Planetary Family." Becomes Her Vision sent her thanks to her Sister through hand signals and then turned to the second moon cycle position.

Her second Sister, Wisdom Keeper, came forward and embraced her, handing her another gift in total silence. Wisdom Keeper's eyes shone on her thirteenth Sister, sending her love, before she returned to her original place on the outer rim of the circle. When Becomes Her Vision saw the gray feather in her hand, she smiled to herself, hearing at that same instant the voice of her second Sister inside her own being.

"This gray feather is the symbol of friendship that teaches us how to *honor the truth* in all things by being a nonthreatening presence in the lives of others. The feather holds the Medicine of high ideals, and like the straightness of the quill, the path of truth will open before us, giving direction, when we honor the truth in all things. From learning how to honor the truth in every Sacred Point of

View, true wisdom is gained, understood, remembered, and then kept in sacred trust for all time."

Weighs the Truth approached when Wisdom Keeper's voice had faded, embracing her Sister and lightly placing her gift in Becomes Her Vision's hands. Weighs the Truth's radiant smile washed over her thirteenth Sister, bringing further joy. Silently, the Mother of Justice returned to her place on the Wheel and her voice filled Becomes Her Vision's senses.

"Sister, this gift is a brown stone to remind you of the soil of our Earth Mother and your connection to her. Through our connections to the Earth Mother, we become self-determined and can find the acceptance we need to weigh the truths of human life. By placing the Stone Person in one hand and leaving the other hand empty, you can weigh the wisdom of the tangible world with the weightlessness found in the Spirit World. Through balancing the two, you will be able to *accept the truth.*"

Becomes Her Vision paused, taking in the full understanding of the words of her Sister, Weighs the Truth, and then she faced the position of the Fourth Clan Mother, Looks Far Woman. When this Sister approached, as silent as the others, Becomes Her Vision was taken by the sparkle in her Sister's eyes. A light shone forth, making Becomes Her Vision understand the gleaming essence of Looks Far Woman's ability to see. They embraced and the gift was given to Becomes Her Vision. Looks Far Woman retreated to her place in the circle.

"This pastel blue mineral represents the gift of prophecy that comes from clear seeing. Like the color of the water that holds our feelings, this mineral can assist you in feeling the truth in what you see. By *seeing the truth*, Sister, you can discover your inner potential, understand your dreams, and trust the truth of your feelings and impressions."

Looks Far's voice faded and Listening Woman appeared with a hug and a gift. Becomes Her Vision understood more about this fifth Sister's gifts and Medicine because she had been able to hear the voices of her other Sisters inside of herself. This newfound ability was the beginning of realizing her personal wholeness. Listening Woman's voice resounded with clear bell-like tones inside Becomes Her Vision's mind when she spoke.

"You listen well, Sister. My gift to you is this rare black shell that comes from the seas of our Mother. In its darkness, it reminds you that the Void of the Unknown is not to be feared but can be accessed and understood through listening to the voice of your Orenda. Through the voices of the Ancestors and All Our Relations you will *hear the truth* and find wholeness."

Becomes Her Vision smiled in thanks as Listening Woman returned to her fifth moon cycle position on the Medicine Wheel. Then out of the mists came Storyteller, the Sister of the sixth moon cycle, bearing another Give-away for Becomes Her Vision. They embraced and Becomes Her Vision looked at her gift while Storyteller returned to her place. Storyteller's resonant, unmistakable voice rang inside of Becomes Her Vision's being, explaining the Medicine of her Give-away.

"It is said that the red color of these flower seeds was created when the birth blood and placentas of the first generation of the Human Tribe were returned to the soil of the Earth Mother. These seeds are my Give-away to you, my Sister, so that you may always be reminded of the seeds of faith that keep us at one with the Great Mystery. Through the lessons of humility, faith, and innocence, we are given the strength to *speak the truth*."

Becomes Her Vision sent thanks to her Sister, Storyteller, through the gratitude beaming from her heart. Then she turned to face Loves All Things as she walked from the seventh moon cycle position to stand in the center of the circle and present her gift. Becomes Her Vision was touched and her heart was filled to overflowing by the embrace that allowed her to feel the unconditional love that poured from the heart of Loves All Things. Thanking her loving counterpart for the hug, she gazed down at the gift while Loves All Things retreated.

"This yellow metal has caused much grief among the Two-leggeds, but that crooked trail was caused by their misunderstanding. They believed it was Grandfather Sun's love made tangible and that whoever had the most metal was loved more than the others. I give it to you as a reminder of the unconditional love we must have for the misguided and the wounded who harm others. It is easy to love the life forms who love us back, but it is difficult to love ourselves. May this golden metal represent the love we need to find for our humanness. To *love the truth*, we must see every life form as a reflection of ourselves, loving all the truths it represents."

Tears stung Becomes Her Vision's eyes as she recalled the life that Loves All Things had led and how her Sister had discovered the wisdom of unconditional love. She took a breath and turned to see She Who Heals approaching with her Give-away. They greeted each other with a warm embrace and Becomes Her Vision accepted the Give-away in her Sister's hands. When She Who Heals was back in her place, her voice permeated Becomes Her Vision's inner knowing. Even through the mists, the iridescent blue shell of Beetle radiated its hues.

"My gift is a reminder that all things return, cycles change, and so do we. The ability of the human spirit to be reborn from the seeming destruction of dire circumstances teaches us that healing is always possible. We learn to *serve the truth* when we remember this wisdom by healing ourselves and then serve others by showing them the tools they need to do the same. Every life form has the potential to heal and to be reborn. Developing intuition shows all living beings how to access those abilities of inner knowing and intuitive healing within themselves."

Setting Sun Woman walked from the ninth position on the Medicine Wheel and stood before Becomes Her Vision, offering her Give-away to her thirteenth Sister. Becomes Her Vision took the gift, hugged her Sister, and sent her thanks, allowing Setting Sun Woman to return to her original place on the Medicine Wheel.

"This green bundle of Sage is the reminder of how to properly use our wills. The Plant People understand that they can depend on the Earth Mother, and that is one lesson they teach us. We must learn how to become dependable by providing for future generations through our human actions and thoughtfulness. This ability to be concerned teaches us how to *live the truth* today and provide for tomorrow."

Becomes Her Vision understood her Sister's words, sent her thanks, and turned to face Weaves the Web as she came to stand in the circle's center. Weaves the Web handed her

Sister a pink flower, smiling as they embraced, and turned to walk back to her tenth position on the Wheel.

"This bloom was once a seed, waiting for the waters of Creation and the loving sunshine to release its creative potential, while it rested in the Earth Mother's body, immersed in warm darkness. The pink is for creativity and the blossom reminds us that through using our hands to fashion objects of beauty, we are really showing ourselves how to use our creativity to manifest our dreams, allowing the buds of our visions to blossom. Through work, we become the builders of those tangible dreams and can create much beauty in our world. Using all of our creativity teaches us how to *work with the truth*."

Walks Tall approached as Weaves the Web's voice faded. She hugged Becomes Her Vision and smiled as she handed her Sister the eleventh gift and received an unspoken thank-you through Becomes Her Vision's expressive eyes. Walks Tall returned to her place in the circle while Becomes Her Vision gazed at the Give-away in her hands. The white piece of bone had been carved by Walks Tall and contained many patterns and designs.

"These are the patterns of magnetism that can teach us what to keep and what to give away. We learn how to *walk the truth* by seeing which patterns of experience we have drawn to ourselves. When we have difficulty on the Red Road, we are being asked to see how the patterns of our talk may have magnetized a difficult situation. This bone gives us the Medicine of structure. We can always change destructive patterns if we release our limitations, maintaining the structure we need to Walk Our Talk."

Becomes Her Vision nodded, remembering how Walks Tall Woman had discovered these truths by her hard-earned life lessons, and sent her Sister another nod of thanks for sharing those lessons. Gives Praise had waited silently while Becomes Her Vision finished her unspoken communication with Walks Tall. Becomes Her Vision turned to Gives Praise and was thrilled by the celebratory hug and knowing smile that greeted her. Gives Praise lifted her eyes to the Sky Nation and held her hand up toward the heavens to offer thanks before she placed the gift she held into her Sister's hand. Then the Twelfth Clan Mother turned to walk back to her place on the Wheel of Life. Becomes Her Vision was admiring her gift when the voice of Gives Praise entered her field of awareness.

"This gift is a reminder of the celebration of life that you represent and the personal thanks that I want to express to you, Sister. You have worked hard to become all that you can be and that effort is a rare gift. The purple of this butterfly wing contains my Medicine and yours. It reminds us of the transformation you are undergoing and the gratitude for your Rite of Passage that is found in the color purple. The healing that all human beings can expect along the Red Road of physical life is available when they celebrate life and *give thanks for the truth.*

"Every one of your Sisters on this Medicine Wheel is grateful for the combined lessons that we have shared with you. At one time or another, all human women will stand on every spoke of this Wheel of the Sisterhood. Every male Two-legged who chooses to heal the female side of his nature will follow. Every human has the ability to become her or his vision through the healing lessons found in the Thirteen Aspects of the Earth Mother. For this Medicine, we are truly grateful."

As the voice of Gives Praise faded, Becomes Her Vision saw the fog clear. Behind what had appeared to be fog was the Great Smoking Mirror. The fiery eyes that the Thirteenth Clan Mother had seen in the vision of the mask that she would one day wear emerged from the mirror like flaming orbs of some giant beast. A booming voice came from the Great Smoking Mirror. The smoke shifted again and then disappeared, enveloping Becomes Her Vision with a sense of heightened awareness as the Great Smoking Mirror spoke.

"Look into the eyes of the Feathered Serpent! This Creature is the Keeper of the Whirling Rainbow Dream of Wholeness. In these dragon eyes of fire, you will see the truth of all that has been and all that will ever be."

Becomes Her Vision was taken aback by the beast appearing before her eyes. A giant Rainbow Lizard with eyes of flame and the wings of Condor came crashing through the Great Smoking Mirror, shattering the surface as if it had been made of solidified smoke. In the eyes of flame, the good and evil of the world parted and all illusions were shattered, revealing the purity of the Eternal Flame of Love. Becomes Her Vision was drawn inside the fire until she became the brilliant flame inside of all things. She turned to see the giant Lizard take flight, circling and circling the Medicine Wheel until it became a whirling rainbow, encompassing all of the natural world.

When Becomes Her Vision found the presence of mind to look around, all of her Sisters were gone. In her confusion, she began searching for them, walking toward the remnants of the Great Smoking Mirror that lay shattered on the ground. As she peered at the scattered shards, she caught her own reflection in the hundreds of pieces of looking glass. The vision of her face changed time and again as she saw each of her Sisters smiling back at her in turn. Something was emerging inside her awareness, while a voice whispered to her from far away. As she gathered strength, the voice of her Orenda pierced through the Clan Mother's confusion, speaking to the Guardian of Personal Myth's heart.

"Self of myself, you are now ready to *become the truth.* All of your Sisters are other reflections of yourself. The smoke-filled illusion that you are separate has now been shattered. Look inside of your being and share with me what you perceive, by acknowledging that we are all one."

Becomes Her Vision saw the chrysalis that she had been wrapped in begin to open inside of the cavernous Inner Earth. It was all happening inside of her. She was stunned as she watched the emergence of a butterfly made of crystal-clear gossamer threads of light. In every position that Butterfly turned, Becomes Her Vision could see all colors, could feel the presences of all life forms, could hear all the rhythms of life harmonizing. Butterfly closed its wings and then opened them, revealing a Crystal Skull. Thirteen times, Butterfly opened and closed its wings, giving birth to the Crystal Skulls of the Thirteen Clan Mothers.

The vision changed and Becomes Her Vision saw Butterfly transform into the shape of a beautiful shimmering woman. Slowly, the radiant form drew her into itself, and in the next heartbeat, she was inside the glittering body of light, looking at her hands as they began to change into human flesh. The sensations of physicality were intoxicating as her flesh became whole, housing all of her knowing, her feelings, and her heart—pounding with unconditional love. The former chrysalis expanded into the vastness of space, encompassing earth and sky. The opening chrysalis was woven from Becomes Her Vision's Orenda. Her Spiritual Essence continued to grow beyond the expanse of her human vision, connecting her to all worlds that existed within the Great Mystery.

Becomes Her Vision became the truth of the awakening dream. She walked the earth and found the other Twelve Clan Mothers, patiently awaiting her arrival. She opened her vision to them and shared the events of her Rite of Passage. The Thirteen Sisters traveled to the site where the Earth Mother had directed them and found a Medicine Wheel that had a Crystal Skull sitting on each of the twelve stones that formed the outer circle, and one sitting on the stone in the center. It was on that site, in the center of Turtle Island, that the Thirteen Clan Mothers built the Turtle Council House.

Becomes Her Vision walked the Earth as the realized dream for two worlds of time, while she and her Sisters shared their Medicines with all of humankind. The Mother of Change learned that the lessons of her Earth Walk would continue, but she had been given a foundation upon which to build her experience. Her chrysalis dream had shown her that the Great Smoking Mirror was right, there was only one woman and only one man on the Mother Planet, but each had billions of faces.

Becomes Her Vision sings to the hearts of all of the Children of Earth, reminding them of the promise of the

Whirling Rainbow Dream and their roles in manifesting that vision. She can be called on to assist any Child of Earth who seeks the light of the Eternal Flame of Love in order to be the truth and become her or his vision. As the Keeper of Spirit Emerging into Form, she teaches us how to bring the truth of the unlimited Spiritual Essences of our Orendas into our human bodies, accessing our unified, unlimited potential to create a dream that all living things can share.

Becomes Her Vision's song of wholeness reminds us: "You are—the moment you decide to BE."

Conclusion
Gathering the Gifts of Woman

To continue weaving the web of the Sisterhood and make it strong, we must first honor the two bylaws that are Native American Traditions—protect the women and never do anything that would hurt the children. These are the un-written laws that kept the Tribes in the Americas strong for hundreds of years. In modern times, we could translate these two laws into meaning that the Planetary Family is restored when the women can feel safe anywhere and anytime. When that occurs, the nurturing of children's dreams is taken care of by women who have become extensions of the Earth Mother and thus Mothers of the Creative Force. Through the nurturing of healed women, the spiritual health and well-being of the next seven generations is assured.

The Sisterhood grows strong when every woman sees every other woman as an equal part of the whole. There is no room for pecking order in a circle of women. "Life, Unity, and Equality for Eternity" is the foundation for the harmonious circle of the Sisterhood. Every woman is asked to do her part by developing her gifts, talents, and abilities. Each woman is acknowledged for the work she contributes to the whole. Every woman is her own judge; the truth of her actions and the integrity of her words is the model she uses as she leads through example. Each woman is required to face the limitations, fears, and challenges within herself and to heal those parts of her self in order to become the living personification of her personal vision.

When each woman honors her Self, more raw, creative energy is available to be used by the whole to effect changes in the way humankind reacts to life. When women are no longer lost, asking others to tell them what they should do or how they should live, there will be great changes in our world. This is not to say that the friendships and bonds of women are not to be used; on the contrary, the support of other women who have walked the same path is paramount. This kind of support is based in truth and delivered with caring—without projections or judging another. That kind of support is healthy and productive, when other women create a safe space in which to share personal thoughts and offer alternatives in a respectful way. The Sisterhood always supports every woman who is willing to surmount her own challenges in order to grow.

Any woman who has taken care of business by becoming strong and her personal best is already standing in the Turtle Council House with the Thirteen Original Clan Mothers. How she continues to develop her talents depends on her desire to see through the smokey illusion of the Great Smoking Mirror. The Mayans say, "I am another one of yourself." Through the Great Smoking Mirror we can look at every life form in the tangible world as representing some gift, trait, or talent that also is a part of our own makeup. When we look beyond the smokey illusions, we can travel past our hesitations and limitations, finding that every one of the Thirteen Clan Mothers is a part of the person we are. Some of those skills may not be fully developed, but they are available to us if we decide we want to use them to grow further.

One way we can balance the male and female sides of our nature is through developing our skills, putting ourselves out in the world in order to make a difference in the lives of others we encounter. Through example, we can show others how to love unconditionally, be their personal best, drop the need to control or belittle, and show compassion. The Legacy of Woman does not have to include the former hurts that have set women against women, women against men, or caused women to destroy themselves through sabotage. The way out of these crooked trails is provided by the Thirteen Original Clan Mothers. When we acknowledge the traits of the Original Thirteen as gifts we can find and develop within ourselves, we have many goals to accomplish and plenty of work to do. There is no need to get involved with the high drama and pettiness that has kept us from achieving human harmony when we are busy working on becoming our personal visions.

To gather the gifts of the Thirteen Original Clan Mothers and to develop them as our own, we must see other women as role models. This is not to put the women who have developed a certain gift on a pedestal, because they too are human and will fall. Every human being is perfect in her or his imperfections and has a right to learn through trial and error. In admiring how another woman uses the gifts she has developed, we can then see how she handles situations in her life. It may not be how we would do it ourselves, but it gives us one alternative to look at without judging it as right or wrong. Being the observer of several women who have certain gifts that we want to develop within ourselves can give us a multitude of new ideas and ways to approach life.

The practice of learning through observing is the way that Native American Tribes have taught Clan or family members to develop their skills for centuries. We are only as accomplished as those we choose as our role models or teachers. When a child showed a skill or talent of some kind, the family would go to the Tribe Member who was the very best at that particular thing and ask if the child could learn from that person. This ensured that the child would learn from the best teacher available and it was the unspoken duty of that teacher to make sure that the student equaled or surpassed the abilities of the teacher. When this was accomplished, the reward belonged to both the teacher and the student for a job well done. There was no jealousy or envy or holding back of some information or technique that would make the teacher superior. That kind of selective teaching was practiced only when separation divided the Indian Nations after the Trail of Tears.

Today, there are many ways to find role models. We can find the information or resources we need through books, seminars, schools, or libraries. We can make it our priority to develop new ways to look at our lifestyles and our environment. We can decide to live in a way that shows respect for the Earth Mother and All Our Relations. We can learn through observing our neighbors. We can develop skills through sharing or helping another accomplish a task. We can ask that the right person or situation be put in our paths so we can observe alternatives. Everything in life is our teacher and everything is alive. The discovery of that aliveness is the adventure that life offers us on a minute-to-minute basis. Our main task is to be aware of every moment in order to take advantage of the opportunities presented.

To gather the gifts of woman, we must be aware of everything in the tangible and intangible worlds. The role models we need are represented in all life forms, not just in women. The feminine principle is present in all things and in the natural world is balanced with a positive male role model, giving us the blending we need to find in ourselves. The receptive observer is the feminine aspect of gathering the information of how to develop a skill. The willingness to take the actions necessary to accomplish that task belongs to the demonstrative male principle. Observing and listening, making sure we understand, and then taking action is the balanced path to developing any talent or accomplishing any goal.

Saying no to anything that is inappropriate or harmful for ourselves or another is one form of taking action. The refusal be a party to pettiness is another way to take action, through nonaction. When we think enough of ourselves to respect our Sacred Spaces and our bodies, we choose the activities that support right action. When our opinion of ourselves is low, we tend to be drawn into situations that ultimately inflict physical, mental, or emotional harm on some part of our beings. These wrong actions come from woundedness. It is then necessary to heal the part of ourselves that is willing to accept any interaction with others as a substitute for self-esteem. In our desire to be liked or admired, we often set aside the standards that we have found will support our growth. The lessons of this crooked trail are hard ones that fall like an avalanche of broken dreams, further wounding the Self. It is the male/demonstrative side of our nature that is willing to risk saying no to protect the Self's identity. It is the nurturing female side that is willing to receive *any* kindness or attention, even if the consequences are not readily seen.

The wounded male side of our nature may insist that we constantly defend, battle, or compete with others to show our worthiness, instead of working together in a supportive way. These reflections of self-importance are seen through the Great Smoking Mirror, making us aware of the pain they have caused in this Fourth World of Separation. If we are constantly defending our right to be, we are defending a deep wound to our sense of Self.

Self-esteem is reclaimed when the feminine principle of nurturing the Self is practiced, instead of expecting our sense of wholeness to come from our relationship to another person. When we care enough for ourselves to take the time we need to give to the Self, we will feel complete. When we feel love for the Self, we will then draw another person to us who can add his or her sense of wholeness to the relationship. The union of two people who have developed the skills of self-reliance and self-esteem is one that will stand the tests of life's experiences.

This type of healing, provided by the Great Smoking Mirror, applies to every human relationship. When two wounded people become friends, the relationship will invariably produce a common ground that will provide many lessons. They may mirror their common weaknesses, lack of understanding, or inflexibility to one another. They could provide a support system for one another or reflect how one is growing and the other has fear of change. In every instance, no matter how the situation presents itself, each individual is responsible for seeing her or his own hurt and for finding a way to heal it without making the other person responsible for that pain. This is the way of the feminine nurturing principle: going within, finding the problem, and remedying it through nurturing the self.

The male principle is then used to affect or change the patterns that caused the person to draw those lessons to the Self. The actions that created the problem are habits that can be broken. If a person always goes along with another's decision and is angry about it later, the anger is really with the Self. If a person is afraid to speak up when something seems amiss, the unexpressed resentment will strangle the relationship.

These and other habits that are limiting can be changed if we use the feminine principle of observing the obvious in ourselves. It is far easier to see the wrong behavior in another than it is to see our own refusal to take right action. We do not need to insist that others do it our way, but we do need to insist upon honesty within the Self in order to support our own well-being. Personal integrity changes as the person grows and develops. It would be unfair to insist that everyone follow one set of rules.

The rigidity within belief systems that makes one faith the true faith and all others false is one of the mainstays causing the Fourth World of Separation to be so destructive. In the Indian Way of the Ancestors, if a person received a dream or vision about a particular way to perform a task, ceremony, or healing, it was never questioned because it was between that person and the Great Mystery. If people chose to dress differently or follow any course of action that did not hurt others, it was accepted as their way of doing things and was not judged. For the most part, families living in a tribal situation did not stick their noses in anyone else's business unless they were asked to. The respect for another's Sacred Space was of utmost importance even if she or he were not behaving properly. The only time anything was brought before one of the Council of Elders was when a tribal Law had been broken that would affect the survival of everyone.

We gather the gifts of woman when we allow all persons to make their own choices about who and what they want to be and then allow them to find a path that suits their personality and unique way of learning those skills. These are the gifts of the good mother who refuses to smother her children but instead gives responsibility according to each child's capacity. This manner of allowing a child to develop the ability to respond from his or her sense of integrity ensures that the children will become self-reliant. The purity of the loving feminine principle is based in unattached guidance giving proper boundaries and at the same time providing a fertile ground for developing the seeds of potential. The Thirteen Original Clan Mothers allow every Child of Earth the opportunity to become his or her potential in this same way.

We can no longer separate the female and male principles within ourselves, because one without the other will leave us stranded on the shores of the future without the means to become our personal visions. Gathering the gifts of woman and bringing those gifts home to our hearts means acknowledging both sides of our nature and investing both sides with goodness. Negative judgments will divide the natural marriage of our *thoughts* (feminine) and *actions* (masculine) that give us the abilities we need to accomplish our goals.

The Sisterhood has been given the task of being the bridge from the Fourth World of Separation into the Fifth World of Peace and Enlightenment. The chasm we are being asked to cross can only be bridged with forgiveness. We all desire the abundance of the Fifth World, but to receive it we must *for-give.* We are being asked to give of ourselves, to forgive ourselves and others, and to allow the abundance of wisdom to flow. Our greatest potential lies within and can be found through forgiving, creating the bridge across the abyss of our woundedness. We are standing at that point in time now.

Every human being who accomplishes the task of becoming her or his personal vision will become a role model for others, whether she or he is aware of it or not. The more gifts we gather and the more skills we develop, the more enlightenment we are able to share with others. This is the road to the Fifth World of Peace, and the Thirteen Original Clan Mothers are the Guardians of that path to wholeness. The time has never been more fertile. The dreams of humankind are nestled in the hearts that are ready to heal the old pain and become the living vision of Life, Unity, and Equality for Eternity.

The History of the Turtle Council House

Many thousands of moons ago when Turtle Island was one land mass and the Children of Earth lived together as one, a call from the Earth Mother went out to all women of the human race. This plea has been echoed through the centuries in the hearts of women everywhere and still reflects the Earth Mother's purest desire for women to take their roles as the Guardians of beauty, harmony, equality, and peace.

In those ancient times, women were uncertain of their roles, and yet they strove to give of themselves in order to preserve the Legacy of Woman on their Mother Planet. It was a time before the religions of the later-established Matriarchy would worship the Great Mother. The beginning of this story takes place in the days when the Earth was new and the steam from her cooling body made tropical environments where the Children of Earth wandered naked, without shame. Great reptiles and mammals roamed the Earth, feasting on the lush vegetation. The human Children of Earth knew no lack because there was food growing in abundance and all of the Children of Earth lived in harmony. It was a time that the Grandmothers call the First World of Love, and the light of Grandfather Sun was the symbol of the constant love that guided the Original People, the Human-beings. The Earth Tribe called Human-beings knew no separation because male and female were honored as equals. For the Human-beings, there was no battle between the genders, because each sex had equally important roles in Creation and both joyously performed their tasks in a loving and good way, supporting all other humans, creatures, and plants.

As the rotations around the sun passed, each of these yearly orbits was marked by thirteen cycles of Grandmother Moon. As new generations were born, the love freely given to all life forms by Grandfather Sun became a source of comfort that marked day from night, Sun from Sleep. His golden light of love brought warmth, because at that time humankind did not understand the mystery of fire or how to contain it. Like the warmth and nurturing ability of the mothers of humankind and the protective, providing roles of the fathers of the Human Tribe, Grandfather Sun's Sacred Fire warmed the hearts of all the Children of Earth.

The five races of Two-legged humans lived in harmony and honored the differences between them as being unique aspects of beauty for many hundreds of generations. The yellow, red, brown, white, and black races of Two-leggeds were not fearful of a scarcity that they had never known. All of their needs were abundantly taken care of until greed changed the orbit of the planet. Something was wrong, very wrong. The Earth Mother could no longer maintain her balance as she traveled across the Sky Nation, circling Grandfather Sun. Slowly she was losing her balance, slipping off her path, and every wobble worried her more. The gold that held her internal guidance system and revolving relationship to the sun was being removed by her human children.

It was during this time of subtle climatic change that jealousy began to rear its ugly head and fear clutched the hearts of the Two-leggeds. Food was not as plentiful as it had been before, because the seasons began to evolve, making changes in the fruit-bearing cycles of the Plant People. The races of humankind began to seek others who looked like their own particular race, causing the first separation of the Tribe called the Human-beings. These Two-leggeds began to believe that Clans or families of the same race should be formed to protect their food stores for those of the same skin color. Grandfather Sun loved all his children equally, without exception, and his heart was saddened by this Crooked Trail that his human children had taken.

The separation continued as gold was chipped from the Earth Mother's body and hoarded. Confused human children believed that gold was the manifested, collected light of Grandfather Sun's love. They believed that Two-leggeds who possessed the greatest amount of this precious metal would rule the others in the Human Tribe. The yellow race of Two-leggeds began to enslave the other races until greed had finally destroyed the ideas of equality that had invested the First World with unconditional love. The male Human-beings were physically strong and began to hunt and hoard the food in order to dominate the females, creating further separation and woundedness.

Misunderstanding of Grandfather Sun's Sacred Fire and the color yellow that represented the Eternal Flame of Love and Light caused the misuse of gold and deterioration of the First World's original intent. The Earth Mother could no longer stand the cries of her children, who had become the Children of Sorrow because love was lost. The First World would have to be destroyed by the same Sacred Fire of unconditional love in order to purify the Mother Planet for a new beginning. The Sacred Fire of Love had been replaced by gold metal, becoming an all-consuming fire of greed, ownership, and control.

Grandmother Moon spoke to her daughter, the Earth Mother, and brought forth an idea from deep within her heart. "Oh, my daughter, do not grieve for that which cannot be changed. There is much love and compassion inside you that can be used to heal the broken hearts of these Children of Sorrow."

The Earth Mother lifted her voice to question the wise Grandmother who wove the tides of her oceans with the feelings of human beings. "Speak to me of the healing my human children need, Moon Mother, for my heart is heavy and my senses are reeling with their pain."

"Daughter, I would speak to you of yourself. You hold all that is good within the feminine. You carry the model of wholeness for all women inside your heart. It is time for us to create the parts of you that will express the hidden human potential. Each time my face comes full one aspect of the feminine healing potential will be revealed. Each of these thirteen parts of the dream of wholeness will be spun of gossamer thread made of my silver light and will move from the Dreamtime into the manifested world to walk the Earth. They shall become the Thirteen Original Clan Mothers, who will be the foundation of the Legacy of Woman. They will hold the Sacred Hoop intact through all the coming worlds. Each will be the Guardian of the secrets of one moon cycle and Keeper of the Mysteries of Woman. Every Clan Mother will represent another part of your spirit and will work in harmony with the others. Together they represent your Medicine and your truth. It is through this Medicine that womankind will once again find the strength of equality. Pass this legacy to your human daughters so that all life may come back into balance."

The Earth Mother's heart was gladdened as she and Grandmother Moon set out to spin the threads of woman. The shimmering fabric of woman was delicate and yet eternally durable, light, and free of form. The individual patterns of the Thirteen Clan Mothers would emerge from this woven light, one at a time, as each of the next thirteen moons passed. The spirit of each would be called forth from the heart of Yeodaze, the Earth Mother, when Grandmother Moon's full light brought forth the hidden feelings, desires, and characteristics of each Cycle of Truth. All women would be called *Yeo*, after Yeodaze, the Earth Mother, and would find their roles through accessing the teachings of the Thirteen Original Clan Mothers. These Thirteen Clan Mothers of humankind would walk the Spirit World and then take their places together as human beings when the manifestation of these magical womankind creations was complete.

During the Clan Mothers' creation process, Swennio, the Great Mystery, smiled upon Mother Earth and Grandmother Moon, for their hearts were pure. The Great Mystery saw the wisdom in a new beginning. The Earth had been raped and defiled by those who would rob her body of the element of gold. These pockets of golden ore guided Mother Earth's lifeforce and maintained her body's connection to Grandfather Sun. The Two-leggeds had chosen a crooked path that had changed the life flow within their

Mother Planet by robbing the golden ore. Mother Earth's body no longer followed the same path across the Sky Nation and continued to dangerously wobble and tilt. These changes in her path caused shifts in the weather that brought the Four Seasons into being. With the changing seasons came the unexpected scarcity of food. All of Earth's Children had to adapt to the shifts in climate. These paramount shifts in the quality of life added fuel to the fire of greed that had been born of the fear of scarcity. When the weight of winter brought ice, cold, and hunger, those who robbed the yellow metal were able to buy food from the hoarders. The hoarded fruits and tubers that had once been freely given by the Plant People were now used as a means to create inequality and control. Greed caused many to starve and others to follow a crooked path, digging for gold to pay for food in order to survive.

The Earth Mother sent a decree into all parts of Creation that was heard by those who listened with their hearts. "I am giving birth to a legacy that will bring forth the best in all of humankind," she cried out. "Never again will the beauty of the feminine aspect be hidden from those who seek Grandmother Moon's light or my gift of nurturing and physical strength to guide their paths. I will give all women of Earth the Medicine they need to birth their children and their collective dreams. Then together with these daughters, I will reverse the pattern of fear that has wounded the hearts of all my children. My promise to the Plant People and Stone People, the Winged Ones, Finned Ones, Four-leggeds, and Creepy-crawlers is that my compassion and love will be present in the Two-leggeds called Yeo, woman. It may take some time and help from other Relations in the

Planetary Family, but woman will find her way, reclaiming for every living thing the love that was lost during this First World's imbalance."

And so it was that the dream visions of the Thirteen Original Clan Mothers became flesh and were nestled in the heart of the Earth Mother deep inside the Inner Earth. The fire consumed the Above World as the flaming purification was followed by ice. Together, these cleansings represented the fire of greed and the hardened hearts that had grown cold from lack of loving compassion. The Clan Mothers, as aspects of the Earth Mother who had taken human bodies, gathered together to dream the vision of the coming worlds when all would be made new. The dream that came out of this Dreaming Circle was later called the Whirling Rainbow Dream. It brought the promise of future wholeness that would manifest during the Fifth World of Illumination and Peace.

The Clan Mothers laid their new human bodies on the Earth in a circle, with their feet to a fire, allowing their bodies to act as the spokes of their human Medicine Wheel. For four Suns and four Sleeps they dreamed. On the first Sun, they dreamed of the illumination that came from the East and how to better understand the opening of the Golden Door that leads to all other levels of imagination and awareness. They dreamed of the lessons of the coming worlds and of how each woman could contribute her talents to make those future worlds full of harmony, truth, equality, and peace. Each Clan Mother's vision was different, for she was given a unique way in which to understand her personal Medicine. The understanding of life and of the breath of life that supports all human beings as they move through their

Earth Walks permeated the senses of the dreaming women, giving them a wisdom of the Knowing Systems they would use in the physical realm.

The dreaming continued into the second Sun, when the visions changed to the lessons of the South. Each woman saw the way that she could use her personal faith to assist in breaking the behavior patterns that had placed the Human Tribe in bondage. The magic of innocence and childlike wonder, celebration, and playfulness filled their dreams with joy as they were shown the pleasures of physical life. Each woman was given a deep appreciation of the simple things that made the Earth a place of beauty. The dreaming continued and the lessons of humility and the consequences of self-importance came into view. Each Clan Mother was shown the abundance that the group could create through *unity* and how they could work together to pass the combined legacy of wholeness to humankind.

As Grandfather Sun rose for the third time, the dream focused on the lessons of the West. The place of all tomorrows, the West or Moon Direction, brought forth the vision of *equality* that was necessary for the future of wholeness to be assured. By honoring the talents and Sacred Spaces of all life forms as well as each other, the circle was enveloped with a feeling of unity while the beauty of each woman's part of the whole was revealed. The preservation of Traditions and the abundance of the Mother Planet came into view as each woman saw her role as a Guardian of fertility and truth. The ability to go within her own heart and to know her truth in order to make balanced decisions became a part of the Whirling Rainbow Dream. The function of Grandmother Moon's cycles and how each woman could find those rhythms within herself whirled through the visions of every Clan Mother. The events that would come later in the story of humankind were revealed as the Whirling Rainbow Dream brought visions of a blending of the Human Tribe far in the distant future. The peace and illumination that had been present in the First World of Love would return when the Earth Tribe had completed its lessons through trial and error.

The final revelation of completion, when all would be healed, had brought the dawning of the next Sun. Grandfather's light covered the Above World in rose-tinted glory once more. The dream then turned to the North and showed the Clan Mothers that *life, unity, and equality* would last for *eternity* as the lesson of each was fully learned. The wisdom of all that had been revealed and how each Rite of Passage brought all things closer to wholeness was implanted in the wombs of all Thirteen Clan Mothers. There the dream would grow and flourish in the warm darkness of their womb spaces, places of balance and vision, the inner Medicine Bowls of these Whirling Rainbow Grandmothers. The North vision then presented the lesson of gratitude, allowing each woman to return thanks from her heart for the vision of wholeness that had been received.

The seeds of the future had been planted in the here and now. The dreams of every human Child of Earth were honored as necessary parts of the whole. These Grandmothers of humankind were forever pregnant with the lessons, the challenges, and the aspirations of the Children of Earth. The dreams of All Our Relations were tied within that Sacred Dream Hoop of Wholeness that would one day come into manifestation. These future dreams and lessons would be birthed when the time was right for the Earth's Children to learn and gather the wisdom. The Rites of Passage, or change, that would mark the birth of each vision had taken root in the present. Each set of life lessons would unfold as it was called forth by the Human Tribe's desire to alter their paths, changing and growing in unity.

The inner knowing and vision that each Clan Mother held would rest inside of her heart. The dream of who she was and what her talents represented was nestled within her womb. The opening of those visions would come when the purification of the Above World was complete. In the following Suns and Sleeps, it would be necessary to give birth to the promise held in the Whirling Rainbow Dream, so that the promise of the lights of wholeness could be seen all over the world. The fire that had provided warmth for their feet during the four Suns and Sleeps of dreaming began to pulse and change form. The heart of the Earth Mother began to emerge as a living, new-flaming sun, deep within the Inner Earth. This heart-fire began to beat a different rhythm that would allow All Our Relations to feel the constant love and deep connection to their true Mother.

The Clan Mothers stood around that pulsing heart and became a part of it once again. The fire of love that each carried traveled up and out of the Inner Earth to create the Aurora Borealis. These rainbow lights sent forth the promise that the Whirling Rainbow Dream was in progress and that the Earth would never again be destroyed by fire. The colors of the Aurora touched the Sky Nation and signaled the beginning of the lessons of healing the world. The Human

Nation would need to learn each lesson on the Medicine Wheel in order to claim the completion of spiritual wholeness. The love of the Earth Mother was present in every colored beam that danced across the indigo, star-studded blanket of the Sky Nation. The dancing colors heralded the message that the Earth Mother's legacy of Life, Unity, and Equality for Eternity had been passed to the Thirteen Clan Mothers. The Sisterhood had been formed. The mission of carrying the Legacy of Woman and the lessons of wholeness to the Children of Earth could now begin.

When the purification of the Above World was complete, twelve of the Thirteen Clan Mothers emerged from the Inner Earth with those faithful humans who had chosen to repopulate the Above World. Becomes Her Vision would wait in the Dreamtime until her twelve sisters had completed their first Rites of Passage, collecting their lessons and taking their experiences into her understanding. Then, Becomes Her Vision would go through her Rite of Passage and join the others when she became the realized dream, taking a human form.

Later, the reunited Clan Mothers would build the first Turtle Council House that would house the Sisterhood. Half of the oval house was to be built below the soil so that the darkness of the womb within would be filled with the rich perfume of the Earth Mother's breath. The domed roof was to be covered with mud and leaves and stones that would form the shell of Grandmother Turtle. The arms, legs, head, and tail of Grandmother Turtle were to be sculpted in soil and covered with tiny Stone People. The future Council House would be built on a site of the Earth Mother's choosing.

There was much to learn about being human. The Rites of Passage each Clan Mother passed through would then allow the Earth Mother to fully understand her human children in a good way, through feeling the human experiences of her thirteen aspects. The Earth Walk of each Clan Mother brought many winters of wisdom, and finally triumph, as Becomes Her Vision became the realized dream of the Legacy of Woman, allowing the Thirteen Sisters to become united as one.

The Turtle Council House stood for many worlds of time while the Clan Mothers taught their human children the love of the Earth Mother. Every Clan Mother had a body that did not age like those of the Human Tribe. When it was time for the Thirteen Mothers to return to the center of Inner Earth without their bodies, the Turtle Council House disappeared from the face of the Earth. Then the Human Tribe was forced to use the tools they had been taught by the Clan Mothers to become the living examples of truth that the Great Mystery had created them to be.

We do not need an archaeologist to search for the remains of the Turtle Council House in the Four Corners area of North America. Now the Turtle Council House can be accessed through our hearts. The Thirteen Original Crystal Skulls hold each Clan Mother's library of wisdom and their spirits are always available to us when we enter Tiyoweh, the Stillness. Today, the symbol of Turtle is a reminder of the fertile legacy that we are being asked to reclaim for All Our Relations.

Entering the Council House of the Thirteen Original Clan Mothers

When I was passed the stories of the Thirteen Original Clan Mothers by Grandmothers Cisi and Berta, I was told that the gifts of the Clan Mothers would forever be a part of the Earth. I was taught that any Two-legged could access the wisdom held by these Grandmothers of the Turtle Council House if she or he had an open heart and a desire to tap into the feminine principle. The aspects of the Earth Mother and Grandmother Moon that took form as the Thirteen Clan Mothers are found in every living thing, in all seasons, and in every location on our planet.

Cisi and Berta told me that just before it was time for the Thirteen Clan Mothers to Drop Their Robes and return to the heart of the Earth Mother without their physical bodies, the Thirteen Crystal Skulls were made. These Crystal Skulls represented the wisdom that was gathered by the Clan Mothers and included all of the love and talents that formed the Legacy of Woman.

I was taught that before the separation of Turtle Island into continents and before the golden ages of various cultures that have made up the Fourth World of Separation, each one of the Crystal Skulls was housed in a place where women gathered to share Medicine. I was taught that most of these sacred sites were in the center or middle section of the one great land mass of Turtle Island. The central section of Turtle Island is presently called North and South America and did include parts of the Atlantic and Pacific Oceans.

Cisi told me that some replicas of the Thirteen Crystal Skulls were made by humans over the centuries to bring pretended power to certain cultures or spiritual sects. The result was disastrous since those societies were seeking to control others through fraudulent means and supposed spirituality. The leaders of the religious cults of various civilizations who sought to enslave the populace through hierarchy, patriarchy, or matriarchy had forgotten the original intent of the Thirteen Clan Mothers. Life, Unity, and Equality for Eternity is the Legacy of the Sisterhood that includes all people and life forms.

Berta told me that the Crystal Skulls were made in the form of human skulls to represent the collected wisdom found in the human potential. The Earth Mother, who is a living being, holds this wisdom because of the passages of her Thirteen Aspects, the Clan Mothers, into human forms.

Berta explained that because of the Earth Mother's mind-set, no outside influence could harm the crystal libraries held in the skulls. The consciousness contained in the Crystal Skulls does not include the human fears that can draw negative influences. Berta said that through the ages, any person who sought to use the Crystal Skulls for evil ends was a fool. The center of each skull contains the reflection of the Great Smoking Mirror. The smoke-filled illusion in front of the mirror is that anyone could send any intention, good or bad, to another person *without having it boomerang back.* The purity and clarity of these clear quartz skulls merely reflects any intention sent back to its point of origin. The joke is on the sender in every case because the only reflection seen in the Skull's crystallized form is the face of the sender. As the Mayans say, "I am another one of yourself."

Cisi and Berta both said that even if one of the Thirteen Crystal Skulls were destroyed by human hands, the total information is held in every one of the thirteen. The wisdom of how all things are interrelated is kept in these living libraries. This set of records also includes how the Earth Mother is related to every other heavenly body in our solar system, galaxy, and universe. It is no wonder that some people who have telepathically connected to one of the original skulls, now known as the Mitchell-Hedges skull after its modern discoverers, have felt that its origin must be another planet or civilization from the stars.

The Stone People are the libraries of Earth and hold all records of the Earth's true history. There are two reasons that quartz crystal was the stone substance used to fashion these skulls. The first is that the Earth Mother's body contains an enormous amount of quartz, which she uses to maintain clarity and focus. All quartz on Earth contains the solidified memory, feelings, and cycles of the Mother Planet's evolving process. Because of the connection of quartz to the element of water, you might say that the internal feelings and thoughts of the Earth Mother are transmitted through these pockets of quartz. Her sense of timing and rhythm are transmitted from these quartz crystals in much the same way that crystals are used inside of some watches and clocks in our modern world to regulate accuracy.

The second reason is that originally in the Turtle Council House, light was reflected under the base of the skulls and would form a rainbow of color through the top of the skulls. The Aurora Borealis comes from the top of the Earth Mother's head, or North Pole, representing the Whirling Rainbow's promise of world peace. The Whirling Rainbow Dream is the prophecy of all races, all nations coming together in the Fifth World of Peace that we are now beginning.

For the human Children of Earth, the skulls are a reminder that the Thirteen Original Clan Mothers dreamed the Whirling Rainbow of Peace at the end of the First World of Love when they were inside the subterranean caverns of Earth. Later, when the Turtle Council House was built, it was half below the soil and half above, representing the marriage of the Natural World and the Spirit World, Mother Earth and Father Sky, the female and male principles. Inside the Turtle Council House, where the skulls were first housed, the sunlight came through the holes in the walls and illuminated each Crystal Skull, sending the combined consciousness of the Clan Mothers into the interior of the structure.

Today, one of the original Crystal Skulls, the Mitchell-Hedges skull, which was discovered in the early 1900s, is being displayed and is traveling to many museums and foreign countries. In the interior of Mexico, I have been in the presence of two more of the originals—one that is guarded by an ancient Toltec and Aztec Medicine Society and another that is in the competent hands of a family of healers. These are not the Crystal Skulls that were once in museums. My other teacher, Joaquin Muriel Espinosa, told me that the Crystal Skulls that have been placed in museums (like the one that was later stolen in Mexico City) are not originals but rather replicas that do not hold the records or mind-set of the Clan Mothers.

Joaquin, Cisi, and Berta all told me stories of how some of the original Crystal Skulls were housed in Mayan, Toltec, Aztec, and Inca, as well as other North American Indian tribal centers. These stories told of how a few of the Crystal Skulls were lost when the oceans reclaimed parts of the land on the east and west coasts of North, Mezzo, and South America at the end of the Third World. My teachers said that the Earth Mother had chosen to ensure that some of the Crystal Skulls would forever be in her keeping, away from her destructive human children. These Elders told me that many humans would dream of the Crystal Skulls and become a part of the Whirling Rainbow Dream of Peace but that only those who had earned the right, through connecting to the Thirteen Original Clan Mothers, would become the Guardians of the actual Crystal Skulls.

Many people on our planet believe that they are connected to the Crystal Skulls through visions they have had or through spiritual messages they have received. Some believe that they are supposed to rediscover the actual skulls. If this was the truth, in fact, those people would have been guided to the actual places where the existing Original Skulls are being kept by the human beings who hold the honored roles of Guardianship. My Elders told me that every human being is connected to the Thirteen Original Clan Mothers and that when a person is ready for that level of spiritual experience, the dreams of the Crystal Skulls, the

Whirling Rainbow, or the Clan Mothers will come to them. This form of initiation is merely an entry point into the Medicine Wheel of the Clan Mothers that will give each individual the right to begin learning the lessons available. The paths to wholeness that are formed by each Clan Mother's spoke on the Medicine Wheel are filled with lessons about developing personal abilities and may take many years to complete.

I was taught how to focus on those lessons and how to persist in my personal growth by Cisi, Berta, and Joaquin. They taught me these seven points of wisdom that I would like to share with you.

1. There are no rules on how to grow or change.

2. All self-imposed rules or judgments are limiting illusions.

3. The Great Mystery cannot be solved, so don't try.

4. Everything you seek can be found inside of you.

5. Laughter and irreverence dissolve the illusions and the fear.

6. Unseen worlds exist within the tangible and cannot be separated.

7. You ARE, the moment you decide to BE.

I feel that I could write an entire book on those seven lessons and so I will leave it to each individual to find understanding for herself or himself.

The manner in which each person contacts the Thirteen Original Clan Mothers is up to that individual. The following exercise can assist those who would like to try it in the way I show others. To take this journey, you must first understand some basic principles.

⩓ ⩓
How to Contact the Thirteen Original Clan Mothers

To enter the realms where the Thirteen Clan Mothers live, we must first seek the loving gifts that they represent inside of ourselves. The Orenda or Spiritual Essence holds those gifts in infinite readiness inside the Sacred Space of each individual. The question of how to define the Sacred Space is answered with our imaginations.

If you can imagine a sphere around you with your body in the center, you will have discovered your Sacred Space. The circle forms the equator of the bubble that stretches above your body into the sky and below your body into the Earth Mother, creating the union of physicality and spirit. The Sacred Space encapsulates all your thoughts and feelings, your body, your spirit, your dreams and visions, and your sense of Self. Inside your Sacred Space, you have a Sacred Point of View that is determined by all that you are and all that you have experienced.

The Sacred Point of View is fed like a fetus by a spiritual or nontangible umbilical cord. Each person has thousands of spiritual fibers that extend into the world from the navel. When the person is open and ready to feel life, these sensory threads spread out like rays of the sun. When a person is tired, hurt, vulnerable, or ill at ease, these same filaments can twine together to become a thickly knotted umbilical cord of light. The relaxed umbilical cord can then be attached to the Earth Mother when the weakened person lets go enough to receive the Earth Mother's healing or energy. If the person is not aware of how to use this spiritual umbilical cord, it may knot up, stopping the life force from entering the body and sometimes causing terror stomach or nausea.

From this place near the navel that we call the Vibral Core, humans sense all things through patterns, rhythms, or vibrations. Inside our bodies, our thoughts, feelings, sensations, and perceptions combine to form our individual Sacred Points of View. Every life form's Sacred Point of View is comprised of personal likes, dislikes, opinions, feelings, thoughts, and/or experiences. Unfortunately for the Human Tribe, we have also adopted hearsay, rumors, fears, the opinions of others, and preconceived notions in our Sacred Points of View. That is one reason why the people of our human race have such a hard time finding personal truths. Our Sacred Points of View are often buried under the opinions we have adopted from others when we did not seek or find what was true for ourselves. These adopted untruths make up the mental matter and chatter that keeps us from respecting our own Sacred Spaces and Sacred Points of View. For this reason alone, it is oftentimes difficult for some people to quiet the mind and enter the Silence or Stillness inside their Sacred Spaces.

My Grandmother Twylah taught me that the Sacred Space can be found in between the *in* breath and the *out* breath. Holding the breath to the count of ten allows us to stop the outer world and to open the door that leads to the inner world of the Self. I developed a way to get to that place within myself so I can connect to my Orenda (Spiritual Essence). By inhaling, holding the breath for a moment, then exhaling, I can calm myself and enter the Stillness. Then I listen to find the small, still voice of love within my heart. The voice of the Orenda, which always speaks from love, stops the outer world's chaos from impinging on my senses. In this place of quietness that exists within myself, I am able to find the Eternal Flame of Love from the Great Mystery that feeds the voice of my Spiritual Essence. In my body, it is located in my heart, but it may be located in a different place for others.

The Orenda is an extension of the Creative Source or Great Mystery. The feeling of connectedness and loving compassion is always there. There is no fear or pain present, just a sense of peace. Getting to that place is a skill like any other and takes practice. For a while, during the development of this skill, a person may simply encounter a feeling of finding that safe space and the Stillness. Later, through developing Swan's Medicine of *surrendering*, a person may begin to hear the inner voice that always speaks the truth with unconditional love. This place inside the Self is where the Thirteen Original Clan Mothers live. The Turtle Council House is the spiritual Self's place of heightened awareness and total receptivity and the seat of the female principle.

It may take practice for some people to let go, getting rid of the adopted mess of chatter that has been collected from others over the years. This mental dusting and house-cleaning is necessary to clear the Sacred Space of other limiting viewpoints. Once this clearing is done, the feeling of total connection and inner peace is earned and found. The next step is finding the feelings, ideas, and viewpoints that belong to the true Self. All of these true parts of the Orenda that are reclaimed will have a very positive influence on any individual's life.

The Orenda, or Spiritual Essence of who we are, hears the call to wholeness and then sends the invitation to those whose hearts are open. We must stop our worldly activities and retreat to hear the Orenda's voice. It is an open invitation and no judgments are made by the Great Mystery or the Clan Mothers if that Child of Earth is not ready. All members of the Earth Tribe will eventually find their ways back home to the loving arms of the Earth Mother, even if coming home means nestling in the Earth Mother's soil after death. For those who want to feel the joy on the other side of physical pain and sorrow, the Turtle Council House is open now.

We enter the Turtle Council House every time we sit in silence and listen in order to receive. Hanging on the walls inside the Council House, we can see the Thirteen Medicine Shields of the Clan Mothers, and next to each shield we can see a Crystal Skull illuminated from the captured sunlight being funneled through the holes in the earthen walls. The ceiling of the Council House is arched like the inside of the Turtle Mother's shell, and there above, the rainbow lights dance as they are reflected from the top of each Crystal Skull.

There are two small ceremonial fires, one burning at each end of the lodge. Above these fires that represent the light of both worlds, the natural and the spiritual, are smoke holes. The smoke holes signify the open doors in both worlds where the illusions and confusions are allowed to escape, when we find clarity through the Eternal Flame of the Orenda or Spiritual Essence. In the center of the highest point in the turtle-shell-shaped roof is a removable circle of thatch that can be opened to the sunlight or to the Medicine Bowl of the night sky. Below this opening is where a person seeking entry would stand, creating the third fire. This fire is unseen because it lives inside the seeker's heart and is only brought to a blazing point through the seeker's reconnection to the Eternal Flame of Love. Rediscovering that fire is accomplished through the male, demonstrative side of our natures. Then, receiving it and giving it a home in the heart is the role of the female principle.

The Wisewomen who have carried the knowledge and wisdom of the ages sit outside on the grass-covered ground, encircling the Council House in an enormous wheel. They are softly singing and giving thanks for another Child of Earth who has chosen to come home. Their voices are as one and provide the strength and support needed to stand in the light of total truth and be healed of the pain found in human illusions.

The Thirteen Original Clan Mothers, whose greatest desire is to see every Child of Earth reclaim the love and inner peace, are calling to all of the Human Tribe. The strength each Child of Earth needs in order to come home is found inside the Orenda where the Sacred Hoop of connection to the Great Mystery and all life is never broken. The Sisterhood provides the support needed to find that connection and the pathway home to the true Self. The silvery webs of the Whirling Rainbow Dream have never been stronger. There is a life net of loving compassion waiting for those who have the courage to face the woundedness and reclaim the love. Our hearts will be cradled in a homecoming tear, our spirits will become at one with our bodies, and we will own the wisdom that we hold in our hearts. We are being asked to become our visions and to use our talents so that together we can create the living dream of world peace.

The gentle winds of change are stirring in the Four Directions to bring the homecoming songs of the Wisewomen to all nations, all races, all creeds. The Rainbow Dream is alive and dancing. The Creature-beings are showing us the road of rediscovering the sacredness of being human. The Stone People are offering to teach us how to retrieve the records of all that has been and the prophecy of all that will be. The Standing People and the Plant People offer us shelter and food for the body and spirit. The Lodge Fires of the Ancestors light our way to the stars by spanning the Great Medicine Bowl of the night sky. The silver horn of Grandmother Moon reminds us that our Orendas fill the Medicine Bowls of our hearts with love; and yet, for some, it is not enough to see these gifts the Great Mystery gives all of the Earth Mother's Children because they are blinded by false needs and old pain.

Patiently, the Thirteen Original Clan Mothers observe this picture of the Earth Tribe, just as if Grandfather Sun had painted it in the evening sky. The Clan Mothers wait, holding the door open for just a while longer. They know that some will Drop Their Robes, others will procrastinate until the door is closed, but some of their children will be bold enough to reach beyond their limitations and ask to be welcomed home. These are the final days of the Fourth World of Separation. The truth of reclaimed love lies beyond the human illusion of fear. The door to the Turtle Council House is open for those who remember and are willing to stand on every one of the thirteen spokes of transformation that support the Medicine Wheel of the Sisterhood. The Legacy of Woman will then be fully reclaimed—Life, Unity, and Equality for Eternity.

Becomes Her Vision, the Thirteenth Clan Mother, speaks to every Child of Earth and softly whispers these words that the Great Mystery put inside the Eternal Flame of Love: "You ARE, the moment you decide to BE."

Acknowledgments

I would like to express my deep appreciation to the people who have supported the completion of this project by assisting me in gathering the needed materials for making the Shields: Sue Woolery, Bird Woman, who tends many beautiful Winged Ones and has graciously shared the feathers of those birds, and Rick Woolery, who has provided me with many feathered pelts and wings, always respecting the spirits of the Bird Tribe in a good way by using the meat for his family and every part of each animal for Good Medicine. I also give thanks for our deep bonds of friendship over the years and the loving compassion they have shown me during hard times.

I would like to thank Sharon (White Arrow) and Ralph Akers for making the small drum-shields that have been made into the Medicine Shields of the Thirteen Clan Mothers. I am grateful for their continued support and friendship, as well as for the manner in which they walk their personal Medicine Paths.

To the staff of HarperSanFrancisco, I owe a deep debt for their continued support of my work. For their sensitivity and encouragement in presenting some of the viewpoints found in the Indian Way of Life, Woman's Medicine, and my personal understanding, I thank all of you.

Special thanks to my editor, Barbara Moulton, who gave me the space to go through my final Rite of Passage by writing this book, allowing me to become my vision. You have become a sister, a friend, and a midwife who assisted me in giving birth to the Legacy of Woman. Throughout the eighteen years of pregnancy that it took for me to pass through the lessons of these Thirteen Clan Mothers, I often wondered how I would be able to share the wisdom passed to me by Cisi and Berta. You have earned your Medicine name, Dreamweaver, because through your understanding of the Grandmothers' dream, it has now taken form, being shared with the sisters and brothers who walk the paths that lead to wholeness. My heart is full.